WEST CORK

THE PEOPLE & THE PLACE
ALANNAH HOPKIN

The Collins Press

Published in 2016 by
The Collins Press
West Link Park
Doughcloyne
Wilton
Cork

© Alannah Hopkin 2008, 2016

First published in 2008 as *Eating Scenery: West Cork, The People & The Place*

Alannah Hopkin has asserted her moral right to be identified as the author
of this work in accordance with the Irish Copyright and Related Rights
Acts 2000.

A CIP record for this book is available from the British Library.

Paperback ISBN: 978-184889-274-3
PDF eBook ISBN: 978-184889-045-9
EPUB eBook ISBN:978-184889-073-2
Kindle ISBN: 978-184889-077-0

Typeset by The Collins Press
Typeset in Bembo
Printed in Ireland by Essentra

Cover images courtesy of Nevil Swinchat
Top: Castletownshend and Reen
Bottom: Caherkeem on the Beara Peninsula

Contents

About the author

Alannah Hopkin was educated in London and has lived in Kinsale, County Cork, since 1982. The author of two novels and other works of non-fiction, she writes for the Insight (Berlitz) and Fodor Guides to Ireland. She is a regular reviewer of books and art for national newspapers and magazines.

Stay up to date with the author at:
htttp://alannahhopkin.com
www.facebook.com/alannahhopkin

Acknowledgements

Thanks to all the people who talked to me about their experiences of west Cork (alas, constraints of space dictated that not all these stories could be included). The idea for this book grew while working on commissions for Joe Dermody, Eoin Edwards, Jo Kerrigan and Fionnuala Quinlan at the *Irish Examiner*; Patsey Murphy, editor of *The Irish Times Magazine*; Liam McAuley at *The Irish Times*; and Letitia Pollard, editor of *Ireland of the Welcomes*: thanks to all of you. I am grateful to Peter Somerville-Large for generous permission to quote from his published works; to John FitzGerald, Librarian, Boole Library, University College Cork; to Cathy Thompson for brilliant copy-editing; and to my agent Jonathan Williams. Special thanks to Aidan for patience and understanding.

The West Cork Region

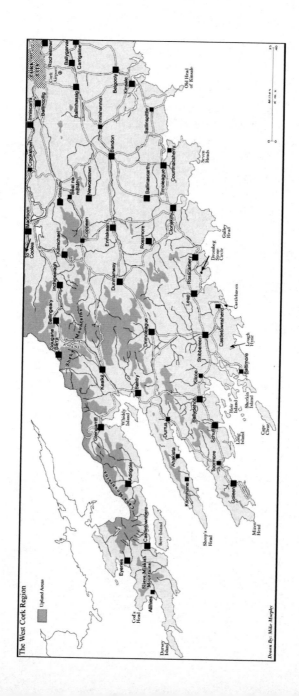

Upland Areas

Drawn By: Mike Murphy

For they dwelt upon a rock in the sea and not in a
    shining metropolis
and lived off the pick of the strand, the hunt of the hill,
    the fish
in the sea, the wool off sheep, and packets full of dollars ...
they were full of sunlight and mist, wind and stone, rain
    and rock,
but the Atlantic Ocean would not pay them a regular salary ...

Lucht an Oileáin
(*People of the Islands*)
David S. Quin

Prologue

There is a story about a charabanc organised back in the 1920s to take a group of working people from Cork city on a day trip through scenic west Cork. They were shown the Pass of Keimaneigh, Gougane Barra, Glengarriff and Bantry Bay before being driven back home. What did they think of the wonders they had seen? Beautiful, they all agreed, but how did anyone make a living out there in the wilderness?

'You can't eat scenery' was the puzzled comment.

West Cork begins on the other side of the Bandon River, less than half a mile from my home in Kinsale. The reason that I do not live in west Cork is because for me it has always been an escape and a haven. West Cork is the place I go to recover from everyday life, to be somewhere different.

I am often tempted to go and live there. I still dream about finding the perfect isolated farmhouse, with a view across rolling green hills to the sea. But I stay in Kinsale. If you move to the haven, where do you run to when you need to escape?

As you cross the bridge over the river, you turn your back on the busy, cosmopolitan town that Kinsale has become and enter a rural community, where (as the promoters of tourism are continually reminding us) the pace of life is slower, the people are friendly and have time to talk, and older values prevail. There is no need to lock your car, because there is hardly any crime, and people still leave the front door on the latch.

Well, that's what it was like 30 years ago, when I first discovered west Cork. But the fringes of rural Ireland, the most westerly settlements in Europe, have been through dramatic changes in the past 30 years. Does west Cork still exist as a place apart, or is it just a romantic dream?

Before I commit myself to writing a book about west Cork, I decide to do some informal research: I will talk it over with Peter and Fran Wolstenholme, ceramic artists, who live in Courtmacsherry. They moved from Yorkshire to County Cork in 1973 and have run a successful business from their home ever since. I could have talked to plenty of others, but it is because they work from home and have close links with the local community that I choose to discuss the project with the Wolstenholmes.

Courtmacsherry is just over half an hour's drive from Kinsale, but it's a totally different place, smaller and quieter, definitely a village, not a town. A straggling line of mainly terraced houses, the village is on the south bank of Courtmacsherry Bay, facing north across the road to the sea. The Courtmacsherry lifeboat, the village's pride and joy, is housed in a shed near the pier. There are still a couple of working trawlers, but most of the deep-sea fishing is done by tourists from day boats, in the summer. At the far end of the village is a sandy beach, and beyond that a walk, partly through woodland, to Wood Point which marks the northern extreme of the inlet. Courtmac (as it is familiarly known) has three pubs and one shop, which also serves as post office, as well as a newsagent and grocer. The hotel, which was built as a summer residence by the Earl of Shannon, is now closed, and holiday homes have been built in the grounds.

For a brief time in the mid-twentieth century there was a branch railway line connecting Courtmac to the West Cork Railway. It carried sugar beet in winter and day trippers in summer. For many people the name Courtmacsherry recalls idyllic summer holidays, with beaches, friendly pubs, fresh fish, and a mildly eccentric but comfortable hotel. A popular bumper sticker sums up its continued attraction: 'Courtmacsherry – A small drinking village with a fishing problem'.

In July and August, like most coastal villages in west Cork, Courtmacsherry can be too busy; it is heavenly in May and June, September and October. But in winter Courtmacsherry is deadly quiet, prone to dull, dark days of low sky and mist, when you are acutely aware of its north-facing character. The only compensation in this season is the presence of thousands of migrant birds, great clouds of golden plover, lapwing, black-tailed godwits, and Arctic shags, fleeing the cold of Scandinavia and Siberia to roost on the mudflats of Courtmacsherry Bay.

Arriving at the Wolstenholmes' small terraced house is like going aboard a well-found ship. As you enter the little gallery with its display of ceramics and fine porcelain (Peter's work tends to feature the birds and fishes of the area, while Fran, the gardener, uses flower motifs), there is nobody to greet you, but within seconds Peter, summoned by a bell inaudible to me, has left whatever he was working on in the studio, and appears, wiping wet clay from his hands, to usher me through to the kitchen.

It is one of those dark Courtmac days, even though the calendar says it is 22 April. Through the back window of the kitchen you can see a large pink azalea blazing in a pot in the yard, and small birds cluster around peanut feeders. I had put my bird feeders away the previous weekend, as winter had ended, and comment on the Wolstenholmes' generosity.

'We've thirteen pairs of nesting birds in the garden,' says Peter. 'I haven't the heart to stop feeding them. And we've a jackdaw with no beak: her whole face was smashed in, so we put down some bread softened in milk, and she learnt to scoop it up. We did that all winter, and now her beak is growing back, at least the top bit is there. And her mate is still with her. They nest in our chimneypot every year.'

Peter is a slightly abstracted man of medium height and stocky build, with short, dark hair and a dry sense of humour. It is hard to believe he will be 60 later this year. He exudes the air of someone well satisfied with the life he has chosen, which is maybe why he seems so much younger. Apart from ceramics, his passions are birds and fishes, both of which abound here. Peter founded the local branch of the Irish Wildbird Conservancy, which makes an annual count of the migrants in the area. He was also involved in the creation of a two-mile waterside footpath that has been laid on the old railway line from Timoleague to Courtmacsherry. It is lined at intervals by ceramic plaques with drawings and information about the various birds you can see on the walk, made by Peter and donated by him to the community project.

The Wolstenhomes' kitchen is much as it was when I first saw it, over twenty years ago – a narrow, quarry-tiled room at the back of the house with a large pine table, simple sink and cooker, looking on to the tidy backyard, with its azalea and bird feeders. Fran is called, coffee is made, and a cake is shared, baked by Fran in a rare initiative inspired by a Spanish recipe in *The Irish Times*. It is a long time since I have had the luxury of taking a coffee break with friends. It reminds me of the early years when I first moved back to Ireland and how amazed I was, coming from a studio flat in central London, that people not only had kitchen tables, but also apparently limitless time to sit around them and talk. I also realise that if the book is to get written, this is the first of many kitchen tables I will sit at in the course of research.

I tell Peter and Fran that I'm working on a book about west Cork and they are my trial research project, since they've been here longer than most other incomers. What does west

Cork mean to them, and how do they feel about it, after knowing the place since 1973, raising a family here, and running a business? These are big questions that cannot be answered directly. Instead, we discuss boundaries, agreeing, as does the Irish Wildbird Conservancy, that west Cork covers the country west of the Bandon River and south of the N22 Cork–Macroom–Ballyvourney–Killarney road.

Peter, who has kept his Yorkshire accent and speaks slowly, as if he had all the time in the world, points out that west Cork is a new term: 'Back in the 1970s, we just said we were living in County Cork. You said you lived in County Cork, or Clonakilty, or Allihies.'

'It's a marketing thing,' Fran adds. 'West Cork Tourism, West Cork Foods, Fuchsia Branding.'

Peter recalls their arrival in Ireland with another couple, Jane and Robin Forrester: 'When we first came over in 1973, we were just out of art school, and we'd seen an ad for a shop and a courtyard in Ballydehob. We went down to look at it, and the place was full of long-haired people living in tepees out on the hill. I had a beard at the time, and I shaved it off the next day, and I said we can't live in Ballydehob. Then we found this old grocery shop in Courtmacsherry.'

Eventually Jane and Robin Forrester moved to Bandon and opened their own pottery, shop and gallery, while the Wolstenholmes stayed in Courtmac and converted part of their house into a holiday home. Their two children grew up and left the area, though their daughter Rachel has now come back: she lives nearby and runs her own ceramics business, making small bird and animal figures.

Put three people around a table anywhere in Ireland, and eventually the talk will turn to property prices. Peter is talking about someone he knows, a local coming back to live in Clonakilty (the nearest town to Courtmacsherry), who has just paid €200,000 for a site: 'He thinks it's worth every penny after London. Clonakilty's a boom town now: everybody wants to live there. His children can walk to school, there's a nice community around them, and he only has a short drive to work in the West Cork Technology Park.'

The West Cork Technology Park? Fuchsia Branding? It is quickly becoming apparent that the romantic in me is going to have to face up to things she would rather not know about.

I am starting to realise that there are as many versions of west Cork as there are people living there. As if to emphasise that fact, I borrow two books from the Wolstenholmes: a copy of the Cork County Development Plan, and another on the folklore traditions of Dunmanus North, both neatly stamped with Peter's name and address and the words 'Please Return'.

'There's no such place as west Cork really,' he says as I go out the front door. 'It's a state of mind.'

That just makes my day. My very first research trip has revealed that I am proposing to write a book about a place that doesn't exist.

As I drive away from Courtmacsherry, through the mist I see a man carrying a newspaper under his arm, walking home along the path beside the mudflats behind two bounding Springer spaniels.

Suddenly I decide that I too want to live in dark, wintry Courtmacsherry, and walk my Springer spaniels beside the silent sea. The dream lasts only for seconds, but I can still feel the excitement and the glow of the moment. Oddly enough, shortly after this visit, I got a call from the supplements editor at the *Irish Examiner*, asking if I'd be interested in working on a special supplement about the West Cork Technology Park. The assignment included an interview with the people who had invented the concept of Fuchsia Branding. The west Cork book was already under way.

Introduction

In the past 35 years west Cork has changed from a depressed, agricultural backwater with a dwindling population into an expensive, sought-after area with a growing population. Those whose parents and grandparents were born and brought up in the area have been joined by incomers from elsewhere in Ireland and from overseas – primarily England, Holland, Germany, France and the USA.

The unique character of west Cork today can only partly be explained by economic factors, such as the effect of the European Union's policies on farming practices, its investment in infrastructure (especially roads and telecoms), and the general effects of Ireland's economic boom. The full picture can be understood only by looking closely at the lives of those who have grown up in the area, and those who have moved from elsewhere to make their living and bring up their children in this corner of the world. Together, these people have created a multi-faceted community in which those who follow the traditional way of life, which is still the dominant mode, have been quietly accepting of other ways of living. Incomers are often motivated by respect for the values of the community they are moving to and make great efforts not to destroy the less pressured, more trusting way of life that attracted them in the first place. 'We all have something to learn from each other' sums up the prevailing attitude.

Ireland is on the western maritime periphery of Europe. Cork is the country's largest and most southerly county. While the northern and eastern parts of the county contain rich farming land, large demesnes with big houses, and towns with charters dating back to Norman and Elizabethan times, the western part of Cork has always been on the far edge of the periphery. Even today, there is no 'town' west of Cork city with an official population bigger than 5,000. Anything under that, in European Union terms, is classed as a village.

There are no generally agreed official boundaries to west Cork. For the administrative purposes of Cork County Council, it begins at Clonakilty, whereas the West Cork LEADER Co-operative (an EU-funded development agency) includes Kinsale, 29 km further east. I prefer the Irish Wildbird Conservancy's definition mentioned by the Wolstenhomes. People who know their wildbirds are to be respected. Whatever definition you choose, the names alone are enough to evoke the place for those who know it: Courtmacsherry, Clonakilty, Rosscarbery, Leap, Glandore, Union Hall, Skibbereen, Lough Hyne, Baltimore, Sherkin, Cape Clear, and the Fastnet Rock, the area's most southerly and best-known landmark, at the outer edge of Roaringwater Bay.

West Cork has three peninsulas that jut into the Atlantic, giving it a long, mainly rocky coastline, with only a few sandy beaches. The Mizen Head is at the tip of the first peninsula (travelling from east to west), with Schull, Goleen and Crookhaven on its sheltered southerly coast, Ballydehob and Durrus at its inland extremities. Dunmanus Bay divides the Mizen from the narrower Sheep's Head Peninsula, which forms the southern extremity of Bantry Bay, leading, as you move inland, to the town of Bantry.

Glengarriff, also on Bantry Bay, due west of Bantry town, marks the landward entrance to the Beara Peninsula, the biggest, most scenically dramatic and least frequented of the three peninsulas. The scenery gets bigger and more magnificent the further west you go, and the number of creative artists per square kilometre increases drastically.

The Caha Mountains run down Beara's spine, with Hungry Hill towering over the village of Adrigole. Castletownbere marks the magnificent anchorage in the lee of Bere Island. Allihies, Eyeries and Ardgroom are the western extremities of the region, the last two overlooking the Kenmare River with views across the water to Kerry's Iveragh Peninsula and the Ring of Kerry.

For most people west Cork evokes images of quiet, fuchsia-lined laneways, rambling up and down hill, past oddly shaped fields and traditional farmhouses, to quiet seaside villages lined with brightly painted cottages. In this version of west Cork, you are always on holiday, and everyone is in a good mood. Front doors are left on the latch, cars give way to each other at intersections, and drivers salute strangers. People on foot have a friendly word for visiting walkers: 'Fine day!' they shout to you as they pass. The sun shines from a clear sky, and white sails scud across the deep blue sea. Later, you watch the sun setting on the horizon from a bench outside a whitewashed 'local', pint in hand, before walking around the corner to choose between steak and seafood at a pleasantly eccentric restaurant in what was once someone's front parlour.

This is the west Cork I discovered as a teenager in the 1970s, mostly in other people's cars, and, when I was really lucky, on other people's boats. It was a place where time seemed to have a different value: there was definitely a lot more of it. Three days in west Cork was usually as reviving as a fortnight anywhere else. And, conversely, a three-day visit could end up lasting for ten, as the pressures of the outside world receded, evaporating in a haze of fresh air and pub fumes. During this same period, Peter Somerville-Large was cycling around the coast from Clonakilty to Ardgroom, revisiting scenes of his childhood, and recalling past inhabitants, in order to write that classic of small-scale travel, *The Coast of West Cork* (Victor Gollancz, 1972).

There is another, less frequented, west Cork, consisting of its inland areas: Bandon, Enniskean, Rossmore, Coppeen, Dunmanway, Drinagh, Drimoleague, Kealkil. These are names that you would recall fondly only if you had family or other connections in the area. One such was the late Pete McCarthy, author of *McCarthy's Bar* (Hodder and Stoughton, 2000). He was born Peter Robinson in Warrington, and considered himself thoroughly English, but his mother, whose name he adopted professionally, came from a farm midway between Drimoleague and Dunmanway. McCarthy describes the childhood thrill of being allowed to hold the reins on the horse and cart, as he and his uncle drove from the farm to the fair day in Dunmanway or Drimoleague – he was never sure which. Both are a little bigger nowadays than the many 'blink and you miss it' villages in Ireland, but even so, it is sometimes hard to remember which one you have just driven through, and which one is coming up. Both straggle along the main road, either side lined by shops and houses of little or no architectural merit, enlivened, perhaps, in summer, by a few tubs planted with brightly coloured flowers.

Then there is the more hilly part of west Cork, to the north and east of the head of Bantry Bay, partly on the border with County Kerry, the wild terrain of the Shehy Mountains and the Gaeltacht area: the corrie lake at Gougane Barra where the River Lee has its source; Inchigeelagh, with the Gaeltacht to its west, running through Coolea, Ballyvourney, Ballingeary; finally, returning towards Cork city through Macroom, Kilmichael and Béal na mBláth, where Clonakilty-born Michael Collins, Commander-in-Chief of the pro-Treaty government forces, was shot dead in an ambush on 22 August 1922.

A century ago if you mentioned west Cork, people would

probably associate the place first with Gougane Barra, where the legendary St Finbarr founded his monastery on an island in a black corrie lake, surrounded by tall hills, having first banished a serpent from its depths. Cronin's Hotel at Gougane Barra and its clientele were featured in the work of writer and artist Robert Gibbings, which was enormously popular in the 1950s. People would have heard in mythology of the Pass of Keimaneigh (the Pass of the Deer), an echoing steep-sided cutting through the mountains. Or perhaps they would think of Inchigeelagh and Ballingeary, promoted by Daniel Corkery to his pupils, the writers Seán Ó Faoláin and Frank O'Connor, as places to immerse yourself in the true Irish culture.

From the mid-nineteenth century until relatively recent times, Bantry and Glengarriff were the chief tourist destinations to the west of Cork city and Blarney. They were usually visited en route to Killarney, crossing the border into Kerry along the tunnel road in the lovely wild hills above Glengarriff. Vickery's Inn in Bantry and the Eccles Hotel in Glengarriff (the latter still going strong) played host to many early visitors, including Virginia Woolf, 'Everybody talks to everybody,' she reported, sounding as pleasantly surprised at this local trait as today's visitors.

Bandon, Clonakilty and Skibbereen grew and prospered with the arrival of the West Cork Railway, but it was not until the private car became more generally affordable in the 1970s and 1980s that the coastal areas south and west of Clonakilty and Skibbereen – Castletownshend, Baltimore, Schull, Barley Cove, Crookhaven – became popular tourist destinations. But they were always low-key places for family holidays, where accommodation was offered primarily in existing houses and cottages (bed and breakfast or self-catering) rather than in grand, purpose-built hotels. And the season was short – July and August, give or take a week or two before and after.

In the old days, country people might visit Cork city once a year (often on 8 December, the Feast of the Immaculate Conception and the traditional day for doing the Christmas shopping), or maybe twice a year, once for the Cork Show, an agricultural show held in August, and then perhaps for a GAA match. Some of the older generation have never been to the city at all, while their grandchildren now often opt to commute 30, 40 or 50 miles to work from their west Cork base.

As a reminder of how much west Cork has changed in so little time, I keep a newspaper clipping on my desk of a photograph from *The Southern Star* captioned 'Main Street, Drimoleague, in the fifties'. The foreground of the photograph is occupied by the dusty, untarred main street. The photographer must therefore have been standing in the middle of the road, without the slightest worry of being run over. And no wonder: there are precisely two cars in the picture, both parked at the side of the road. There are four, possibly five, people: an old woman near a telegraph pole on the left of the road, one or two individuals beside one of the cars, and a couple of small children, who seem about to cross the deserted road. A pub–grocery, marked by hanging signs for 'Players Please' (cigarettes) and Guinness, is open for business; all the other shops have reverted to private use or are boarded up. The village had only recently been electrified, and probably still has no running water. The place is tidy. It is just that it is eerily empty.

The majority of the people who were born in Drimoleague are probably working in Birmingham, Cricklewood, Boston or New York, or numerous other places around the globe to which they emigrated. The population of rural Cork declined steadily from the Great Famine until the late 1980s, when a small reverse trend was established.

Unlike the bright, self-confident village of today, Drimoleague in the 1950s looks like the place you would least want to visit in the universe – let alone migrate to.

Introduction

The increased population figures in west Cork came about through a combination of factors, which are still being analysed. Incomers were certainly important – among them, young people from predominantly middle-class backgrounds, not long out of college, who decided in the late 1970s to opt out of the rat race and live a simpler life, closer to nature, in a beautiful, unspoilt part of the world, where land and housing were still affordable. These, and their older counterparts, were called affectionately 'blow-ins', as in 'Who's your man?' 'Ah, he's just a blow-in.' The implication being that there was nothing to worry about – like seeds on the wind, these strangers would blow away again as quickly as they had blown in. Some did, but others took root.

Since the 1980s, jobs have been increasing steadily, enabling many locally born people, who would otherwise have left for Dublin, London or New York, to stay in the area and raise families of their own. The number of farmers is shrinking, but jobs in tourism, the service industries, the pharmaceutical industry and information technology are steady or growing. There has even been a significant contribution to the population figures made by people who had one or more parent from the area, were born and educated abroad, but eventually decided to live where they really wanted to be, instead of staying in a city they did not want to live in while progressing pointlessly up the professional ladder. We are sometimes called 'blow-backs', to distinguish us from blow-ins, who have no previous connection to the area. I prefer the term 'returnees'.

My own story is a classic 'returnee' case study. My mother was born in Summercove, a village on Kinsale Harbour a mile outside town. For me as a child in the 1950s and early 1960s, holidaying in Kinsale, the west of the county was an exotic, faraway destination. If a trip to, say, Clonakilty, was planned, my mother would pack a rug, a picnic basket, and a flask of tea, convinced that the car would break down on the way. All too often it did. Today I think nothing of nipping over to Clonakilty, a pleasant half-hour drive from Kinsale, to visit friends, or go to the Farmers' Market or to walk on the beach at Inchydoney.

People did not travel for pleasure so much before the 1960s. To travel usually meant to emigrate, as my mother did in 1933. 'There was nothing for us in Summercove' was her way of putting it. She and her sister took the steam packet from Cork to Fishguard, to study nursing at St Mary's Hospital, Paddington, coincidentally next door to the terminus for the Fishguard train. Her sister came home, but my mother married an English doctor, and lived outside Ireland for most of her life. My grandmother died in the early 1950s, shortly after I was born, and I cannot remember her, but we kept her house (no one else in my mother's family had any use for it) and used it for holidays. In the early 1960s my parents were faced with the expense of installing running water (electricity had arrived in 1951) at a time when we were about to move to Dallas, Texas, and would unable to visit Ireland. This, plus complications caused by the absence of title deeds, made them decide to give up the house. Then we came back to London and visits to Summercove resumed. We stayed in rented houses until 1974, when my mother bought another house in the village. Since leaving school, I had spent most of my time travelling and living abroad, seldom visiting Ireland, but from 1976 I started spending as much time as I could in Kinsale and, in 1982, I sublet my flat in London for six months, to see if I could make it work full-time. Twenty-five years later I'm still here.

West Cork attracts well-travelled people who have seen the rest of the world and decided that this is as good as it gets. Parts of west Cork are only half an hour from Cork Airport, which has direct flights to many UK destinations and several European capitals. The first wave of outsiders to buy in west Cork was mainly holiday-home owners and retired people.

There is a still a large contingent of Dublin business people and politicians, as well as London media people, with second homes in the area. In the late 1970s, the low price of land and the mild climate attracted urban people keen to experiment with self-sufficiency and alternative lifestyles, Dutch and German, Irish and English.

Today the trend is increasingly towards people in early to mid-career, successful business people, turning their back on the corporate culture in order that they and their children can enjoy a balanced and more fulfilling lifestyle in beautiful, unpolluted surroundings. For the price of a modest Dublin-semi, they can buy a prime waterside property in west Cork, and live in relative splendour. They are well organised and acutely aware of both the drawbacks and the advantages of such a radical change. They are also determined to succeed both professionally and personally in their new lives, while respecting and, in time, enhancing the community they are moving into.

But there are shadows too, like the one cast by the murder in 1996 of Sophie Toscan du Plantier, a well-connected Paris-based film-maker. The violent murder of a woman who had assumed that she was safe in her relatively remote holiday home alone, shocked and outraged people far beyond the immediate area of Schull. For the first time people living remotely, alone or in couples, felt the fear and suspicion that are commonplace in urban Europe.

One of the first people I talked to about this book was the film producer David Puttnam, currently President of UNICEF, whose home is now near Skibbereen. He explained how his liking for beautiful but remote places began when he was making a film in western Scotland, *Local Hero*. 'That's what interested me about your project. The title is a line from that film.' I managed to hide my surprise, and he continued. 'It's what someone says to the American oil man who wants to ruin this absolutely beautiful place: 'You can't eat scenery'. Yet these days, west Cork is buzzing with activity – artisan food producers and craftspeople, writers, artists, IT personnel, even people like Jeremy Irons restoring crumbling fifteenth-century castles. You might not be able to eat scenery – but you can do just about anything else.

1

Long Ago – The Early History of West Cork

Every year on the day of the winter solstice I drive to Drombeg Stone Circle off the road between Rosscarbery and Glandore, hoping to watch the sun setting in alignment with the stone altar. Twenty years ago there would be half a dozen people there; in 2006 there were over 200.

Drombeg, locally called the Druids' Altar, is a well-preserved circle of fourteen stones, with two uprights, known as portal stones. The traditional way to enter and leave a stone circle is through this portal; otherwise, some say, you will have bad luck.

Directly opposite the portal stones at Drombeg is a recumbent stone, usually presumed to be an altar stone. Behind this stone and to its left is a view of low hills, spreading back for maybe ten miles. Drombeg is on a low plateau, peaceful and sheltered, with open views to the north and west, and, when visibility is good, distant sea views to the south. There is a natural geological V-shaped gap in the hills, and at the setting of the sun on the winter solstice (around 4.30 p.m.) the last rays are supposed to fall through this gap in alignment with the recumbent stone and the portal.

Once, just before the sun went down, a huge flock of rooks flew past, heading to the woods to roost for the night. Then there was silence. It is a strange and memorable experience to stand there, some 6,000 years after those stones were first put into place, and wait for the light to disappear behind the same low hills that our ancestors once viewed. Who were those people who used to gather here at this same time of year, waiting for sunset, looking out at the still grey hills?

Settlers first came to west Cork around 6,000 BC. These Stone Age people lived by hunting, fishing and gathering, according to archaeological evidence. Much of the country was covered with primeval forest of oak, interspersed with holly and birch, or with ash, hazel, and yew in limestone areas. Around 3,000 BC a wave of settlers are thought to have come from Galicia. If you set sail from Galicia in a primitive boat, the tides and currents would most likely bring you to the shores of west Cork. The Galicians were part of the migration west across the Mediterranean from the Middle East in search of new lands. These migrants were farming people, who made clearings in the forest to grow crops, moving on to new lands when the productivity of the fields was waning. Pig-keeping was an important part of the economy, and herds of swine roamed among the trees. Eagles and wolves thrived in the wild until the mid-eighteenth century, when the last recorded wolf in Munster was shot.

Metalworkers and prospectors reached Ireland about 2,000 BC, and soon succeeded in their search for copper deposits. Nearly all the mines in west Cork show evidence of prehistoric mining. The Bronze Age descendants of these Stone Age settlers were the builders of Drombeg Stone Circle and west Cork's other megalithic remains: standing stones, wedge tombs and cooking pits. West Cork's megaliths are relatively small-scale: it is their unspoilt scenic locations – coastal plateaux, open fields, often with long views – that make them memorable.

The region's megalithic remains began to be properly documented in the 1950s. Only in 1992 was a major survey completed by a team of archaeologists from University College, Cork (UCC), for the Department of Environmental Heritage and Local Government. This found that Drombeg was a Bronze Age ritual site, with carbon dating of 1,124–795 BC. The circle contained a burial urn at its centre, with the bones of an adolescent. Beyond these facts, all is speculation.

While there have been no great finds of Celtic metalwork in west Cork, the area is unusually rich in ogham stones. Out of a total of 358 ogham stones on record from Ireland, 252 are from Munster and 247 of those are from Cork, Kerry and Waterford. A collection of 28 of Munster's inscribed ogham stones, dating from the mid-fifth to the late seventh century, are on display in University College, Cork.

Ring forts, or circular earthenworks (raths), which surrounded the huts of the farmers of early Christian Ireland, are extremely numerous throughout west Cork. In the Clonakilty area alone, the Cork Archaeological Survey recorded 48 circular earthworks or possible ring-fort sites. Many were left untouched for centuries because of superstition: the local people thought that they were the home of fairies and it was believed that bad luck would pursue anyone who interfered with these places. This extended to stone monuments as well as to ring forts. Even today, where small fields have been turned into vast prairies, the ring forts often still stand untouched, usually marked by rings of trees, clearly visible from the air.

Those early settlers in their stone-built or wooden huts with tightly corbelled or thatched roofs would have been damp, but never really cold. Because of the Gulf Stream and its southerly location, the coastal areas of west Cork are frost-free all the year round. Further inland, the temperature seldom falls below zero. They chose sites that had a good view of the surrounding country, were easy to defend and, if possible, were near a source of fresh water. These places, which often have the word *lios* (liss, fairy fort) or *dún* (dun, fort) in their names, have been in continuous use for hundreds, sometimes thousands, of years.

Christianity probably arrived in Cork well before St Patrick brought it to the north and east of Ireland, traditionally in ad 432. The Old Head of Kinsale is marked on the map of the world produced by the Egyptian Ptolemy in the middle of the first century ad. This map also shows Cork Harbour, the River Shannon, and the Mizen Head, and was presumably based on information gained from sailors who had returned to the Mediterranean from Irish waters. St Ciaran of Cape Clear Island is referred to in the *Annals of Innisfallen as Primogenitus Sanctorum Hiberniae* – 'the first born of the saints of Ireland'. According to the *Annals*, he returned from Rome to his native Cape Clear Island on 5 March 402. St Ciaran's Day is still a holiday on the island. The origins of Cork's more famous saint, Finbarr, do not have such strong local roots. Saint Finbarr is reputed to have banished a monster from the black waters of Gougane Barra, set up a hermitage there, and a famous school at Cork in the sixth or seventh century. Latest scholarly opinion holds that legend has been mingled with the widespread cult of Finbarr, a teacher of Colmcille, who founded a church at Movilla, County Down, and whose life was first written around 1200.

The pre-Christian inheritance is also evident in the cult of St Gobnait, patron saint of beekeepers. Her shrine and Holy Well in Ballyvourney are regular places of pilgrimage today: the bushes are still decked with rosaries and ribbons; the well's water is still believed to have healing powers; and today's pilgrims continue to observe the patterns, or 'rounds', old forms of worship that distinguished Irish Christianity from mainland continental practice. Another famous County Cork saint, St Fachtna, founded a monastery and school at Rosscarbery around AD 590. This attracted pilgrims and scholars from Ireland and Europe, until the Danes destroyed it in the ninth century.

Prior to the Norman invasion, the region we have defined as west Cork formed part of the Kingdom of Desmond (south Munster), ruled by MacCarthys based in Cashel. There were Ó Laoghaires, Ó Céilleachairs and Ó Tuamas in the Lee valley. Fighting was endemic among the Irish chieftains. Its effect on west Cork was memorably summed up by Lee Snodgrass of the Mizen Archaeological Society in a talk dealing with the years of inter-tribal warfare: 'The O'Mahonys were pushed south and west by the MacCarthys; the O'Mahonys, in turn, pushed the O'Driscolls south and west to Baltimore and then Cape Clear.'

The O'Mahonys built twelve castles in a ring around the Mizen Peninsula. The O'Driscolls had castles at Baltimore, Ringarogy and Cape Clear. Both families were involved in a lucrative endeavour, charging dues from herring fishers from Spain (Galicia again), Portugal, and France in return for salting facilities, landing, and mooring places. This is the reason why there are so many castles set dramatically on cliff edges along the coast, looking out to sea.

All these early inhabitants of west Cork seem to have been colonisers of one sort or another who came to the area from other parts of Europe or from other parts of Ireland. The term 'native Irish' is used comparatively, referring to those immigrants who had been here longer than the newer arrivals, particularly in the case of the Norman invasion. The intensity of tribal warfare glimpsed is one of the reasons traditionally given for the lack of resistance to the Anglo-Norman invasion. Dermot MacCarthy's submission to King Henry II caused further disagreement among the MacCarthys. The Normans took advantage of this to establish their own power and territorial claims.

By about 1215 the Normans were building castles, specifically fortified tower houses, some of them on the site of old Irish forts, many of which were then unoccupied. For example, Myles de Courcey chose a place near the site of Dún Cearma, on the narrowest part of the peninsula of the Old Head of Kinsale, to build Dunmacpatrick Castle in the thirteenth century. Castles previously belonging to MacCarthy, O'Mahony, O'Neill, O'Driscoll and O'Sullivan were now held by the new Norman overlords: Barry, Carew, Roche, de Courcey, Barrett, de Cogan, Hodnett, and others. There are over 400 castles and fortified houses (dating from around 1600, after the Elizabethan wars) in County Cork, about one quarter of these, approximately 104, in the west Cork area.

The assimilation of the Anglo-Normans, who inter-married among the native chieftains, was rapid, although for generations people continued to boast of both bloodlines – Anglo-Norman and 'native Irish'. Piaras MacÉinrí, head of the Centre for Migration Studies in the UCC Department of Geography, points out that mainstream Ireland has imagined itself in mono-ethnic, mono-cultural tribal terms since the foundation of the State, even if this has never corresponded to the realities: '…a counter-history is now needed, that tells the history of the country and its multiple peoples and diasporas, not in the tribal sense of a "core nation" beset by successive invasions, but in terms of an accretion of encounters and syntheses over many centuries making us the already multi-ethnic, non-tribal nation we are today.' (When this conclusion from an academic paper was reported in *The Irish Times*, MacÉinrí received virulent hate mail.)

The ports of Dingle and Kinsale had strong maritime links with Cornwall, France and Spain, in contrast to Dublin, which was closer to England and Wales. Once Henry VIII had broken with the papacy, fears grew amongst the English loyalists that the coast of west Cork and Kerry would be used by England's enemy, Catholic Spain, as a back door into England. The baronies of Carbery, Bantry and Berehaven, and Muskerry (baronies which contained roughly that area that we have defined as west Cork) remained in the hands of native Irish dynasties throughout the fourteenth and fifteenth centuries. A landing of Spanish and Italian forces at Smerwick on the Dingle Peninsula in 1580 strengthened the English determination to crush rebellions in Munster. The 1583 Desmond rebellion was followed by the start of 'plantation'. Land was taken from the rebellious warlords and given to English colonists, who could be relied on to be loyal to the Crown. This process started in the north and east of the county. Small areas at Kinsale, Bandon and Bantry were 'planted' in the mid-sixteenth century, after the Earl of Desmond's revolt, and further grants of land were made after the Battle of Kinsale in 1601.

By the end of the sixteenth century, Kinsale was an important naval base, a walled town that had received a royal charter in 1334. The Battle of Kinsale was a resounding defeat of the combined Irish and Spanish forces under O'Neill and O'Donnell. Six Spanish ships that had landed in error at Castlehaven were sunk or otherwise dealt with by six English warships. In the wake of the battle, the land to the west of Kinsale was sacked and laid waste.

After the defeat at Kinsale, Donal Cam O'Sullivan Beare's mercenaries retreated to his castle at Dunboy near Castletown-bere. Sir George Carew (1555–1629), provincial president of Munster at the time, had the responsibility of restoring law and order to west Carbery. As the historian Hiram Morgan succinctly puts it, 'His mixture of brute force and skilful diplomacy quelled Munster within a year' (Sir George Carew' in Sean Connolly ed. *The Oxford Companion to Irish History*, Oxford University Press, Oxford, 1998, p. 70). Carew arrived in Rosscarbery on 4 May 1602 with 4,000 men, and next day they went to inspect Castlehaven Castle and harbour. The following day he and his regiment visited Baltimore and Sherkin Island. Each soldier had a ration of two pounds of beef on flesh days and eight herrings on fish days, which had to be requisitioned as they moved on. The English troops confiscated cattle and horses and laid waste what remained. It took them until June to reach Dunboy Castle. The castle held out under siege for six months, and eventually its defenders, heavily outnumbered by the English forces, were killed when they blew it up rather than surrender. (The full story can be read in *Pacata Hibernia*, ed. Standish O'Grady, London, 1896.) Donal Cam escaped and, on 31 December 1602, began his long march from Glengarriff to Leitrim. Of the 1,000 people who set out, only 35 reached their destination.

In 1607, the clan chiefs left for Spain, an exodus known as the Flight of the Earls, and the old Gaelic world order was over. The emigration of Gaelic leadership continued after the victory of the William III at the Battle of the Boyne and the Siege of Limerick in 1691, when some 14,000 individuals, mainly from the minor nobility, gentry, and professional classes (known collectively as the Wild Geese), left for Europe.

By 1641, 22,000 English Protestants had settled in Munster, most of them to the east, south and north of Cork city where the land was of better quality than in the west. In 1641 an alliance of Irish – including MacCarthys, O'Donovans, O'Driscolls and O'Mahonys – and Anglo-Normans reacted to land confiscation by massacring large numbers of Protestant settlers in both Munster and Ulster. Fighting dragged on, interrupted intermittently by temporary truces, for the next seven years. Among the houses and castles left in ruins by the rebellion were Rathbarry Castle at Castlefreke, O'Donovan's castles at Castledonovan (Drimoleague) and Raheen (Union Hall), Cormac MacCarthy Reagh's castle at Kilbrittain, and

Coppinger's Court, a massive fortified house between Glandore and Rosscarbery.

In order to quash these rebellions, Oliver Cromwell was sent to Ireland in 1649. Between August 1649 and May 1650 his troops marched west from Cork through Kinsale, Bandon, Dunmanway and Skibbereen to Glengarriff. From this time until the Act of Union, the presence of the law (in the form of permanent garrisons of redcoats, as the English troops were called) in the Baronies of Carbery, Bantry and Berehaven, and Muskerry, ended at Kinsale. But, in case of further rebellions, subjects loyal to the crown could take refuge in Bandon, a walled town, known as the Derry of the South.

Bandon, or *Droichead na Banndan*, dates its foundation from 1604 when the bridge across the Bandon was rebuilt by Henry Beecher, Richard Skipwith and William Newce. Richard Boyle, the Earl of Cork, received its formal charter from James I in 1613. Its massive walls enclosed 27 acres and had four gates which stood until 1688. One section of the wall can still be seen on the west side of the town. Bandon was intended as a safe refuge for the English settlers, or planters, who had been granted tracts of fertile land along the valley of the River Bandon, and south and west of the town down to Clonakilty, in an attempt to 'plant' the area with subjects who would be loyal to the Crown in times of trouble. Protestant settlers from as far away as Clonakilty took refuge in Bandon in times of trouble. At the same time, Richard Boyle founded Enniskean and Castletown Kinneigh to the west of Bandon and Clonakilty to the south.

The first Bandonians came mainly from Somerset. Their names can still be found in the town today and have also been given to local places: Becher, Bennett, Deane, Newce, Coombes, Poole, Bernard, Frost, and Reen. Bandon Grammar School, one of the oldest schools in the country was founded in 1641, and is still thriving, with over 450 pupils of all religions being educated in a strong Church of Ireland ethos. Until the relaxation of the Penal Laws in the latter part of the eighteenth century, no Catholics were permitted to live in the walled town of Bandon. When Charles Smith, author of the history and gazetteer *The Ancient and Present State of the County and City of Cork*, passed through in 1750, he wrote 'In this town, there is not a popish inhabitant, nor will the townsmen suffer one to dwell in it, nor a piper to play in the place, that being the music used formerly by the Irish, in their wars.' He also notes that Bandon could raise a militia of a thousand men. To this day, people like to quote the saying 'Bandon, where even the pigs are Protestant'. Such sectarian attitudes are history now. In 2004, the town's 400th anniversary was marked by an Ecumenical Service of Light, in which the town's various religious communities took part.

Because it straddled both sides of the river, Bandon had two churches and two market houses from the very start. Christchurch, Kilbrogan, on the northern side of the river, dates from 1610. It was deconsecrated in 1973, and is now the West Cork Heritage Centre. St Peter's Church of Ireland stands on a hill on the opposite side of the river. The Methodist church was built beside the river on the south bank in 1821. John Wesley and his brother Charles preached in Bandon on several occasions and there is a strong Methodist community to this day. The Society of Friends (Quakers) was introduced to Bandon in 1655 and had a Meeting House behind South Main Street, which was demolished in 1999. The Masonic Lodge adjoining the Courthouse was taken over by the Kingdom Hall of the Jehovah's Witnesses, and the Masons now meet at Riverside Hall, in Allen Square.

In 1795 Lord Bandon guaranteed the lease of a plot of ground at Gallows Street for the building of a Roman Catholic Chapel, and Lord Bandon's estate paid the ground rent of £20 per annum. In 1856 the foundation stone of The Church of the Immaculate Conception and St Patrick was laid, and the church was formally opened in 1861. Designed by a successor of A. W. Pugin, it is an imposing, hill-top building in the Gothic Revival style, with an impressive dark interior, lit only by stained-glass windows, and epitomising the pre-Vatican II era, when churches were truly awesome places.

Today Bandon is often referred to as 'the gateway to West Cork', but it is very different from the brightly painted, flower-bedecked holiday destination promoted as West Cork. While its urban population stands at around 1,500, it caters for a rural population of about 6,000. Bandon is a sober place of grey cut stone – a place of schools (six primary, four post-primary), churches and hardware stores. The last are fast disappearing in rural Ireland, yet Bandon has five: one beside the mart, one beside the bus stop, two old-fashioned ones in the town centre, and a large Co-op on the edge of town. Bandon and its hinterland, especially the Kilbrittain area to the south, are now popular commuter destinations, with Cork city half an hour's drive away.

Clonakilty, with its award-winning floral displays, brightly painted shop fronts and cheerful riverside warehouse conversions is closer to the kind of place tourists expect to find in west Cork. Clonakilty too was founded as a Protestant settlement in 1613 by Richard Boyle, the first Earl of Cork. It became a centre of the linen industry and flour milling. Today, like Bandon, it is popular with commuters, who find the 45-minute drive to Cork well worth it in terms of local amenities, which include good schools and numerous beaches. (While there are people commuting from as far afield as Bantry and Skibbereen, the normal Cork-city commuter belt ends in an arc that can be drawn through Clonakilty, Macroom, Mallow, Fermoy, and Youghal, all within 45 minutes of the city in good conditions.)

At the same time that he founded Clonakilty, the Earl of Cork gained a charter for Baltimore, the least successful English settlement in west Cork. A prime location on the shore of Roaringwater Bay proved also to be its nemesis. On

20 June 1631 two shiploads of Algerian pirates, piloted by a Hackett from Dungarvan, raided the settlement, killing two people, and carrying off 111 others, only two of whom were ever seen again. It has generally been assumed that these exotic raiders were given information about Baltimore by O'Driscoll émigrés seeking revenge on the English who had driven them out of their home. The chief consequence of the raid was the founding of the town of Skibbereen twelve miles further inland, on the River Ilen, by the few English settlers who were left. Understandably, they were keen to rule out the possibility of being attacked again from the sea.

Both Skibbereen and Baltimore were 'Beyond the Leap', hence the absence of any forces of law and order. These days Leap, pronounced 'Lep', is a pleasant village strung out along the roadside of the N71 on the way to Skibbereen. At the end of the village, the road goes downhill and passes an estuary on the left, which is in fact the topmost point of Glandore Harbour. Beyond it is Myross Woods, one of the few remaining wooded areas along this coast. A dramatic hand-painted sign situated on the roadside as you leave the village heading west pictures a large white horse, with a rider crouched on its back, jumping across a grassy ravine and its waterfall. This is the Leap, after which the village is named.

Before the modern road was built, you could not proceed any further west by road unless your horse knew how to jump the 'Leap' – the gap at the top of the glen of Myross. Anyone fleeing from the forces of law and order could take this road, confident that his pursuers' horses would not be able to negotiate this formidable obstacle. Leap marked the entry to the wilder shores of the Barony of Carbery, and the impene-trable countryside around the edges of Bantry Bay, the Barony of Bere and Bantry, where eagles and wolves ran free until the mid-eighteenth century. Hence the expression 'Beyond the Leap, Beyond the Law'.

❖

Richard Tonson was Collector of Revenue for the port and district of Baltimore during the mid-eighteenth century, and his area included Roaringwater Bay and all of Bantry Bay. Most of the time he worked alone, with 'shilling-a-day men' sworn in as constables and hired as needed, but Tonson also had a network of well-paid spies around the coast, which kept him informed of smuggling activities. Just as there was money to be made in smuggling, so was there money to be made in intercepting the contraband, as the Exciseman was entitled to a generous cut of the proceeds. Records of a raid by Tonson on Berehaven in 1732 show that not only were the Catholic Sullivans involved, but that the Puxleys – supposedly loyal planters who had come to Berehaven from Cornwall via Galway – were also leading figures in the illegal import– export trade. Ironically, the lands granted to the Puxleys included the remains of Donal Cam O'Sullivan's castle at Dunboy that had been blown up after the Battle of Kinsale.

A sign of the times is that only six years later the two families had parted company, and were effectively on different 'sides'. The Sullivans were now exporting men as recruits for the Irish Brigades in the service of the Catholic monarchies of Europe, while the Puxleys were now sworn in as Revenue Commissioners, working to stop the smuggling trade. Morty Óg O'Sullivan was an officer in the army of the Empress Maria Theresa of Austria and was subsequently made a colonel on the battlefield at Fontenoy. John Puxley served in the Duke of Cumberland's cavalry. But both fought at Culloden, on opposing sides. The feud between the two families intensified when both soldiers retired from active service and returned home. This culminated in 1754 when John Puxley was shot dead by Morty Óg O'Sullivan. The latter was hanged for this crime.

In the early to mid-eighteenth century many Catholics living in remote areas, including the Beara and Iveragh Peninsulas, sent their sons to France or Spain to be educated, a privilege denied to Catholics under the Penal Laws. They were often put into the care of distant relations who had left Ireland after the Siege of Limerick. Many prospered abroad, and it is in this period that the ancestors of families such as Hennessy, Barton and O'Higgins left Ireland.

Those fortunate enough to be commissioned (an expensive business) were often subsidised by earnings from the smuggling of wool and brandy. Many never came back to Ireland; why would they, when the professions were barred to them and their land had been confiscated? As the European wars of the mid-eighteenth century used up more and more cannon-fodder, the forcible impressment of recruits into the European armies became as much of a hazard in some areas (including the Beara Peninsula) as was the forcible impressment of able-bodied men into the British navy.

Another example of the difficulty of settling back into the unremarked status of a provincial after being an officer in the Irish Brigades, is the case of Art O'Leary, a landowning member of the Iveleary clan and an officer in the Austro-Hungarian army, who was shot while on the run in 1773 as the result of a feud with the High Sheriff of Cork, Abraham Morris. The poem written by his widow, Eibhlín Dubh Ní Chonaill, *Caoineadh Airt Uí Laoghaire*, is generally acknowledged as one of the greatest poems written in the eighteenth century. Eibhlín Dubh was an aunt of Daniel O'Connell, the Liberator.

The Last Colonel of the Irish Brigade by Mrs. M. J. O'Connell (first published in 1892) is a rich source for detail on the old Catholic households in Kerry – equally applicable to Cork life at the same time. She writes of eighteenth- and nineteenth-century life at home and abroad based on letters and other papers kept by the O'Connell family. Derrynane, their family home, was just across Kenmare Bay, almost directly opposite the O'Sullivan stronghold at Eyeries on the Beara Peninsula. (Fishermen would row between the two coasts, a couple of hours each way, up until the 1950s, because there was more market for fish on the Kerry peninsula than on the northside of Beara.) The O'Sullivans and O'Connells intermarried and were closely related. In the O'Connell book, smugglers are referred to as 'traders', and smuggling is seen as an acceptable way for respectable people to make a living, given the unfairness of English tariffs and the remoteness of the coast. The young men destined for the Brigades learnt French and Spanish at home, coached by tutors who were also usually priests, and could therefore say Mass for the family. Because the Catholic religion was effectively outlawed for the first three quarters of the eighteenth century, there are very few records available, which makes this account of a hidden history, albeit a partial and clumsily put-together narrative, extremely valuable.

There is no lack of records of Protestant west Cork at the same time. The list of priests and rectors of the old Castlehaven church from 1403 to 1604 documents the replacing of native Catholic society with a new Protestant one: O'Callaghan, O'Driscoll, and Cormac are supplanted by Basse, Pratt, Stukely. The old church at Castlehaven was replaced by St Barrahane's Church in 1761 and a plaque there gives a detailed history of the Townsend family. It tells us that Richard Townsend, a Cromwellian officer, aquired the cliff-side O'Driscoll castle in a place known as Glen Barrahane, overlooking the safe anchorage of Castlehaven. Castlehaven was one of the three finest harbours west of Kinsale, along with Baltimore and Berehaven. In 1732 Thomas Somerville was appointed rector of Castlehaven and Myross. Somervilles and Townshends (the 'h' was added in 1870, with permission of an English Lord Townshend, presumably because it looked more distinguished) lived and intermarried in the parish, eventually joined by Admiral Sir Josiah Coghill (1773–1850) who, with his wife Anna Maria Bushe, created a veritable dynasty of Coghills. Peter Somerville-Large, one of his descendants, has written: 'The Ascendancy usually chose to build their mansions far away from villages or town where barefooted peasants walked the muddy streets. But at Castletownshend ('CT' to the initiated), the Protestants were all herded together side by side in the English manner.' Only one Somerville ever made much money: Thomas Somerville, son of the original rector, became a very successful merchant, trading (legally, of course) with Newfoundland and the West Indies. He bought land, and built two beautiful houses which stand to this day, the Mall House and Drishane, and also the stone-built warehouses and quays necessary for his trade.

The population boom of the late eighteenth century is closely interlinked with the potato. Ireland's population grew from about 4 million in 1781 to about 4.4 million in 1791. There were crop failures causing famine and widespread hardship in 1724 and 1731, but their cause was not understood. By the mid-nineteenth century, the poorest people in the country were living almost entirely on two or three meals a day of boiled potatoes, eaten communally, directly from the basket in which they were drained. On the coast they were supplemented by shore foods: mussels, periwinkles, limpets and seaweeds. Herrings were cheap, as was buttermilk. Salted pig meat was used occasionally as a relish. Because pigs were also fed on potatoes, pig meat became the most widely available and the cheapest meat. Turkeys, geese, ducks, and hens were also fed on potatoes, and thrived, In late summer, the old potatoes, dug the previous season, would run out before the new ones were ready to be dug, giving July the name of 'hungry month'. Some had oatmeal or cabbages to fall back on, but, understandably, they missed potatoes. It is said by many people that the potatoes grown after the Famine were never as delicious as those grown before it.

The Great Famine of 1845–47 was the watershed of the nineteenth century in west Cork, as in the rest of Ireland, marking the end of a period of rapid population growth, and the start of more than a century of population decline. The areas worst hit by the potato famine were overpopulated rural districts, including coastal west Cork. When the potato crop failed, owing to blight, there was nothing to fall back on. It is hard to imagine today, as you drive past such fertile land and food-rich seas, that anyone could starve to death in this area, but that is to forget the density of population and the poverty of resources. There were so many people competing for so little food that contemporary records state there was not a scrap of seaweed left on the shoreline from Baltimore to Ballydehob. In my childhood, many of the older generation refused to eat mussels, referring to them as 'famine food'.

The Beara and the Mizen Peninsulas lost three quarters of their population from famine and emigration in the ten years between 1845 and 1855. The population of Ireland dropped from 8.5 million in 1845 to 6.5 million in 1851. The fact that grain was being exported to England while people starved to death served to fuel nationalist hatred of a government that had allowed such a thing to happen – for the British government, with its strong belief in laissez-faire politics, responded slowly and was reluctant to provide free food, expecting men barely able to stand for hunger to labour on the road-building and other projects for a pittance.

As the audio-visual presentation at Skibbereen's Famine Centre points out, Poor Relief was not a social welfare payment: it was a minimal intervention to prevent people from dying on the side of the road. Many miles of roads and stone walls, many bridges and causeways were built during this era, to provide an income to otherwise penniless labourers, so that they could feed their families, but it was often too little too late. Justice of the Peace Nicholas Cummins of Ann Mount, Cork, wrote a famous letter to the Duke of Wellington, published by *The Times* (London) on Christmas Eve 1846, about the horrors of the time and inspired a collection of over £470,000 from private individuals for famine relief. But this was also too little too late.

The historian Patrick Hickey, currently parish priest of Timoleague, has written an account of these events that is both studious and readable: *Famine in West Cork – The Mizen Peninsula, Land and People, 1800–1852* (Mercier Press, 2002) Over 7,000 of Schull and Skibbereen's population of 43,266 died during the Famine, and over 1,000 emigrated. Another angle is covered by Eoghan Harris's play *Souper Sullivan*, which deals with those who tried to persuade people to change religion by tempting them with soup, an issue fuelled by sectarian tension, which is extremely charged, politically and emotionally.

The shadow cast by the Famine is a long one. The failure of the potato crop recurred in 1890–91, once more creating great suffering. Even today, potatoes can only be reliably grown commercially if they are sprayed at the correct time during the growing season. As Peter Somerville-Large observed in 1972, 'West Cork never recovered from the potato famine of 1847, and its effects linger like clouds of fall-out.' Among these effects was a rapid loss of the Irish language. In 1843 it was used by over 90 per cent of the people; 40 years later, this was down to 35 per cent. Today the only Irish-speaking districts in the county are Cape Clear Island and the area around Ballyvourney, Coolea and Ballingeary.

Famine was followed by economic depression and continued emigration, for the next 100 years or more. The trend of falling population was reversed only in the 1980s.

2

Farmers and Food Producers

'Farming is such an honorable profession,' says Beara Peninsula farmer Norman Steele. 'It makes a great life. It was a great way to live when the children were growing up. It's a shame that it is disappearing.' The milk from Norman's herd of 27 cows went into Milleens, the prize-winning soft-rind cheese made by his wife, Veronica, on their farm near Eyeries. 'That was a huge herd for the area,' he says, 'by far the biggest around.' Alas, after 27 years, in 2003 the herd was lost to BSE. All the cows had been born on the farm, and Norman didn't have the heart to start again. Before he was a farmer, Norman was a philosopher: he taught Wittgenstein, among other things, at Trinity College, Dublin. The philosopher speaks: 'While it is true that I moved from professional philosophy to farming, the metamorphosis was never total in either direction. It is easier to think, when living a pastoral life, and as I become older I am devoting time that was formerly spent in milking cows to more cerebral matters.' The habits of a lifetime die hard. Norman still rises at six, as he did when he had a herd to milk, and spends three hours reading and writing before facing into the day. The Steele's youngest son, Quinlan, has taken over the cheese-making, with a passion, leaving Veronica free to help her two daughters with the grandchildren, five living locally, and two in London.

Milleens was one of the first and the most successful Irish farmhouse cheeses. Other people in west Cork were experimenting with cheese-making at around the same time: Jeffa Gill at Durrus, Helene Willems at Coolea, Giana Ferguson at Gubbeen, and Bill Hogan and Sean Ferry. They formed Cáis, the Irish Farmhouse Cheesemakers' Association, to promote the cheeses and further the education of cheesemakers. Milleens is a pungent product, with a lingering aftertaste, a cheese for the discriminating palate. Myrtle Allen recognised its qualities at once, and put it on the menu at Ballymaloe House in 1976. So did Declan Ryan, then of the Arbutus Lodge, and Gerry Galvin at the Vintage Restaurant in Kinsale. The great chef Anton Mossiman tasted it at the Vintage, and ordered two 1.6 kg cheeses a week. Says Norman: 'I used to post them to the Dorchester in London in wooden boxes. I posted all the orders out back then. It was part of the fun, we knew all the customers personally, and what they wanted, and we matched the cheeses to the people. We had distributors coming along wanting to buy everything we could produce, but that wasn't how we wanted to do it.'

Even before the BSE catastrophe, the Steeles were buying in milk since the demand for Milleens far exceeded the amount they could make with the milk from 27 cows, and this is how the cheese continues to be made. 'We're buying in milk from the neighbours, so it is very similar. Their cows are eating the same stuff as ours did. We have superb pastures, with herbs and mixed grasses and hedgerows, so the milk is more interesting than the milk from cows that only eat rye grass.' And the neighbours enjoy knowing that their milk is going into a very special product, sought after by connoisseurs all over Europe, rather than contributing to the butter mountain. To keep the Steele's land in good trim, a young dairy-farming neighbour makes silage on it, and rears his heifers and dry cows there.

❖

One thing I missed when I moved from London to Kinsale was street markets. There was Bantry, and that was about it. But there has been progress in the past few years. In addition to Bantry, Clonakilty, Castletownbere, Inchigeelagh, Kinsale, Macroom, Schull, and Skibbereen all have farmers' markets on one morning a week, which encourages farmers to sell direct to the consumers. The markets vary, but the idea of the grower going to market once a week has not yet caught on among traditional farmers: there are some, but not many. There are generally more bakers, cake-makers, pickle-makers, and vendors of pre-cooked, homemade convenience foods at these markets than there are sellers of local carrots, potatoes and cabbages. The markets are predominantly middle-class, both in terms of vendors and shoppers. They are expensive too, though the foodie mantra is that you get what you pay for. Some suppliers are said to be making four-figure sums every week trading at farmers' markets: but in reality very few, I reckon, are making a good living from it.

It took me a long time to get a grasp on the 'foodie thing'. I like cooking and eating, and I grow some salads and herbs, but food is not a major obsession. The Slow Food movement originated in Italy, and initially grew up to defend traditional methods of food production against EU regulations. Today, it is an international movement of people who are interested in the promotion, production and consumption of good food. It supports makers of artisan foods, and attempts to preserve their skills.

An invitation to a Slow Food Picnic provoked an impatient reaction: I just don't have the time for Slow Food. I reread the invitation:

West Cork Slow Foods
Annual Summer Picnic – Sunday 19th August
A revival of the Somerville and Ross tradition:
Climb up Lough Hyne and treat yourself to a scrumptious
picnic while gazing at the spectacular view.
Meet at bottom of Lough Hyne to collect your
pre-ordered picnic at 1:00 pm
We aim to start the climb at 1:30 pm

'You must come,' says Giana Ferguson of Gubbeen Cheese. 'There's usually about 100 of us. This is the fourth year we've done this. Even in the rain it's fun. You'll meet some very interesting people!'

I didn't want to offend her, but I couldn't feel anything but dread at such a prospect. If I go to Lough Hyne, one of the most beautiful spots in west Cork, I like to be alone. I get cross if there's even one other person there, let alone 100. But the final clincher was the menu: 'The West Cork Cheese Picnic: Selection of local cheeses by Durrus, Gubbeen, Milleens, and West Cork Natural Cheese. With Inner Pickle's Roasted Red Pepper and Garlic Pickle; Jim and Pagan Cruit's white yeast bread; organic potato salad with green beans and pesto; organic mixed greens with Desmond cheese and cider vinaigrette; raspberry mousse by Glenilen; a quarter bottle white wine from Febvre & Company.'

I was fine with the cheeses, but Inner Pickle made me feel slightly sick, and when I came to 'Jim and Pagan Cruit's white yeast bread', I knew I would not be going. Why do they do it, these foodies? Why does everything have to be named after somebody – Giana Ferguson's Gubbeen Cheese, Jim and Pagan Cruit's white yeast bread? I'm sure Pagan is a fascinating person – I've never met anyone called Pagan before – but what's all this got to do with bread and cheese?

Everything, as it happens. John McKenna, one of Ireland's leading advocates of artisan food, lives in deepest west Cork with his wife, Sally. Together they edit *The Bridgestone Irish Food*

Guide (Estragon Press, 2007); he explains: 'The personalisation of food has a double dividend: it gives the food character, most fundamentally the character of the person who creates it – just as an artist paints the way they do, a writer writes the way they do – food is no different. It is a canvas for expression. The second dividend is that this character of the artisan is the truest statement of what is nowadays called a luxury brand. Luxury can only truly exist when something is handmade by its creator, otherwise it's not luxury. So Yves Saint Laurent goods are not a luxury, they are simply overpriced. But a handmade cheese, made on the farm by the person who milks the cows, is the purest form of a luxury, as is a handmade loaf. It is food as art, and the most valuable kind of art, because it is designed to give pleasure, and to be shared, not to be collected or hoarded.'

Denis Cotter, whose cooking at Cork's Café Paradiso redefined vegetarian food, records a similar phenomenon in his cookbook *A Paradiso Year* (Cork University Press, 2003), when he recalls the animated discussion of potatoes around the family table in Macroom: their flouriness, size, dirtiness, even the character of the man who dug and sold them. The integrity of the food producer and the integrity of the food go hand in hand.

The West Cork LEADER Co-operative Society has done much to encourage this sector, using their Fuchsia Branding scheme to create a regional identity that will help to promote high-quality local produce. In addition to makers of Milleens, Durrus, Carrigaline, and Gubbeen farmhouse cheeses, the farm-based enterprises they promote include: Gubbeen Smokehouse products; Glenilen cream and yoghurt, Drimoleague; Scarriff Lamb, Bandon; Skeaghanore Duck, Ballydehob; beef from Dexter cattle at The Traditional Meat Company, Dunmanway; salad leaves, lettuce, and potatoes from Anthony Boyle in Skibbereen; Valley View Free Range Eggs, Bandon; and more. Then there's smoked fish: Union Hall Smoked Fish, Ummera Smoked Products, Timoleague (who also smoke bacon and chicken), and Woodcock

Smokery at Castletownshend. And finally artisan food products that are handmade in small factories and off-farm workshops, such as: Beara Preserves, Castletownbere; Gwen's Chocolates, Schull; Coolmore Foods, Bandon; RGL Patisserie, Dunmanway; Clona Dairy Products, Clonakilty; Irish Yogurts Ltd, Clonakilty; Heron Foods, Bandon; and even Sonia Bower's Inner Pickle, Rosscarbery. The Fuchsia Brand is also awarded to the accommodation and catering sector and the craft sector, creating a cluster of high-quality products and services associated with the region. A study carried out by researchers at UCC and University College, Dublin (UCD), showed that in 2005 the total direct value of output related to the Fuchsia Brand, including goods, services, and value-added, amounted to €106.97 million.

West Cork's artisan food producers tend to be very small businesses. There are currently about 50 food producers using the Fuchsia logo, but only twelve of the Fuchsia-branded businesses are farm-based. Skeaghanore Duck, for example, employs two people full-time (the owners), and two part-time, producing farm-reared fresh duck.

Artisan food is no doubt a good thing for the area and is being sensitively developed and promoted. But west Cork also has a very successful agri-business, Carbery (Milk Products) of Ballineen. The company was established in 1965 on a greenfield site and currently employs about 300 people. The plant produces about 30 per cent of Ireland's cheese, including, ironically, the Dubliner brand, as well as cheddar, mozzarella and Red Leicester. It is also a major manufacturer of flavours and food ingredients, the latter utilising the whey from the cheese-making process. The plant also uses milk to produce the alcohol that is used in Bailey's Irish Cream. It has a turnover of about €200 million.

'Agriculture should be simple, but has become incredibly complicated.' John McKenna is speaking again, this time in the opening address to *A Taste of West Cork Food Festival* in September 2007. He pointed out how agri-business, agrichemical, and agri-industry remove the 'culture' from agri-culture. But it can be put back.

The culture of agriculture is thriving on the 250-acre farm near Schull, Gubbeen, where Giana Ferguson makes her cheese. Gubbeen has won prizes all over Europe; her son Fingal is carrying on the artisan food tradition at his smoke-house on another part of the farm, where he cooks and butchers the pigs his father Tom raises on the whey left over from the cheese-making, creating a wide range of continental-style charcuterie. Giana and Tom's daughter, Clovisse, started growing herbs for the smokehouse, and has expanded her plot into an organic vegetable garden, while their adopted daughter, Rosie, handles everybody's paperwork.

Giana says she has always been acutely aware of the importance of different food traditions, having grown up with both the garlic-flavoured cuisine favoured by her father's Hungarian family, and the cucumber-sandwich tradition of her mother's English background. She is, in manners and accent, very much a well brought-up London girl, Kensington to be exact, even after 30-plus years in rural Ireland. She is a good talker, a natural PR person, and has done much to promote the artisan foods of west Cork and the Slow Food movement. She has a degree in History of Art and was working at the ICA (Institute of Contemporary Art) in 1973 when she suddenly took off for Ballydehob. 'I just had to get away; it was a sort of claustrophobia brought on by the art world. I stayed with some friends in Ballydehob who let me pitch my tent in the garden, and I lived in an outhouse when it rained. I got a job in a bar, and one day Tom walked in, and I thought, "there's trouble".'

What she liked about Tom was that, at the age of 23, he knew who he was, in a way that none of her London friends did. 'Tom's family were Protestants who would have come over to Carrickfergus during the Ulster plantation, and somehow moved ever further west and south. They survived in west Cork, in the same way that my mother's family, who were kind of impoverished gentlefolk, struggled on in those old houses in England. You hold fast to what you believe in. There are more Protestants in west Cork than just about anywhere else in Ireland. They survived through all the troubled times by behaving themselves, keeping their heads down.' And, she might have added, working very hard, as she and Tom have done. She worries about Clovisse's future as an organic gardener, a tough profession for a slim, frail-looking woman. 'I think she'll make a living,' says Giana, admiring the prolific herbs and vegetables. 'I don't think she'll get rich, but her life is rich indeed.' Fingal was born in 1977 and there are hopes that he will soon take on the herd of 117 cows, as well as continuing to run the smokehouse.

It's interesting that the majority of indigenous artisan food producers are from the Protestant tradition and I'm glad that Giana drew attention to the large number of Protestant farmers in west Cork. It's a tricky issue for an outsider to raise; one is constantly aware of old wounds only recently healed, and so one treads warily. The Protestant farms are a legacy of the large grants of land that were given to settlers in the latter part of the seventeenth century, especially around Bandon, Clonakilty, Skibbereen, Bantry, and as far west as Schull, where the Fergusons farm. This was usually the better land, more fertile and easier to work than the rocky coastal fringe, and the hilly inland areas. In contrast, Norman Steele says there is only one Protestant farm in the Allihies–Eyeries area – that of the Hodge brothers, descendants of a family that came from Cornwall to work in the copper mines, so a different case. The lands granted in the seventeenth century gave people big farms, so their descendants were wealthy and usually well-educated. Apart from essential chores, Protestant farmers do not generally work on Sundays. Until the mid-twentieth century, a Catholic farmer who wanted to work on a Sunday (to bring in the hay, for example) had to ask permission of the parish priest.

Protestant farmers are more inclined to experiment and

innovate, as at Gubbeen. Vets, farm inspectors, and other people who have daily contact with farms can usually tell at a glance whether the farm is run by a Protestant family or a Catholic one. One of the few people to have written about this is Maurice O'Callaghan. In his story, *The Lord's Burning Rain* (Destiny Books, 2005) he describes an encounter between a self-styled 'Black Protestant' (uncompromising in matters of faith), and a young boy from a Catholic background. Says Maurice: 'I think people are often afraid to talk about it. I feel freer, because my mother's side was Church of Ireland – the Goods of Bandon – so I have a leg in both camps.

'You can generally tell a Protestant farm because the houses are that bit bigger, and the farmyards are better. They are tidier, and they have a bit of architecture: entrance arches and arched windows. The ceilings in the houses are generally higher, because the average Protestant farmer was that bit wealthier. You had gradations of Protestant farmers – squires, squireens, "strong farmers", and the smaller farmers. They kept their heads down. Protestants and Catholics went to different schools and, while Protestants were happy to do business with Catholics, they didn't mix socially when I was growing up.'

Even today, despite the homogenising influence of television and radio, there is still a distinct Protestant accent characteristic of the west Cork area. At its most pure, it is a wonderful accent, slow and considered, with a roundy burr, less sing-song than the average Cork accent, at once solemn and humorous. A trained linguist could probably explain why, but I swear you can hear echoes of the Somerset origins of these people's ancestors.

The Irish landscape is a major attraction for visitors: 82 per cent of people in a recent Tourism Ireland survey cited the scenery as a prime reason for their visit. In west Cork this figure would probably be higher. The appearance of the landscape, most of which is farmland, matters a great deal to people who are not farmers and they may have very strong opinions on the visual effects of farming activity, even though they do not work the land. Our increasingly urbanised society has an idealised view of the countryside as 'natural', when in fact the rural landscape is a construct that has evolved down the years and is determined by the social and economic aims of the people who manage the countryside.

While 10.2 per cent of the population is employed in agriculture nationally, this rises to 21 per cent in west Cork, almost double the national average. We live among farmers, but we are not part of their lives, and they are seldom part of ours. Farmers' decisions about which crop to grow, what land to leave fallow, and what animals to rear is manifest to the rest of us as changes to the scenery. Beet, for example, which has been part of the landscape for most people's lifetime and seemed likely to remain, disappeared suddenly in 2005, when sugar beet processing plants throughout Europe closed down. But beet fields had not always been part of the landscape: it was only introduced as a commercial crop for sugar-making in 1922. Flax, a giant, spiky, non-native plant, was grown commercially in the Clonakilty area up until the 1950s – and was even used in the construction of early aeroplanes. Many of the fields that once grew beet now have a tall crop of sweet corn rustling in the breeze. Others lie idle, gradually being reclaimed by the bog. Experiments are currently under way with bio-fuel crops – willow, miscanthus grass (also known as elephant grass), and oil seed rape – all of which will have a big impact on the look of the west Cork countryside if they prove viable locally.

Alice Taylor's memoir of an Irish country childhood, *To School Through the Fields* (Brandon Books, 1988), describes the experiences of the generation who lived through the changes brought about by the arrival of electricity, running water, and the internal combustion engine in the mid-twentieth century. Publisher Steve Mac Donogh believes it is one of the biggest-selling books ever published in Ireland, with about 450,000 sold of the Brandon edition. Alice grew up on a farm near Newmarket in north County Cork. In her day, children walked to school. Distances of three miles and more in each direction were not unusual. Alice was lucky: she could see her home from the schoolhouse, and had to walk only a short distance across some fields.

Alice's memoir struck a chord with everybody who was old enough to have gone 'to school through the fields'. It helped that Alice is a natural storyteller with a warm personality; her first radio interview, with Gay Byrne, lasted a record 42 minutes, and her first appearance on *The Late Late Show* was of a similar length. All over the country voices were raised in a loud cry of, 'I went to school through the fields too!'

For a few weeks in May 1988 it seemed as if people spoke of little else but 'Alice's book', I witnessed a fiercely competitive conversation at the garage in Ballinspittle, as the men, all in their fifties, vied with each other over who had walked the furthest distance to school. I asked Alice if she could identify the key to her book's extraordinary success. She said, with typical astuteness, 'It's got people reading books who never read a book before. The lads up on the tractors have a copy of it in their back pocket.'

The kind of farm described in Alice's memoir, a small mixed farm as owned by Old MacDonald of the nursery rhyme, had been the dominant way of farming for centuries. While the EU has affected all of us, it has had the biggest impact on the lives of farmers. The Common Agricultural Policy (CAP) influenced what farmers produced, how they did it, how much they produced, and what they earned from that produce. In the 1970s peripheral areas like west Cork were woken from their long somnolence and dragged into the twentieth century where things were done differently. The creameries of old, where the farmers would pass the time of day while waiting to deliver their milk and collect the whey, have either closed down or been converted to agricultural retail outlets selling fencing posts, animal fodder, and bags of fertiliser. Nowadays the milk is collected by a stainless-steel tanker. The driver siphons it in directly from the storage tank, without any human contact, before driving off to the next farm on his route. The four west Cork agricultural co-operatives that ran the creameries – Bandon, Drinagh, Lisavaird, and Barryroe – are now big, diversified businesses. Barryroe, for example, had a turnover of €50 million in 2003.

Changes in farming methods have been accompanied by changes in the social and economic life of the farming community. It is easy to forget just how low standards of living were in parts of rural west Cork before entry into the EU. People from mainland Europe who knew the area in the 1960s have remarked on the lack of sanitation among rural dwellers in those days. German-born Marie Therese Schmitz and her husband bought Whitehall, a large eighteenth-century house on Roaringwater Bay, in 1962. She says:'When we came here first, the people were terribly poor. They all slept in one room – father, mother, grandfather, aunt, and six to eight children. And they had no facilities, not even the little house in the backyard; they just went behind the ditches. That was the expression, 'behind the ditches'; it was incredible. They were very, very poor. But they were very nice people.'

Schull-born veterinary surgeon Frank O'Keeffe has witnessed these changes first hand. Between 1962 and 2003 he practised in Kinsale, with a practice that spanned both sides of the River Bandon. He was also President of the Veterinary Council of Ireland from 1986 until 1988. At the beginning of his career most farms were traditional mixed farms, and all but the biggest farms still worked with horses. He says:'It was the most interesting place to set up practice. You had the traditional Irish family farm, around 50 acres, and they kept about twelve or fifteen cows, about 30 sheep, and five or six sows. So you had all the species, and there were still horses working on the farm. The bigger farms had tractors, and hired them out to the smaller ones. Each farm had at least one horse, and they were worked particularly for scuttling beet, and for bringing in the potatoes that they all grew.'

The level of knowledge that these farmers showed of their herd impressed Frank enormously: 'In those days the farmer walked the cattle in, morning and evening. As a result, they knew the herd in every detail. When you visited them, their description of a sick animal was so detailed and well observed that you could almost be reading from the textbook: the history and the symptoms were exactly as written down. They had reared them right through from calves, and their powers of observation were immense. The animals were individually tied up, you moved from cow to cow with the electric milking machine and the bucket. The stockmanship was fabulous.'

Most farmers left school at thirteen or fourteen. Only a few would go on to technical school and acquire skills such as welding or carpentry. This was before free secondary education. Frank discovered a great thirst for knowledge among his clients, which was catered for by Macra na Feirme (the young farmers' association) which organised lectures for their members: 'I used to go and give lectures at 8 p.m., at each of the five different local clubs. You'd get about 50 farmers, young and old. I went through husbandry of the different species – cattle, sheep, pigs – talking about disease prevention, vaccination, basic hygiene, and good practice. I gave my time freely around, because there was no other system.'

Macra also has a social side, with dances, amateur dramatics, field days, and agricultural shows. This was very important and Frank, like many people, can name several couples who met through Macra and subsequently married. He also saw the GAA playing a crucial role in rural life in the mid-twentieth century: 'It was great for building a sense of community and local identity. People travelled to matches and got to know people from other parts of the country. The annual dinner dances were great events, with speeches and singing and recitations. People got involved in training the under-age teams – it got people off the street corners, gave them a sense of purpose, and it was all voluntary. Like Macra, the GAA was great for teaching things like team spirit, leadership, and public speaking.'

In 2007, there are about 24,000 dairy farmers in the country. This is predicted to fall to around 10,000 by 2010. There will be fewer but bigger dairy farms. Frank witnessed the start of this process: 'When intensification came along, in the early 1970s, the traditional farm with fifteen cows scaled up rapidly to 50 or 60 cows, and at the same time the price of milk went up. The increase in farm income was enormous. And people used it very well, to raise their standards. From being very much the underdogs, farmers became people who were proud of themselves, who could afford comforts that they had never had before. It was wonderful to work through it, when I look back on the transformation.'

The change in farming methods also led to changes in the social life of farmers and their families. Like many people, Frank O'Keeffe has fond memories of old-style harvests and threshing days, when the whole community would get involved in turn in threshing on the neighbours' farms, the work rewarded with a communal meal and sing-song. 'It was a marvellous occasion, a lovely social occasion, and a great feeling of fulfilment, as the year was coming to a close, the days were getting shorter, and all the grain and straw were in for the winter.'

The communal threshing is a loss that seems to haunt Frank and others of his generation, and typify all that they regret in the modernisation of farming. We were talking in the midst of the haymaking season, a bad one, hot sunny spells alternating with thundery showers. Said Frank: 'I was watching a combine harvester yesterday, working out in a 45-acre field – a brand-new combine, cutting a swathe about 25 feet wide, one man sitting up on it, and another man driving alongside him with a trailer, and the grain was pumped from an arm on the harvester into the trailer. They never stopped to talk, they just kept going. Then a guy came in with a baler and baled all the straw. Three silent men were doing the work that used to be done by a whole crowd of people, in a wonderful festive atmosphere.'

There is silence down on the farm: no more gossipy visits to the creamery. No more harvest festivals, just three men in a field. No more fair days, up at crack of dawn to drive the herd to market, falling in with other neighbours along the way, with the long day of dealing followed by convivial hours in the pub; instead, there's a chipper outside the Bandon Mart. No wonder depression, suicide and alcoholism are rising among farmers; there is now a west Cork branch of the Samaritans advertising in local health centres.

The contrast between the bigger farms – concreted yards, gravel cattle tracks, bright new galvanised buildings, giant tractors, and specialised farm machinery – and the apparently abandoned smaller farms, with ramshackle half-ruined buildings, unmade approach roads, and untended land overrun by brambles and nettles, is a striking feature of the west Cork landscape.

Small farms in scenic areas are increasingly being sold off as holiday homes, or to hobby farmers, their owners moving to the new estates around Courtmacsherry, Bandon, Clonakilty, and Skibbereen. This trend seems set to continue, with projected farm numbers for west Cork by 2010 estimated at 2,300 full-time commercial farmers, 2,707 viable part-time farmers, and 2,757 non-viable farms, most of which will be managed under the Rural Environment Protection Scheme (REPS). The REPS phenomenon has meant that by 2007 about one fifth of the smaller farmers in west Cork were being paid to manage the land in an environmentally friendly way: many of those apparently semi-derelict farms are in fact being carefully managed to encourage wildlife and biological diversity.

The emphasis on productivity and efficiency that dominated the Common Agricultural Policy in the 1970s and 1980s has been succeeded by policies that reflect the need for sustainability and environmental accountability. Public indignation at the environmental damage being caused by overintensive farming coincided with changes in international trade agreements, until a point was reached at which it made more sense to dissolve the relationship between direct payments and production of milk, beef, pork or whatever – to 'decouple direct payments', as the jargon has it – and pay farmers to look after the environmental health of their land. A farmer who has a quota for raising beef cattle is now being paid a sum indexed to his quota *not* to raise beef cattle, greatly to the amusement of the urban community.

Pat McCarthy inherited a farm at Kilgobbin, near Ballinadee. He farms the 75 acres with the help of a REPS grant, but he does not live there – he now lives on another farm, belonging to his wife, 21 miles away near Dunmanway. There is a small barn, a concrete yard, a couple of stables, and several other stone buildings in disrepair. There is electricity and one tap with a hose. The house is rented to a Latvian who works in Bandon. Some of the land is rented out to a friend of mine who keeps a couple of horses there. In the winter a local farmer rents the barn and rears sucklers. Wheat is grown on a couple of other fields, and sometimes cattle are grazed. One year there were sheep. We call it 'the farm', and that is what it is, but it doesn't seem quite the right word, so far removed is it from the archetypal farm of old.

Pat, who has a degree in Dairy Science and a diploma in Environmental Studies, is also the Environmental Manager at Carbery (Milk Products) near Dunmanway. Like everyone in the farming community, he divides Irish farming into before and after Ireland's accession to the EU in 1973. The farm he inherited had no milk quota, so Pat went into suckler production, building up the numbers in order to get a suckler quota. His job at the time, as a manager with Bandon Co-op, took him frequently to England: 'The farmers in the UK thought all Irish farmers were just honing in on the EU subsidies: they grew grain, they milked cows, they raised cattle because of the subsidies. And they have a point. Irish farmers are very grant-conscious; they go into a thing for the grant. A lot of people are building slatted sheds they don't need at the moment, because there's a big grant.'

The REPS scheme has encouraged part-time farmers to do less, says Pat: 'It's made farming more laid-back. You're paid to be understocked. If you look around the country, you'll see a lot of empty farms and overgrown fields, fields going back to bogs.' I tell him I hate seeing this happen, that it seems such a waste to let good land revert to bad land, and he corrects me: 'Bogs are important for cleaning the water table.'

Pat has just sold a site near the road: 'Up to about ten years ago, anybody who sold a site was a bad farmer, and it was a shameful thing to do. But as sites got ludicrously expensive, a lot of farmers were advised by their accountants to sell a site, because it made financial sense. I took three years to get planning permission, but I've sold it now, for €200,000. I used to let that field for €160 an acre. The site is 0.6 acres, so that site was grossing €100 a year for letting, but now it will probably make about €9,000 a year in interest. Fair enough, if you hold on to everything, everything will get dearer, but with the interest I can make improvements to the farm, so it made sense to sell the site. When I got this farm in 1989, when the house was derelict, if I'd sold the whole lot then to pay off all the debts, I'd have been lucky to clear the same money I did with that site.'

Selling sites is a handy way for farmers like Pat to make money, but it still goes against the grain: 'When you've sold the site, the land is gone. There's been 700 years of occupation here, so it's in the blood. Most Irish people want to own their own land, and they don't want someone else owning what they once had. Part-time farmers will not sell to big farmers – nor will they work for other farmers.'

Pat is aware of the contradictions of the system, and he is not happy about them: 'The irony is that we're being paid not to produce food, while in other parts of the world people are starving for lack of food.'

I think back to the words of another farmer, Norman Steele, who had a more traditional experience: 'Farming is such an honourable profession. It makes a great life … It's a shame that it is disappearing.'

3

The Coast of West Cork Revisited

When I first discovered the coast of west Cork, I thought I had found paradise, like many others before me. It seemed to be a place of infinite delights, where time had stood still, waiting for me to come along and explore. I was in my late twenties when I graduated from dinghy sailing to 'real' boats: yachts, in which both your bum and your feet stay dry and you can spend the night aboard, travelling on the following day. Sailing for grown-ups. I did not realise it then, but I was being introduced to sail cruising on a stretch of water that is regarded by those who know their sailing as one of the finest cruising grounds in Europe.

There are few pleasures to equal sailing out of Kinsale Harbour in fair weather and heading west at the Old Head of Kinsale, with the prospect of several days' cruising ahead. As you sail along parallel to the coast, the boat is often accompanied by porpoises, playing silently around the bows. Seabirds are constant fine weather companions: gannets, comorants, and black guillemots, to be studied through binoculars. There is little commercial traffic: the occasional coaster, heading for Kinsale or Ringaskiddy, can be spotted steaming along the horizon. Sometimes there are one or two trawlers working singly or in pairs, but mainly there is sea and sky and plenty of both. From the sea, the land looks almost uninhabited. The coastline is dark green above slate or sandstone cliffs; the big landmarks west of the Old Head lighthouse are the headlands and rocks – Seven Heads, Galley Head (with another lighthouse), Toe Head and the Stags, the Kedges, and the Lot's Wife beacon, marking the entrance to Baltimore.

Many people are content to explore Roaringwater Bay and its islands, the Fastnet Rock, Barlogue Creek, and the lively villages of Baltimore, Schull and Crookhaven, never going beyond the Mizen Head, at the western extremity of Roaringwater Bay. People often used to say, 'I draw the line at the Mizen', as if to go further were to leave civilisation behind. Those comments reflect the fact that sailing the waters beyond the headland is suddenly less about simple fun – and more a test of concentration and skill. But the rewards are Bantry Bay, with good anchorages on Bere Island, and shelter in Berehaven and Glengarriff.

Glengarriff is where the Irish Cruising Club was founded, on July 13 1929, by a small flotilla of five yachts, cruising in company. One of these boats was skippered by Harry Donegan of Cork, a great yachtsman of his time, who edited the first edition of the book that is now the bible of this coast, *Sailing Directions for the South and West Coast of Ireland* (Irish Cruising Club, 2006). This began life as *The South and Southwest Coast*, the west coast being a far trickier and less hospitable place for small boats.

I've never owned a boat myself. When I did most of my sailing along this coast, I was very lucky in my friends, most of whom were much older than me and have now sailed on. They were easy-going, uncompetitive sailors, out for the sheer pleasure of it, not to show off or compete. Sailing was very much a male preserve, even in the late 1970s, and I soon found out that if I offered to be 'cook', I was usually welcome. Not much was expected of the cook: cold ham and tomatoes, with sliced white bread and butter, were acceptable at lunch or supper. Breakfast was traditionally a fry. On English boats, baked beans and spam were still in favour. Cup-a-soup had just been invented, and we thought it was brilliant. The sea air is great for sharpening the appetite.

My first 'long passage' was from Kinsale to Glandore, about three hours with a decent wind. People sailed by local knowledge, using visual landmarks rather than plotting a course, although they would of course carry the relevant charts and a well-worn copy of the *Sailing Directions*. GPS systems were still very expensive and not very reliable. The dominant opinion, especially among the old codgers, was that satellite navigation wouldn't catch on. All the boats I sailed on had a radio receiver, but not all had radio transmitters. Life jackets were always aboard, but it was considered sissy to wear one: I can remember using them only on English boats. Depth sounders and automatic logs were just being introduced, but I did several trips on an old nineteen-footer (about as small as an ocean-going yacht can get), which had nothing in the way of navigation equipment, or indeed 'facilities'. Instead of a toilet, it was 'bucket and chuck it', or cross your legs till you got ashore. Engines were unreliable: you could never be sure they would start when you wanted them, and they certainly could not be relied on to get you out of trouble. The nineteen-footer had an outboard, but one person I sailed with had bought a new fibreglass 23-footer, the nicest cruising boat he could afford, and was going to buy the engine the next year. Predictably, this being west Cork, he never got round to it. But we managed.

There was no marina between Kinsale and Dingle. Even now, there is only one, at Lawrence Cove on Bere Island. At the smaller ports, you just turned up and dropped anchor. There were seldom any moorings to be had. If the weather or the holding was in any way dodgy, you would lay a kedge, a second anchor, and always leave someone competent on board. There were alarming stories of boats dragging their anchor for miles out to sea, under bare poles, while the crew snored away below. Fog was a serious hazard, especially for those who didn't have a log. If it came down unexpectedly, you frantically tried to take sights with your hand-held compass before it closed in, so that you had at least a vague idea where you were.

Pubs loom large among the yachting fraternity, not just for the alcoholic beverages, but because they are warm and dry and you can stand up straight, something which is not possible in the saloon of a small boat. Also, a great deal of informal exchange of information goes on in the pub, and you learn of the whereabouts of friends and acquaintances on other boats. Yachtsmen tended to favour particular pubs in the coastal villages: Mr O'Brien at the Marine Hotel in Glandore; Bushe's Bar in Baltimore; Johnny Regan in Schull, a good old-fashioned pub where the bar came up to a standing man's nose; Mary Ann's in Castletownshend; and Nottage's in Crookhaven. These were places where people gathered late into the night, being well off the normal 'beat' of the enforcers of licensing laws. In Glengarriff, Doc Ryan's was the place to go, the owner being a great raconteur and a lover of practical jokes. Castletownbere – a busy fishing port with a big fleet, where Spanish, Catalan, French, and Breton were spoken on the quays – was different from the smaller ports of call, and made a welcome change. As well as shops, it also had a really great café–restaurant. We would talk all the way in of the T-bone steak and chips we were going to order in Murphy's Restaurant. In those days Castletownbere had over twenty bars, but for most yachtsmen there was only one place to go: MacCarthy's Bar, a family institution, provisioner to trawlers and sailors of all descriptions, which has since become famous worldwide.

I first sailed round the Fastnet Rock Lighthouse in August 1979, making a special detour en route from Baltimore to Cape Clear. There is an old belief that the Fastnet Rock sets sail every May Day, and if you're up early enough you can catch it on the move. Looking at the distant lighthouse through the refractions of a heat haze on a dead calm early morning, I could understand how this belief originated. In Cape Clear, we tied up alongside the quay, across from the place where the mailboat docks and, since there was no wind, we stayed on the island, sunbathing, swimming, and walking, using the boat like a caravan, as a place to sleep and cook. A week later I had to leave this heaven and go back to a basement flat in Pimlico. It was not the first time I had thought of moving to Ireland permanently, but this was the strongest impulse yet.

My self-pity evaporated on Wednesday 15 August, when one of my sailing companions rang me at crack of dawn, distraught. A gale had hit the boats in the Fastnet Race, causing an, as yet, unconfirmed toll of damage. I had heard the news on the radio, but it had not occurred to me that some of these boats were based in Cork and Kinsale, and were crewed by people I knew. My friend, Alex, knew far more of them. He had sat up all night at the marina, in the company of other sailors, listening to his friends' Mayday messages. At that stage he still did not know who had perished and who had survived.

One of the survivors, paediatric surgeon Barry O'Donnell, a former President of the Royal College of Surgeons of Ireland, wrote a short account of the race, which has become a classic of sailing literature (it was published in *The British Medical Journal*, Vol. 281, 20–27 December 1980). He was aboard his 37-foot production sailing cruiser, *Sundowner*, with an experienced crew of eight, including his two sons. All bar one, and the skipper, were under 26 years old. They had spent the previous week racing at Cowes in order to settle the boat, and set off confidently towards Land's End on the first leg of a race designed to take them as far south and west as the Fastnet Rock, around it, and back again to Plymouth.

The Fastnet race takes place every other year, and this was the eighteenth race since the inaugural one in 1925. It normally takes anything from about three days, depending on wind and sea conditions. Up until 1979 there had only ever been one race death. In 1979, 302 boats crossed the starting line, but only 85 finished. Barry O'Donnell was one of 194 boats that retired. Twenty-three boats were abandoned, five were lost, and fifteen people died. Another 173 people were taken on board other boats or rescued by helicopter.

The disaster was caused by a combination of factors, chiefly a sudden deterioration in weather, a deterioration so rapid that, because of its time slots, the BBC shipping forecasts failed to broadcast the serious gale warning it merited, although gale warnings did go out on other frequencies. Aboard *Sundowner*, the barometer was under close scrutiny. It began to fall off Land's End, and fell an unbelievable 40 millibars in 24 hours. A fall of one millibar an hour is dangerous, and this was double that rate. The experienced crew and skipper on *Sundowner* did not wait for a weather forecast to tell them to prepare for the worst. By 23.00 hours, *Sundowner* was heading for the open sea under bare poles (all sail taken down) and trailing warps (to slow her down). The fastest speed the boat recorded was sixteen knots; the boat's previous record was 9.9 knots. The wind reached a speed of 72 knots. According to O'Donnell, the darkness and the noise were the most terrifying aspects of the gale.

He attributes his boat's survival to three important decisions: not to abandon ship; to have someone on the helm all the time, rather than lash it; and to have all the crew wearing full safety gear – harnesses and life jackets, and a safety line when on deck. Many of those who perished did so because they abandoned ship for their life raft, when they would have had a far better chance of survival by staying with their boat. Inflatable life rafts were a relatively new piece of equipment, and it seems that people overestimated their usefulness. O'Donnell writes: 'Use the life raft after fire, explosion, or collision; otherwise stay with your boat.' Another mistake people made was to leave the cockpit hatch open to allay claustrophobia. O'Donnell points out that with the hatch closed, the saloon turns into a large air bubble, which will both keep you afloat, and help you to survive should the boat turn turtle.

He also points out that statistically the most dangerous 50 yards in the world are those you spend in your dinghy from the quay to the boat. Every year people are lost in the course of this passage. Most people who sail can name someone who has died that way, but very few of us know people who have died at sea in a big storm, unless it was the Fastnet Race of 1979.

Nine years before the Fastnet Race disaster, Peter Somerville-Large had been cycling along the back roads from Clonakilty to Allihies, via Bantry Bay, researching his classic travel book *The Coast of West Cork*. His account is especially valuable because it is a record of west Cork at the very start of the development of tourism. Most of the people he encountered along the road were elderly, and had sad tales to tell of neighbours who had emigrated – in one case an entire fishing village, Croagh, had disappeared, leaving only one old man to contemplate their ruined cottages. Somerville-Large notes that during the late 1960s, west Cork had started to benefit from tourism: 'After seeing it for the first time, many visitors return to buy houses with views of the sea, finding compensation in the beauty of their surroundings for wet weather and Ireland's expensive economy. Their presence is one of the few signs that the long era of stagnation which resulted in so many people leaving may conceivably be coming to a close.'

He was travelling at a time when emigration was still the only option for many people. The scarcity of people in the black-and-white photos taken by Somerville-Large recalls the emptiness of the picture of Main Street, Drimoleague, which I keep on my desk. There is nobody at all in his pictures of Glengarriff, nobody in the main street of Castletownbere, nobody at the Dursey Sound, just an upturned *namhóg*. The only kind of people who would choose this place for a holiday were people with a curiosity about a forgotten corner of Europe, and a liking for wilderness, solitude, and rain. Mr Somerville-Large, an old-fashioned type, cycled with an umbrella: the one thing that has saved west Cork from being overrun by mass tourism is its weather.

One measure of change since Peter Somerville-Large's bicycle journey is the present state of some of the larger buildings he mentions. Castlefreke, then an ivy-covered ruin, is now being painstakingly restored by descendants of the Lord Carbery who left it for Nairobi's Happy Valley in 1919. Kilcoe Castle, then a ruin described as being 'in an excellent state of preservation', is now a fully restored home. Dunboy House near Castletownbere, then a ruined shell grazed by cattle, opens in 2008 as a luxury hotel with timeshare suites. When I asked Peter Somerville-Large what he missed most about the old west Cork, he answered with one word: 'Ruins.'

Peter Somerville-Large's west Cork coast, as seen from a bicycle, ran from Clonakilty to Ardgroom, via Allihies. Today the most sought-after areas of coastal west Cork are Kinsale, Glandore, Castletownshend, Baltimore, and Schull, all good, sheltered harbours with attractive houses overlooking the sea, and a selection of characterful bars and (generally) expensive restaurants.

Anyone who knew Baltimore and Schull in the 1960s and earlier would be amazed at their transformation. Gerry Wrixon, former president of UCC, used to spend holidays with his uncle, Father Michael Cleary, who was the curate on Sherkin Island in the 1950s. He remembers being alone in Baltimore Harbour on a blue summer day, with his brother and his uncle, in a small boat fishing for mackerel, and wondering, even as a child, why there were not more people enjoying this idyll. Baltimore continues to be a favourite holiday base, but in July and August you will never find yourself alone. In the high season, about ten ferries share the harbour with two sailing schools, a sailing club, several line-fishing boats, two diving firms, a yacht charter company, a yachting sales and services company, and a thriving fleet of fishermen – as well as visiting yachts and thousands of other casual visitors.

As I travelled around Roaringwater Bay in the summer of 2007, I was increasingly aware of the presence of RIBs (Rigid Inflatable Boats), buzzing to and fro at great speed, as well as larger, very fast, fibreglass boats. The second marina in Kinsale is almost entirely occupied by the latter, which come in various sizes from medium to very big. I decided to do some research in the bar of the Kinsale Yacht Club, and I learnt the following: thirty years ago, mass-market power boats didn't exist; there were only motorboats that chugged along at an average of about five or six knots. Today you can do a steady 30 knots, given the right sea conditions, thus allowing you to nip down to Baltimore or Castletownshend for lunch. My informants, being yachtsmen, could not resist adding that the best part is missing in a motorboat, be it slow or fast. 'These boats have a place, but they are different. They are all about getting there. You miss the pleasure of the voyage by getting there too fast. What we go out for is the sailing, not the arrival.'

The boats are being managed like serviced apartments. Before arriving in Kinsale, you can arrange for the fridge to be stocked, the ice put in the ice-maker and the heating turned on if needed: 'All you do if you own a powerboat is step in, turn on the ignition, and out you go, you're at sea in two or three minutes. And the less experienced owners can go in convoy. You can get the benefit of sea-going experience while you are learning.' But the suspicion is that the novelty of owning a powerboat soon wears off. 'The truth is, we can see that they don't get used much. You know that saying about a boat: the two best days of owning a boat are the day you buy it and the day you sell it.'

Everyone at the Kinsale clubhouse agreed that there had been 'an explosion' in the number of RIBs in west Cork. Where once it had taken half an hour to sail from Schull to Heir Island, people were nipping across in their RIBs in minutes or, because of their shallow draft, casually going up to Ballydehob for a cappuccino. These days, the yachtsmen coming ashore in their dinghies were climbing across five or six RIBs in order to reach the pontoon at the pier in Schull. 'RIBs have outgrown the infrastructure, there are so many of them. They're sports cars on the sea. People get a bit of a feeling of well-being, because they have the wind in their face, they feel they've had an experience. Children love them, and older people find them exciting.'

The yachtsmen have also noticed that around Roaring-water Bay RIB-owning and holiday home-owning go together. The sheltered waters favour the nippy little boats, while their shallow draft means that rocks are not the hazard they are for keel boats. And, of course, everyone has GPS aboard their RIB, so they always know where they are. 'There is less palaver in going to sea in a RIB, less trouble than a sailing boat. You just hop in and go. But a quay needs a good slip with the RIB culture – they need to come out of the water regularly to be kept clean. People keep them there for the two or three weeks of the holiday, then take them home to their backyard.'

The retired film producer David Puttnam lives in a house with land running down to the Ilen River, not far from Baltimore, and keeps a semi-rigid inflatable in his boatshed. The main traffic on his completely unspoilt stretch of the river comes from the Skibbereen Boat Club, who glide silently past in their rowing skiffs. Talk of building a school for powerboat owners on the same stretch of the river has him seriously worried. 'I'm hyper-conscious about not being a NIMBY, but to have powerboats down here would be a nonsense. Anyone who writes about this place immediately refers to its tranquillity. The other day we saw our first kingfisher. West Cork has to decide how it's going to approach the twenty-first century; it will have to make up its mind what its Unique Selling Point is. If the USP is tranquillity, it will have to be protected against another way of life that could take over.'

The tranquillity referred to by Puttnam is epitomised by an ever-growing fleet of traditional wooden boats in Roaring-water Bay, carefully built replicas of local mackerel and lobster boats. This fleet celebrates its return to the water after the winter laying-up with the Baltimore Wooden Boats and Seafood Festival on the last weekend of May. It is early in the season for sailing, but the date is chosen to encourage people to push on with the maintenance and get the boats back in the water. I went to the festival in 2005, on a fresh, breezy Sunday morning. Crowds were milling around outside Bushes Bar looking out over the sheltered harbour as a cluster of small wooden boats with tan-coloured sails scudded past, lifting at the bow and heeling over until their leeward gunwale was awash as they raced against each other.

Nearby a marquee was put up for local food producers, who had combined with Baltimore's restaurants and bars in a Seafood Festival: a feast of oysters, mussels, langoustines, smoked salmon, smoked mackerel, and fresh fish, comple-mented by locally produced artisan foods.

The lobster boats – the smallest under sail that day – are lively craft: tough, uncompromising work-boats, with low gunwales designed for fishing, not leisure, but capable of a nifty turn of speed. They are light and manoeuvrable, perfectly balanced, but demanding skill of the helmsman. The mackerel boats, although bigger, are also fast, as speed was important in the old days: the sooner you got the fish into harbour, the better the price paid. The crews wear full oilskins, catching the tops off many a wave as the boats slap their way through the light swell across the wide harbour, then gybe dramatically around the markers with loud clunks and much flapping of sail.

The picture is strangely familiar, as if photographs of west Cork taken in the early twentieth century, featuring small wooden fishing boats, have suddenly been brought to life. In a way, that is exactly what has happened.

Races like these, hotly contested between working boats on a rare day of leisure, were highlights of local regattas up until the 1950s. Then changes in the fishing industry, chiefly the invention of affordable diesel engines, meant that many of the existing sail and oar-powered fishing smacks were converted to diesel, decked in, given a wheelhouse, and otherwise modified. As the wooden boats started to age and became uneconomic to repair, they were abandoned in muddy creeks and inlets and left to rot.

And there they would have stayed, lost, along with the lore and expertise that went with them, had it not been for a handful of enthusiasts who literally dragged the rotting bones of these wrecks out of the mud, just before they disintegrated entirely. In 1996, none of the mackerel smacks and lobster boats sailing in the 2005 Baltimore Wooden Boats Festival existed in a viable form, and their design and sail plan were on the verge of extinction. Though many more people were eventually involved, three key figures prevented their demise: all-round maritime enthusiast, Nigel Towse; traditional boat builder, Liam Hegarty, and local historian Cormac Levis.

Nigel lives on Sherkin Island where he runs a mussel farm. He has a background in boats and seafaring. Born in Bognor Regis, he spent time in Suffolk, where his interest in traditional wooden boats was first kindled. But it was music –

he plays the accordion – that brought him to west Cork. A self-taught shipwright, who admits to owning 'too many boats', Nigel first restored a traditional mackerel yawl, *An Rún* (the secret). *An Rún* and her sister ship, *Shamrock II*, owned by Liam Hegarty, were the first boats to resurrect a lost chapter of west Cork's sailing history. Both are exact replicas of the style of boat traditionally used by fishermen from Long Island, off Schull.

Liam Hegarty learnt traditional shipwrighting from his father, and he now runs Hegarty's Boatyard at Oldcourt, on the estuary of the River Ilen near Baltimore. Hegarty's Boatyard is a key element in the revival, providing the expertise to build wooden boats the old-fashioned way, with oak keels and frames, larch planking and stone for ballast. To walk into the boatyard is like going back a century in time. Boats are moored alongside stone-built sheds dating back perhaps 300 years. Whole tree trunks lie around, waiting to be sawn up. A rotting wooden hull has been there so long that beech saplings are growing up between its thwarts. In another stone barn, Fachtna O'Sullivan works with an adze on the hull of a wooden yacht, leaving the earth floor ankle-deep in wood shavings. It is a small business, with Liam, Fachtna, and two others permanently employed, and any number of contractors on site, depending on the jobs in hand. The main business is still the repairing and refitting of commercial fishing boats, wooden or steel. But when that goes quiet, the wooden boat work fills the gap.

Skibbereen schoolteacher Cormac Levis had been doing research into the much smaller Heir Island lobster boat, described in his book *Towelsail Yawls* (Galley Head Press, 2002). These 24-foot, gaff-rigged sailing yawls had been used from the second half of the nineteenth century up to the 1950s by the islanders, who travelled hundreds of miles between May and October every year in pursuit of lobster. The lobstermen slept and cooked aboard, throwing a 'tent' over the mast to create cover. The tent was *teabhal* in the local Irish dialect, pronounced like the English 'towel'. It could also be rigged as a spinnaker when running before the wind; hence the Heir Island boats' nickname, 'the towel-sail yawls'.

Because of the fragility of their boats, the lobstermen learnt to read the weather by what Cormac calls 'inherited wisdom', and their movements were watched carefully by settled communities and yachtsmen alike: if the lobster boats took shelter, bad weather was certainly on the way. It was a tough life, away for six or seven weeks at a time, shooting and hauling the pots all day long. The hardship of living on an open boat at the mercy of the elements for weeks is hard to imagine. Three men would cook, eat, and sleep on the little boats, fishing by day. And once they got wet, they stayed wet.

For boat owners and spectators alike, it is the link with the region's past that makes these boats so important. Says Nigel: 'They belong to west Cork, that's the thing. It's to do with heritage. If people just wanted a sailing boat, it wouldn't matter what they had, but if you have a house down here because you love the place, you're going to want a boat that has the same kind of connection with the place. You can look at pictures, read books, but to get your hands on a wooden boat in the same style, and be able to indulge yourself in that way, is a unique attraction. That is what this festival is about; it's about Baltimore and Roaringwater Bay and its maritime heritage.'

4

Living Offshore – The Islands

There are seven inhabited islands off the coast of west Cork, not counting the smaller privately owned islands. In Roaringwater Bay there are four islands with regular ferry services: Cape Clear, the only Irish-speaking island, 45 minutes from Baltimore by ferry; Sherkin Island, a ten-minute hop from Baltimore; and Heir Island and Long Island, with their own piers at Cunnamore and Colla respectively. Bantry Bay has Whiddy Island at the head of the harbour, between Bantry and Glengarriff, and Bere Island off the coast of the Beara peninsula – both accessible by car ferry. Finally, there is Dursey Island at the tip of the peninsula, reached by cable car. The islands' permanent population, which had been declining until the 1980s, is now steady and in some cases growing.

While Bere, Whiddy, and Dursey in Bantry Bay have little or no contact with each other, the islands of Roaringwater Bay have in common the use of Ballydehob as their traditional marketplace and fair venue, although each island has its own strong identity. The people were fishermen – mackerel or lobster – and small farmers, sometimes both. Cattle swam to the nearest mainland point, and from there were herded to market.

Like the rest of the country, the islands' populations peaked in the pre-Famine years: it is believed that land hunger in the years of potato dependence was responsible for the increase. At that time Cape Clear's population grew to around

2,000 and even the smallest, most inhospitable, islands were inhabited. The island communities did not die in such great numbers during the Famine as did the people on the mainland coast. The mainland people sold their boats during the first year of blight and could no longer fish. On the islands, the women and children lived on wild food (sorrel, sea kale, samphire, nettles, berries, seaweed) and shellfish, leaving the Indian meal – maize imported as a famine-relief food – for the men who had to work in order to earn Famine Relief. During the Famine, the population of Heir Island fell from 358 to 288, at a time when whole villages were being decimated on the Mizen Peninsula.

After the Famine, new houses were built on the islands by the Congested Districts Board, and most islands had a National School. The populations remained steady until the early twentieth century, in spite of stories of people being forced to move to the mainland by priests afraid of what people might get up to on the smaller, churchless islands. Long Island, for instance, had a population of about 300 up until the First World War. But it was economic stagnation that kept people living there: few seem to have had any sentimental attachment to their island homes. Long Islanders were given the choice, in the 1950s, between continuing to live on the island, or being re-housed nearby on the mainland at Colla: most people chose the latter option, a fact that will not surprise anyone familiar with the long, dark, west Cork winters. There are now only five people living on the island: even the ferryman, John Shelley, prefers to live on the mainland.

The island schools started to close in the 1970s. While Cape Clear and Sherkin still have National Schools, the island children must move to the mainland from Monday to Friday for secondary education. Whiddy and Bere are close enough to towns with secondary schools for the children to go in daily by ferry.

The introduction of a higher standard of living on the mainland made people less inclined to stay on the islands.

Women didn't want to marry into an island-based family, or stay on an island where they didn't have mod cons. Those who stayed tended to be elderly or unmarried, or both. Incomers from other parts of Ireland and abroad started to arrive at the same time that the schools were closing, and they have been largely responsible, along with returning natives, for the reversal of population decline. A surprising number of blow-ins who have moved to live on the islands have taken root. Islands attract a particular kind of person, independent and resourceful: people who recognise their like-minded neighbours, perhaps without ever acknowledging the fact.

Cape Clear is different from the other islands in that it is bigger, it is further from the mainland, and it is officially Irish-speaking. Most first-time visitors to Cape Clear, the furthest island offshore, sit white-knuckled, while the mailboat helmsman, always an O'Driscoll, casually steers full steam ahead through a narrow passage between exposed peaks of sharp black rocks, all the while catching up on the local news, *as Gaeilge*, with his passengers. I always remember a story told by John M. Feehan, the founder of the Mercier Press, and a keen single-handed yachtsman. He was being piloted through a tricky patch between Heir Island and the Skeames by a local boatman, and he asked his pilot if he was sure he knew where all the rocks were. 'I'm not sure I knows where the rocks is,' the pilot answered, 'but I bloody well knows where they isn't.'

Cape is the most southerly point of Ireland, about three miles long by one mile across. When I first visited in 1978 it had one pub, a grocery, a youth hostel, the bird observatory, and a couple of B&Bs. Now it has a selection of B&Bs and holiday homes, a campsite, a Heritage Centre, the Cape Clear Co-op, several craft outlets, and a Tourist Information Office, indicating the importance of visitors to the island's economy. In high summer the population swells to around

500, peaking at around 1,200 on August Bank Holiday week-end, not counting day-trippers. Two summer colleges attract Irish language students and there can be 100 tents in the campsite on a busy weekend, while yachts anchor in both the south and north harbours. Séamus O'Drisceoil, a former manager of the Co-op (founded in 1969) and an active promoter of the west Cork islands, is reluctant to quote a figure for the winter population: 'The winter population figure of around 130 is a worst possible case scenario, as it excludes people who are frequent visitors and regard Cape as their home: people who have family on the island and strong connections, but, for whatever reason, have to work on the mainland and keep a base there too.' There are about a dozen children of secondary school age on the island, who go to Rosscarbery as weekly boarders.

It's a good place for walking, easily explored in a day, and a local guide can be hired in advance. An alternative option is *Walks of Seven West Cork Islands* by Damien Enright (Merlin Press, 2005), a book written at the request of the authority promoting the islands to make visitors aware of the their quiet attractions. Cape Clear has, for example, a ruined O'Driscoll castle, Dún an Óir, and several standing stones, in addition to the places associated with St Ciaran – his well, and the remains of his church – which are visited on his Saint's Day, 5 March. Cape Clear's antiquities give it the feeling of having been inhabited for a very long time, and it is also rich in folklore. The views of the surrounding bay and the other islands are endlessly beguiling, and a constant challenge to one's powers of orientation, since the other islands all look different from different angles. The one thing you can be sure of getting right is the Fastnet Rock, with its lighthouse off on the horizon, fourteen miles to the southwest.

The Bird Observatory, founded in 1959, was the first in Ireland. Cape Clear often reports the arrival of large flocks of migrants, and rare birds sometimes arrive, having been blown off course, in their turn attracting 'twitchers', who thrive on such events. There is also a goat farm with a shop selling yoghurt, ice cream, and other goats' milk products. The owner, Ed Harper, is an Englishman, resident on the island since 1979. He has not let his blindness hinder him from rearing goats, and until recently he used to run courses, to pass on his expertise.

Most island people make a living from several different jobs – fishing, building, bartending, working on the mailboat, on the roads for the County Council, for the Post Office, or the Co-op. The mailboat takes 45 minutes each way, to Baltimore and back, but there is a faster boat that can do the trip in 30 minutes and is scheduled to allow people to commute to work on the mainland. But Séamus O'Drisceoil reports that more and more people are working from home on the island, which has two competing sources of broadband. He says: 'We've had broadband in the school and the Health Centre since 1999. Like everywhere else, the computer has become an ever more important part of people's working day. People who wouldn't have considered themselves teleworkers are now spending more and more time at the computer.' Internet and broadband have been important in attracting incomers who can bring their jobs with them to the island. There are two translators working in French, and one Irish-language translator. A fourth was lured away to Brussels. Another couple work from home offering computer support and software.

An excellent account of life on Cape Clear in recent years, *Cape Clear Island Magic* (The Collins Press, 1994), has been written by Chuck Kruger. Born in 1938, he moved there with his wife, Nell, in 1992, having impulsively plunged all their life savings into the purchase of a small farm on the island. Both had an epiphany the first time they took the ferry to Clear. They found themselves in tears, in spite of the fact that they were talking to other people at the time – they had simultaneously recognised Cape Clear as a place where they could die. Chuck comments, 'I should add that neither of us is particularly anxious to die, nor are we particularly lachrymose.' It was a third life for the Krugers, who had started out as high school teachers in Philadelphia and St Louis, then moved to Switzerland to study psychology at the C. G. Jung Institute in Zurich, where they lived for 22 years. On Cape Clear, Kruger fulfilled a long-standing ambition to become a full-time freelance writer and poet. The island has been his chief inspiration, and he has repaid it by recording not only its myths and legends, but also the rare quality of its everyday life. He sums up the advice he was given by islanders on moving permanently to Cape: 'Learn to do things for yourself, to be independent, self-reliant: then you will survive the rigours of the island – and be able to appreciate its peace.'

Sherkin Island, only a ten-minute ferry ride from Baltimore, is sheltered and very pretty, with narrow fuchsia-lined lanes and a choice of big sandy beaches. It has a strong appeal to incomers, many of them followers of an alternative or artistic lifestyle: long skirts, face jewellery, long hair, and beards abound. The number of full-time residents has risen from 83 in 1997 to around 140 in 2007. (Before the Famine about 1,200 people lived on Sherkin.) The usual collection of island cars are parked on the quay: rusty old bangers, held together by baler twine, that travel the twelve miles of road. Cars kept for island use are exempt from the NCT, but many residents choose not to have a car, just a bicycle. Shop-owner Mark O'Neill is generous with lifts on his tractor, when holiday-home owners with their bags arrive for the season. In the case of thriller writer Julie Parsons and her husband, John Caden, the luggage includes two howling cats in a travel basket. John and Julie, who live in Dun Laoghaire, have spent several years restoring a traditional farmhouse, 40 minutes on foot from the pier, and are both passionate about the island.

Other visitors are drawn to Sherkin because of its Marine

Station. An independent enterprise, set up in 1975 by Matt Murphy and his late wife, Eileen, generations of students have spent time at the Marine Station, working as volunteers between April and November in return for their board and a small allowance. The Station, which occupies sixteen acres in the northwest of the island, carries out long-term monitoring surveys of the shoreline's flora and fauna, and publishes educational books for children and adults.

Like Cape Clear, Sherkin has benefited from the European policy of using communication technologies to overcome the disadvantage of peripheral location. In 1999 a study entitled *The Southwest Islands Telecommunications Hub – Exploring a Joint Technology Strategy* (Sherkin Island Development Society) was launched. The report recommended establishing a system of accredited computer-skills training for islanders, and the promotion of flexible part-time employment opportunities to complement existing, seasonal employment patterns. Already islanders were studying for their European Computer Driving Licence (ECDL) on public computers in the Community Hall and there was a demand for an e-commerce solution for the island, offering online ferry and accommodation bookings. There was also, more unusually, a demand for a distance-learning programme in art. The programme was to be piloted in partnership by the Sherkin Island Development Society (SIDS) – chaired at the time by Liam Chambers – and the Dublin Institute of Technology (DIT), represented by John O'Connor, Head of the School of Art, Design and Printing.

The artistic community at Sherkin was certainly growing and two people in particular were catalysts for growth: Majella O'Neill Collins (also known as Madge), an artist with a BA from Limerick School of Art, who had married into the island and had been giving art classes to her neighbours for some years; and Bernadette Burns, artist and lecturer at DIT, who has a home on Sherkin. Madge, a forceful, warm-hearted character, nicknamed 'Queen of Sherkin', was already making a good living from her large oil paintings of the sea, inspired by the view from her Sherkin studio. One of her pupils, Kordula Packard, a former choreographer from Germany, had started marketing her landscapes and still-lifes on the Internet and opened The Packard Gallery in her house in the summer. A well-established Danish abstract artist, Claus Havemaan, has a home on Sherkin, and takes part in the island's summer show. Islander Seán O'Neill produces accomplished abstracts, and Scottish artist, John Simpson, reinvented himself in mid-career by moving to Sherkin in 1998. Artists F. X. Murphy, Jo Jeffreys, and Jo Ashby are also considered part of Sherkin's artistic community.

The three-year distance-learning programme in Art and Culture combined live teaching with video-conferencing, email, and web communication, to give people access to an accredited course while holding down jobs and living in their own homes and communities. It has attracted international interest among academics. In the first three pilot years, students spent a minimum of 30 days on the island each year. Seventeen people completed the three-year programme, which was marked by an exhibition at the West Cork Arts Centre in 2003. There was then a hiatus, partly caused by an arsonist burning down the Community Hall and destroying all its computers, and partly by tensions between the community and its development society.

Happily, in 2007, a four-year degree programme in visual arts was validated by DIT, and John O'Connor is now organising the delivery of its final year to those who have completed the three-year pilot course. So far, fourteen of the seventeen original students, many of whom are already exhibiting and working in arts centres, have confirmed they will take up the option of completing their BA. People came from all around west Cork to take part, including John Desmond, the chef from Heir Island; Nigel Towse, boatbuilder and mussel farmer on Sherkin; Geoff Stephens, who looks after the Office of Public Works' properties on Sherkin; Lorraine Bacchus, from Dunbeacon, Durrus, co-director of the West Cork Literary Festival; and Gill Good, an artist who rents out guest accommodation in Ballinadee, near Bandon. Sherkin's artists show their work every summer in the Community Hall and usually at a mainland venue too.

Heir Island is pronounced 'hare', but not because of any association with the Irish hare, *Leptus timidus hibernicus*. Its name in Irish is *Inis Uí Drisceoil* and it was named for the heir of the O'Driscolls, to whom it belonged at one time. Heir is only minutes from Cunnamore Pier, about ten minutes south of Skibbereen, down a narrow, windy boreen. It is reputed to have a sunnier microclimate than the neighbouring mainland: they say you can sit in the sun on Heir and watch it rain on Schull. The summer population of about 120 goes down to about 30 in winter, and these people inhabit only ten of the island's approximately 50 houses.

I first went to Heir to go to dinner in its renowned restaurant, Island Cottage: a tiny place, but so popular that people book weeks in advance. The friends who invited me make a pilgrimage every year, driving the hour and a half from Kinsale to Cunnamore Pier for the 8 p.m. ferry (which is run especially for restaurant patrons), returning to the mainland again around 11.30 p.m., and driving back home. It has to be a very special meal to be worth all that trouble, and it is. The chef, John Desmond, has had a long career and taught at La Varenne cookery school in Paris. His partner, Ellmary Fenton, is an experienced restaurant manager.

On arrival, you can enjoy the sea view from the cottage's conservatory. Ellmary serves a four-course set menu (no choices) featuring local produce, including wild food from the island. We dined on marinated wild salmon, roast duck leg with *gratin dauphinois*, tossed green salad with French dressing, and Gubbeen cheese. Then there was a slight delay, during which we could hear a metal whisk at work in the kitchen before being rewarded with a hot Grand Marnier crêpe soufflé with blackcurrant *coulis*, as good as any to be had in the finest establishment in Paris. At the end of the meal, the diners rose as one and applauded, while the chef, in full whites, made a brief appearance.

I was surprised to discover that I knew the ferryman, John Moore, who took us over to Heir Island. Back in the early 1980s, we were neighbours in Kinsale. He was Mister Corporate Career then, commuting every day in a suit, while his beautiful wife, Patricia, looked after the two babies. I knew they had a house on Heir Island, because they disappeared there for most of the summer, but the last I'd heard John had been promoted and they had moved to Galway city. Now here he was, working on a ferry, the *MV Thresher*. What on earth had gone wrong?

When I eventually caught up with John and Patricia, I discovered it was more a question of what had gone right. John had bought the house on Heir in 1971, when he was in his early twenties, before he married Patricia in 1979. They never missed a Christmas in the house on the island, and John had always wanted to live on Heir full-time. He saw his opportunity when the islander operating the ferry and the shop wanted to retire due to failing eyesight. John and Patricia were already building a sailing school and converting a pair of existing houses.

In order to keep an income coming in, Patricia took over as postmistress, a not very onerous job that came with the shop, while John took over the ferry in partnership with Richard Pyburn, a resident of Heir, whose family came to west Cork to work in the copper mines several generations back. Both sons have now left home, so Patricia has no more school runs, but she still makes regular trips to the mainland. 'You have to get off every now and then, or you go a bit strange,' she says. What pleases John is that the sailing school allows them to make a living, but is completely compatible with the very special environment of the island. Not only that, but their home is as comfortable and stylish a place as you would find anywhere in Ireland. It just has better views.

Day trip to Heir Island, 12 August 2007

I accidentally run into a friend, Daphne Daunt, on the three-minute ferry ride to Heir Island in August 2007. Daphne and her family have had a cottage on Heir for 21 years. Her summer break has been interrupted by trips back to the city, but she is able to travel with just a small handbag, because she has everything she needs in the cottage.

Daphne keeps a wheelbarrow at the quay for luggage and shopping. Her daughter, who is accompanied by her small child, has an overnight bag and a box of fresh food. The cottage is only a five-minute walk, and Daphne invites me for coffee. The one-storey cottage is small inside, with low ceilings and attic bedrooms at either end. As much as possible of the original tongue-and-groove interior has been retained and painted in off-white and Wedgwood blue. The main room runs right across the house and so has windows facing both north and south. There is a wood-burning stove for winter evenings and plenty of books. When I leave to go for a walk round the island, Daphne tells me to drop in if I need anything, or if it rains: 'Even if we're not here, the door will be on the latch.' Her daughter adds, resignedly, 'If it rains, we'll be here.' There are only three things to do on Heir, according to Daphne's daughter, who spent all her childhood holidays here: go for a walk, go to the beach, or, if it rains, read.

When I walk down to the nearest beach two RIBs are arriving, laden with squealing kids and picnic gear. The profusion of wild flowers is remarkable. There are small blue butterflies, wrens in the hedges, shags drying their wings on the rocks offshore, and some cattle beyond the bridge which I know is called 'Paris' by the locals (probably a corruption of 'pallace', or fish palace, a building in which oil was extracted with large presses during the pilchard fishery in the late eighteenth century). A couple of families are still farming, and there is one fisherman's cottage, marked by nets, fish boxes, and all sorts of flotsam and jetsam. The other houses are all well-maintained holiday homes, most with expensive patio furniture. I pass a building with a plaque: Heir Island School, 1900. It closed in 1976, and sat vacant for many years. Through its tall windows I can see the heads of a family of holidaymakers, sitting down to Sunday lunch.

I pass a large white bull, in among a herd of cows, and two fields with donkeys and foals. I spot the sire in a field on his own, looking over a wooden gate. I see donkeys as a good sign on an island, ever since I read about the day they took the last pair of donkeys off Inisheer in the Aran Islands. They were removed to facilitate the increased traffic at the airstrip, where they used to graze. There are no airstrips on the west Cork islands.

I walk right to the end of Heir, the Dún, which takes about 40 minutes. The absence of traffic noise makes me feel light-headed, disoriented. As I walk, the clouds clear away and the sun appears. The road is more grass than tarmac, then, beyond a stile above an impressive vertical 60-foot cliff, the path disappears into a carpet of low-growing flowers.

The usual Roaringwater Bay game of 'spot the island' begins: there is one opposite, with long sandy beaches, but is it Horse Island or Castle Island? I can identify the white beacon at Baltimore, the back of Sherkin, Cape Clear looking much closer than it should, the Fastnet Lighthouse apparently floating on the horizon, the white sails of a regatta fleet racing out of Schull. Sea and sky are a deep blue. I have rediscovered the time warp, a quiet world, peaceful and remote, where time seems to move more slowly: the old west Cork.

I find a soft, heathery place at the end of the island, looking down on the Skeames and the Gascanane Sound. As I unpack my sandwich, a couple of walkers turn up, and sit down directly above me, so that their hiking boots are only inches from my head.

'Sorry,' says the man. 'Won't be long.'
English.

Whiddy Island in Bantry Bay acquired a new passenger ferry in 2007, the *Ocean Star*. Ferryman Tim O'Leary bought it from the O'Malleys of Clare Island, County Mayo. His Yorkshire terrier, Lucky, goes with him back and forth. Like all the island ferries, it is subsidised to make it viable, as there are only about sixteen people left on the island. Others come from the mainland to work at the oil terminal. The land is rented out to off-islanders for grazing cattle. Tim, who is from an old island family, is hoping the faster, more comfortable boat will tempt day-trippers out from Bantry. He is advertising an evening cruise around the harbour and trips around Whiddy. Attractions on the island include the Bank House (a simple pub–restaurant), an overgrown tennis court, and a concrete crazy golf course that has seen better days. The quay has a vandalised car and a couple of dead bicycles. The best walk leads to the lake, but I opt instead to walk to the back of the island to look at the oil depot, part of the national oil reserve. These are the tanks that can be seen from the road as you drive between Bantry and Glengarriff. Apart from one spectacular field of purple loosestrife and orange montbretia, it is an awful walk, parallel to a tall chain-link fence topped with barbed wire, the air permeated with the smell of diesel, and signs advertising the presence of Bantry Bay Terminal CCTV.

I wanted to see the oil tanks up close because of the *Betelgeuse* disaster. In 1967 the availability of deep-water anchorage in the shelter of Bantry Bay, one of Europe's largest harbours, led Gulf Oil to establish an oil terminal at the western end of Whiddy Island, large enough to accommodate giant supertankers. It opened in 1970, functioning as the transatlantic landfall for European energy supplies, and was meant to herald a new era of prosperity, not just for Bantry, but also for Ireland as a whole. Crude oil was to be shipped from Whiddy by smaller tankers to Gulf's refineries in the UK and continental Europe. The French tanker *Betelgeuse* caught fire at the jetty on Whiddy Island on 8 January 1979, resulting in a huge explosion that caused the deaths of 41 crewmen on the *Betelgeuse*, one of their wives, and eight local workers at the terminal. A Dutch diver died later during the salvage operation. Nowadays, Conoco Phillips maintains a single mooring point offshore at the terminal, capable of handling vessels of up to 300,000 tons, and there is a jetty where smaller ships can discharge.

In the wake of the disaster, attempts were made to develop a mussel industry in Bantry, which has been moderately successful. One of west Cork's leading businessmen pointed out to me a couple of years ago that, while mourning the loss of life entailed, we should really be thankful for the *Betelgeuse* disaster, because it was the last time anyone tried to introduce heavy industry in this region. The lack of such industry, and the unspoilt scenery of west Cork, have been key factors in the area's new prosperity.

Bere Island is about seven miles long by about three miles wide and runs parallel to the eastern coast of Beara. I took the ferry over from Castletownbere and met the ferryman, Colm Harrington. He tells me that a lot of native islanders are coming back to Bere and building, with an eye to retiring there. Maeve Harrington (no relation) is another ferry passenger that day. She works in Germany and spends five or six months a year in her house on the island. 'Ryanair is a great thing,' she says of her lifestyle. 'It isn't everybody who'd come back to a place like this. People find it lonely. They miss the noise and the lights. It gets very dark in the winter.' Maeve and her friend, Phil Harrington (no relation), are off to Dursey Island for a day trip.

'Why so many Harringtons?' I ask Colm.

'We're all Vikings!' he says. He's a huge, chunky man, with a good-natured smile. But even so, I refrain from telling him the story I heard from a man who does the live commentary at Gaelic games. He was covering a football game on Beara up near Allihies and was familiarising himself with the names of the players before the match. To his horror, every player on both teams was either a Harrington or an O'Sullivan.

Colm inherited the job of ferryman from his father, who did it the hard way, in an open boat. The key to Colm's contentment is the fact that his new ferry, bought in 2005 from the Hebrides, is big enough to take a large lorry: 'Before it was a day's work to bring in a lorryload. Now animals are transported in lorries, and building materials go in lorries: we can bring in ten lorries a day. I've a load of ready-mix concrete coming in later.'

Sure enough, I pass it on the road on my way back to Bantry.

Bere and Whiddy are different from the other islands, because they were British army bases. Maeve told me that her grandfather, who died recently aged 95, was one of the first Irishmen to know the rules of soccer, because it was a garrison game: 'They laid out a golf course too, and a rugby pitch. The army kept the island very anglicised, but they also created a lot of employment.'

Bere Island, with about 210 residents, is a friendly, welcoming place, where the values of a bygone era prevail. People waiting to travel over on the ferry leave their shopping and their bicycles unattended on the boat, while they see to other business in town, knowing there is no petty crime. While accessible by car ferries at both east and west ends, Bere Island has all the good characteristics of an island, with thriving wildlife, and peace and quiet. There are two villages (each with a bar), beaches, walks on the Beara Way, a cycling route, and old army batteries and barracks to explore. There is plenty of simple accommodation and very few tourists. Best of all, there are people to talk to, who are still curious about strangers, and introduce you around. Some have deep roots; quite a few are incomers, older and more conventional than the people who have settled on Sherkin. One couple from Wicklow intended to move to Adrigole, but changed their mind and settled on Bere Island instead. They said it was less isolated and more of a community.

I too was impressed by the strong sense of community spirit. Everyone I met wanted to tell me about West Cork Rural Transport, and what a difference it had made to the older people. Thanks to this initiative, the island has a minibus, and every Friday it calls to the front door of all the older folk to take them in to Castletownbere to do their shopping. They don't even need to get off the minibus: it drives on to the ferry, and ten minutes later it drives off again, and delivers them to the door of the supermarket. And when it is time to go home, the minibus returns them to their front door. 'Old people love living on an island,' Phil Harringon explained. 'They are happy to be surrounded by water because if gives them a sense of safety.'

5

Losing our Head – Environmental Activism

The headland known as the Old Head of Kinsale had been open to the public as far back as anyone can remember, even though most of the land was a privately owned farm. The road running from the fourteenth century de Courcey castle to the black and white lighthouse on the tip of the rocky promontory was a famously bracing walk – the best hangover cure I ever found. But the public is no longer allowed to walk there. Now you will find that the Old Head Golf Links, one of the most expensive golf courses in Ireland, affords its unique cliff-top location and magnificent views to paying visitors only.

I still walk the public road out to the monument commemorating the sinking of the *Lusitania* off the Old Head in 1916. Sometimes a visitor stops me and asks why there is no access to the headland, where the golf course is. It's hard to know what to say, although I vividly recall the sequence of events leading to loss of public access. The Old Head was classified as an Area of National Scientific Import-ance and as an Area of Visual and Scenic Importance in the County Development Plan (1986). In 1978 the Office of Public Works issued a Preservation Order for the promontory fort and castle, under the National Monuments Act. An Foras Forbartha listed the Old Head as an outstanding landscape in the National Heritage Inventory. But when it came to a big commercial investment, none of this counted for anything.

When I saw 230 acres of land advertised for sale at the Old Head in the late 1980s, I remember that it struck me as odd: it's not the sort of place you'd think anybody owned, individually. The road the public walked did not form part of the property for sale: it belonged to the Commissioners for Irish Lights. Local residents believed that because we had always walked it, it was a traditional right of way. In fact, Irish Right of Way law, unlike its English equivalent, is virtually non-existent.

The land was the property of a local farmer, Michael Roche, though this fact was little known outside the immediate area. It was rough, exposed land, and with all the visitors (an estimated 200,000 a year), it was not much use for anything. According to an interview he gave to journalist Mary Leland in July 1992, Michael Roche said he had asked Bord Fáilte to consider buying it, but they refused. The Office of Public Works declined to offer for it, and the offer made by Cork County Council was so low that it could not be taken seriously. In 1990 John O'Connor, of Ashbourne Holdings Ltd, bought the site. At the time no planning permission was required for a golf course, but permission was needed for a clubhouse. When this was granted by Cork County Council, the Cork branch of An Taisce (of which I was then Honorary Secretary) decided to make an appeal against the decision to An Bord Pleanála.

John O'Connor, the chief partner in the Old Head of Kinsale Golf Course, a Kerryman who had made his fortune in property development in the USA, initially reassured the public that access would continue. However, Mr. O'Connor changed his mind. He barred public access from the very start and took the matter of the public right of way to the High Court and on to the Supreme Court where, in 2005, after a ten-year legal process, he secured a ruling that there never was a public right of way on the Old Head of Kinsale.

Losing our Head – Environmental Activism

The Friends of the Old Head was formed in summer 1992. Although the group was poorly funded, archaeologists, historians, writers, artists, and environmentalists rallied to the cause. A meeting held at Acton's Hotel, Kinsale, in September 1992 was attended by over 300 people and revealed a clear division between those who opposed the golf course and those who supported it. Opponents were generally professionals based in or around Kinsale town, many of them incomers. Not a single commercial venture in Kinsale came out against the golf course, but neither did they support it. Those in favour of the golf course were from the farming community in the Old Head–Ballinspittle area, and they were adamant that you couldn't stop progress. They stood at the back of the hall, banging their sticks on the floor, stamping their feet, and chanting 'Michael Roche must get his money'.

This polarisation was sharp and uncomfortable. Both sides were motivated by their passion for a place, but one side saw a commercial development as a benefit and felt strongly that a local farmer should be allowed to sell his land if he wished. The other saw only the loss of a unique, unspoilt environment and much-loved amenity – an amenity which, in fairness to Mr. Roche, had only been made available through his granting of access over the years, though hardly anybody knew that fact.

The golf course is a commercial success. From March to October it claims to employ 250 people: for the rest of the year it is closed, but says it employs 100 people. Desmond O'Grady's poem, 'The Old Head Said to Me', was written at the time and he closes with this thought:

> A country that will not preserve for its people
> the heritage it fought to recover from the usurper
> does not merit the title of nation.
> *That's what the Old Head said.*

❖

Fortunately, the other headlands of west Cork have managed to retain public access, often thanks to landowners like Michael Roche, who quietly ensure that traditional access is perpetuated. The Beara Way is a 196 km waymarked path, running from Glengarriff to Dursey Island, via Bere Island and Castletownbere, and back up the northern coast of Beara to Kenmare. It passes through some impressive coastal and mountain scenery, and much of it is off-road. Since opening in 1998, it has attracted numerous visitors to the area. It was developed by Beara Tourism, in an initiative led by Jim O'Sullivan. As a former telecoms linesman for the area, he knew the territory. Jim stresses that the path exists only through the kind permission of the landowners. Like everyone involved with waymarked paths, he welcomed the Minister for the Environment's 2007 confirmation that farmers will receive a monetary acknowledgement for their co-operation in strimming, checking markers, and looking after stiles on the routes. 'It's going to make life much easier. Landowners are like any other group of people: some are easier to deal with than others.' About ten people are employed on path maintenance through a LEADER scheme, but Jim says this is nothing in comparison to the financial spin-off to the wider community in terms of the walking route's ability to attract visitors to the area.

The Sheep's Head Way near Bantry was set up by a farmer, James O'Mahony of Kilcrohane, who also enjoys walking, and opened in 1996. Its character is summed up by the words from Seamus Heaney's poem, 'Peninsula', whose last line is inscribed on a bench near the Peakeen Loop: 'Water and ground in their extremity.' The path goes right out to the lighthouse at the tip of the peninsula, past glacial rocks strewn over the coarse grass, a spot so remote that it can give you the shivers – not from the cold, but from its 'extremity', as the poet noted. James O'Mahony explains why he got involved: 'We developed the Way to keep the old paths open – bog paths, burial paths, school paths, fishermen's paths – the rights of way to the sea. We wanted to preserve the past before we had too many foreigners who put up 'Do Not Enter' signs on paths which have always been open.'

The area around Kilcrohane, towards the narrow tip of the peninsula, has wide-open sea views and attractive stone-built farmhouses, most of them painted white. There are hardly any local farmers left out there at all: nearly all the houses are owned by incomers.

The Sheep's Head Way has not had the problems with people blocking off paths or demanding payments for access that have beset other waymarked paths in Ireland. James O'Mahony comments: 'The Sheep's Head Way is a success because farmers, landowners, and local people developed it: and people are proud of it: they feel it is their own.'

The Seven Heads Millennium Walk from Timoleague through Courtmacsherry to Travarra Strand, a seashore walk of about ten miles, is smaller in scale, and is the result of a community effort. The main sponsors were Barryroe Co-op and West Cork LEADER, but there was a big input from the local community in terms of voluntary work over several years. This was the project for which birdwatcher and ceramic artist Peter Wolstenholme designed information plaques. Other members of the local community gave financial support or physical help, forming work parties. The chairman of the Seven Heads Walk Committee was Michael Holland (born at Kilsillagh, Butlerstown, in 1919, now deceased; also a founder member of the Barryroe Co-op). He was a man of unusual vision, and was conferred with an honorary Master's Degree at UCC in 2002, in recognition of his exceptional contribution to the community.

It was the granting of permission for a bungalow at a hitherto undeveloped site on the seashore near Allihies that turned Tony Lowes into an environmental activist. Tony Lowes was one of the first incomers to settle in the hills near Allihies at the tip of the Beara peninsula. He was born in New York into a wealthy family and studied at Trinity College, Dublin. Around 1968 he bought a dilapidated farmhouse and a few acres at Cod's Head on Beara, with superb views of the sea and rugged cliffs. There he met and married Christa, a weaver from California. Together, they raised five children, living without electricity by choice. It was not until 1991, when Tony's elderly mother came to live with them, that they hooked up to the national grid. Overnight the family went from Tilley lamps to satellite TV and Tony went online.

Tony Lowes formed a west Cork branch of An Taisce in 1990. From his remote base on the Cod's Head Peninsula near Allihies, he did much to radicalise An Taisce. At one point, property developers in the local business community decided to take on An Taisce West Cork by joining it, and using the democratic process to outvote those who were rejecting their planning applications. Someone described them to me at the time as 'a crowd of pint-drinkers in bad suits'. Head office in Dublin found a way within An Taisce's constitution to annul their memberships owing to conflicting interests.

Tony has since become the founder of the Irish Environmental Network. This was incorporated into the Friends of the Irish Environment, which was founded in 1997. Its specific aim is to use existing EU law to campaign on environmental issues in this country. 'Before we came along, no one referred cases to the European Court of Justice for advice,' he explains. Lowes makes submissions and appeals on behalf of local groups who lack such expertise. Christa sadly died in 2004, but Tony has remarried. He and his wife, Caroline Lewis, are also involved in the Irish Natural Forestry Foundation, doing the back-room paperwork for complicated challenges to the Irish government's interpretation of EU law on forestry grants.

❖

Ian and Lynn Wright are classic blow-ins, having been simultaneously self-sufficient smallholders and artists. Ian, who was once a star student at London's Royal College of Art, still has a cheerful cockney accent after 30 years in west Cork. He celebrated his sixtieth birthday in 2007: 'We arrived here from north London back in the early 1970s on the hippie trail. People were very good to us. We arrived here with a fiver, and we were living in the back of a Land Rover. We got our first overdraft to buy a cow. We did the self-sufficient thing for years, killing pigs, and milking cows, living on fifty pence a week. And out of that we developed the ceramics.'

As an artist, Ian is known as 'the tits and bums man', having made his name with ceramics modelled from plaster casts of curvaceous women. He works now in cast cement, because it is quicker. He sells mainly through the Private Collector Gallery in Innishannon, where his life-size nude, the rear view of a woman leaning against a door, has become a local landmark. They also work as consultants for other people, building lakes and ponds, and advising on land management for the benefit of wildlife.

Ian and Lynn bought thirteen acres on the outskirts of Skibbereen while prices were still rock-bottom, and many years later, a small inheritance enabled them to buy 70 acres of woodland on higher ground near Ballydehob.

The land around their cottage has been turned into a wildlife reserve that provides as many different habitats as possible. The approach has been consistently low-tech, low expense and common sense. The first of several visual highlights is the lake, built by Ian and Lynn, which covers about a quarter of an acre, and has a small island. The island is important because it is fox-proof: 'We've had moorhens hatch there this year, and our own domestic ducks, and also wild mallard. You get kingfishers, and we had an otter just two days ago.' The visiting otter is spoken of with reverence, as if he were royalty – which, in this context, he probably is. Even though the lake was stocked with brown trout, rudd, and sticklebacks, and now consists of what Ian calls 'fish soup', it would not support an otter. The edges are softened by water plants, which were brought in by the bucketload from bog land that was being drained. At the top of their hill is a smaller lake, the Sky Pond: 'This one was made in four hours with a digger. We literally scraped the bog off and made a dam. If you create a dam and lift the water up, you get a far more natural edge than if you dig a hole, and it's a very easy, cheap way of doing it.' As we stand there, swallows dart down to drink, and a clutch of about twenty dragonflies hover. Some are as big as hummingbirds; you can hear their wings rattle. The dog stands at the water's edge casting a perfect reflection in the water, as does the whole of the sky. What was once a tatty piece of bog is transformed into a place of contemplative beauty.

The thirteen acres are crossed by narrow footpaths, created by strimming, which let the light in. Already, after only twelve years, the native trees form a canopy overhead. Mushrooms and woodland plants have appeared of their own accord. The bird life is remarkable: 'We've recorded over 70 species of bird, and over 23 species of butterfly. We are using this place to show what you can do without huge input. Once you get the habitat right, everything just turns up. None of these birds or butterflies has been introduced.' Above the woodland, the land opens out into grassland: 'This field is our pride and joy – we call it the seed bank. It's never had nitrates on it, and it hasn't been ploughed in 60 years. We had the guy who runs the Botany Department at Trinity College, Dublin, in last week, with a bunch of German scientists, collecting the seed, which they take away and propagate. We've had carpets of flowers, and clouds of butterflies in here.'

From the highest point you can look out at the surrounding farms. Where the Wrights' fields have a variety of colour and vegetation, from the browns of bog, the different greens of alder, ash, oak, spindle, and blackthorn, to the blues, yellows, greys and pale green of the wild-flower meadow, the land around them is a uniform shade of bright green. Nitrogen green, Ian calls it: 'All of that was twelve little fields up until a few years ago, when they used EU grants to remove all the ditches. That clearance has created a green desert, and led to a devastating loss of habitat. Initially we lost the snipe, we lost the grasshopper warblers, and so many other birds. But now they've all come back – to our place. The birds are having to adapt to using smaller and smaller sites.'

Ian and Lynn are aware that most farmers could not afford to manage fields as they do, but they urge people to consider leaving headlands and other awkward corners unsprayed, to create pockets of different habitat. 'Many people own a few acres, which they might rent out to a farmer, just to keep it tidy, but they don't seem to think of letting it go wild, and managing it as a nature reserve instead. If you manage it, even by doing as little as strimming a path through it, it's like framing a picture, the path leads you into it, and lets you appreciate it. The return is massive, in terms of bird life, insect life, wild flowers, even lichens and mosses.'

The same principles, writ large, apply to the Wrights' 70-acre mountainside-holding near Ballydehob. At 400–700 feet above sea level, the parcel of land had planning permission for 100 per cent Sitka spruce. Ian appealed to Europe, in order to secure grant aid for an alternative-planting scheme. They now have permission – and the all-important grant aid – to plant 60 per cent broadleaf.

Already, after only four years' work, the contrast between the varied growth and curving road of their site, and their neighbour's straight-edged Sitka spruce plantation with its barren earth, is remarkable. The Wrights used the earth scraped off while building the road to make ditches, which are already covered in growth, providing a habitat for wildlife. They have created a series of ponds by building dams, with the same machinery that built the road. Forty acres have been planted as forestry, and the other 30 are being managed under REPS. Already it is an attractive place to walk. The hen harrier has returned, one of the ponds is covered in water lilies, and the valley is a sea of bog cotton. In contrast, nothing grows under the Sitka spruce, which is destined for clear-fell, leaving an ugly scar.

Says Ian: 'We wanted to prove that by using the grants available for commercial forestry, you can have a plantation that is both commercially viable and environmentally friendly. His battle for EU grants to grow native broadleaf trees was one of the key factors leading to the foundation of The Irish Natural Forestry Foundation (INFF), which operates at the Manch Estate near Dunmanway. Lynn Daley, INFF's Education Manager, relishes the fact that INFF is part-funded by the Forestry Services of the Department of Agriculture, the same body against which it actively campaigns.

Set up with funds from West Cork LEADER and private sources, and using 100 acres of land belonging to the Conner family, INFF is now a thriving experimental forestry initiative, with a busy educational programme. The old woodland borders on the fork of the rivers Bandon and Blackwater now have experimental plantations of native hedging and predom-inantly broadleaf trees. Different planting projects investigate, for example, the efficacy of tree shields, and the effect of injecting root systems with myccorhizas – fungi that help the plant gain nutrients from the soil. INFF hold regular open days, when the public can take a guided walk, or simply wander freely through the plantations. There are also open days for foresters and farmers, courses in hedge-laying, woodland establishment and management, as well as a schools programme.

In 1999 Baile Dúlra Teoranta, a company granted charitable status and set up by a group of like-minded friends, bought 30 acres of land near Castletown Kinneigh, Enniskean, with the aim of setting up an eco-village to study and teach sustainable living. This is now The Hollies Centre for Practical

Sustainability. It took three years to get planning permission. Ambitious initial plans for sixteen energy-efficient houses were scaled down to two houses and a study centre, and building began in 2002. One of the leading figures behind the village was Rob Hopkins, an English pioneer in the concept of Permaculture, who taught the Practical Sustainability Course at Kinsale Further Education College. While working in Kinsale, he launched the Kinsale Energy Descent Action Plan, the first attempt to design a timetabled strategy for weaning a town off fossil fuels.

Thomas and Ulrike Riedmuller built a cob house at the Hollies – clay, sand, water, and straw, using no cement – to a passive solar design by Ballydehob-based architect, Jeremy Baines, and moved in with their three small boys in 2006. From 2002 to 2004 Rob worked to add his own cob house to the Centre, but three months before completion it was destroyed by an arsonist. In September 2005, Rob, with his wife and children, moved to Totnes, Devon, and he began a PhD at Plymouth University. This will allow him to develop his ideas about Energy Descent Action Plans. Speaking in November 2007 he was philosophical about the move: 'Given that the house had no insurance, and that we never found out who had done it, we felt we couldn't rebuild. Plus the fact that it really felt like a kick in the stomach for something we had spent ten years working towards. That decision made, we thought long and hard about where to go. The decision to come home was based on the opportunities for the kids that are available here – and perhaps on some deeper level, after the fire we just wanted to come home.'

Meanwhile, the educational and open day programme at The Hollies is thriving. Both children and adults enjoy the hands-on, down-to-earth approach. Organic gardener Paul O'Flynn has created an impressive vegetable garden, but much of the site is still scrub. The Riedmullers' house is a wonderful construct, curved in shape, with a compacted earth floor, and mainly glazed on the southern side. The cob acts as a heat battery, and heavy curtains prevent heat loss at night. The exterior needs regular limewash, but so far there has not been any significant erosion.

Thomas Riedmuller, who gives brilliantly lucid guided tours of the site, explained the Centre's aims: 'What we're trying to do here is to learn and teach a wide range of skills using local resources to meet local needs.' Traditional builders and tradesmen, as well as those interested in sustainable living, attend the courses and open days. There were 22 people on a recent nine-day course in cob-building. Cob houses have been built in Galway, Meath, and Kilkenny by people who learnt the technique here. Many people have expressed an interest in coming back to rebuild Rob Hopkins' house. Its shell was recently cleared out by volunteer working parties, and the cob walls are still standing after three years' exposure to the weather.

Many people assume that west Cork must be a Green Party stronghold. But this is to underestimate the power of tradition when it comes to casting a vote. The Green Party has an able candidate in Quentin Gargan, who contested the general election in the three-seat South-west constituency in 2007. Gargan, who moved to west Cork from Dublin in 1999 at the age of 43, lives on a farm at Ardnashee, five miles from Bantry with his partner, environmental campaigner, Clare Watson, and their two children. They built an eco-house powered by a wind turbine and solar panels. The house is made of straw bales, lined with wool, with rooftop lawn, and heat-exchange ventilation, in addition to a wind generator and solar panels. They have regular open days for people interested in their sustainable living project.

In 2003, Gargan and Madeline McKeever were arrested for selling home produce on the street in Skibbereen. A subsequent court case found that their market stalls were legal, to the benefit of other would-be market traders. Gargan is a spokesman for Bantry Concerned Action Group, a campaign that highlights the dangers of overhead power lines. His Green Party campaign was conducted by electric car, with meetings organised by local Green Party members throughout the electoral region.

The Cork South-west constituency extends east to Ringabella, and includes the Kinsale, as well as the Bandon, Bantry and Skibbereen electoral areas of Cork County Council. In 2007, Quentin Gargan received only 2,860 first preference votes for the Cork Southwest Constituency. In contrast, the successful candidates, P. J. Sheehan and Jim O'Keeffe (both Fine Gael and both first elected to the Dáil in 1977), and newcomer, Christy O'Sullivan (Fianna Fáil), each received over 10,000 votes by the time second and third preferences had been allocated.

6

The View from the Big House

West Cork has one of the finest stately homes in Ireland, Bantry House, with its elevated location at the head of Bantry Bay, looking across the sea to the Caha Mountains and the Beara peninsula. It was the first house in Ireland to open its doors to the public in 1946, when the stately home business was just beginning.

Richard White, a local landowner, was created Earl of Bantry for his loyalty during the threat of a French invasion in 1796–97. At the time he lived in a small Queen Anne house on the same site, Seafield. This was renamed Bantry House and was extended in 1820 by adding two drawing rooms. The second Earl and his wife furnished it with treasures acquired on their European grand tour, including four panels of Royal Aubusson tapestry made for Marie Antoinette; some Chinese lacquer, Buhl and other fine furniture; and an eighteenth-century Waterford Crystal chandelier. They also further extended the house, adding two wings, the stable yard and the Italianate formal gardens, and terracing the land in front of and behind the house.

Bantry House is still lived in by direct descendants of Richard White. Visitors are often amazed to discover that the tall, diffident man in a blazer taking their money at the entrance desk is Egerton Shelswell-White, or as the Italians call him, 'Milord'. Besides being a showplace, Bantry is also home to Egerton and his wife, Brigitte, who have brought up four children here. They are unusual among stately-home owners in that they have lived other lives: Egerton is a musician, a brass player, and lived in America during his first marriage; Brigitte was born in Austria, trained as a picture restorer in Vienna, and ran a successful picture-restoring business in Toronto before moving to the Bantry area.

The house and gardens are open to the public from March to the end of October. The library of Bantry House is also used for classical music concerts, and for the West Cork Chamber Music Festival. There is a modest café–restaurant, serving local artisan food, but so far Bantry has refrained from adding the golf course, spa, suites, and executive homes that now surround so many big Irish houses.

Estates that once extended to Castletownbere are now reduced to 100 acres, about 46 of which are gardens and accessible woodlands. The history can be studied in the Bantry House Archive, which Egerton and Brigitte donated to UCC in 1997. During the Civil War the house was used as an emergency hospital, treating the wounded from both sides. Egerton's mother, Clodagh Shelswell-White, recalled, 'Sometimes the screams were awful, but it was worse when they stopped.' During the 'Emergency', the house was the headquarters of the Irish Army commanded by Captain Buttimer.

Maintaining the building is a constant challenge. Because the house is open to the public, tax relief is available on repairs, maintenance, and restoration, including staff wages, but the house receives no grant aid, and, with some 30,000 paying visitors a year, is currently running at a loss. The B&B wing, which opened about twenty years ago, helps to boost the income. Brigitte designed and supervised the decoration of six first-floor rooms overlooking the terraced gardens, with a billiard room on the floor below, and a basement breakfast room.

To the conventionally minded, Egerton and Brigitte

might seem an unlikely couple. She is vivacious and elegant, while he, her senior by some years, is a quiet, benign presence. When I first met Brigitte, she was 'cloud-pruning' a box hedge on a sunny morning. I'd never heard of cloud-pruning, but she demonstrated how it removes years of old, lower growth to reveal the top sections of the box as a series of freestanding 'clouds'. It is a dirty, dusty, slow job, but that would not deter someone used to the painstaking work of picture-restoring.

Brigitte and Egerton live in a first-floor apartment within Bantry House, created by Egerton's mother, Clodagh, when the house was first opened to the public. Now a series of interconnecting rooms above the dining room, it has taken a lot of work over the years to turn this into a home for a family with four children. We talk in the large kitchen, which is also a pleasantly lived-in family room, with three large cats making themselves at home in front of the Aga. Brigitte has been studying her gardening books, getting the order for spring bulbs together. 'I've missed the boat again this year for daffodils. I should have ordered them last month. You need thousands – 3–4,000 really – and people to plant them, if you're going to make any kind of display.'

Egerton, divorced from his American wife, met Brigitte at a dance at the Reendesert Hotel in Bantry. They were both with other people. Brigitte, then 34, was living in Ballylickey with her boyfriend, an artist. Naturally, she had visited Bantry House: 'When I came home, my boyfriend asked how was it, and I said it's a lovely house, but it's had it, it's over, it's too run down. I was completely wrong, but that was the very first impression. I just thought golly, so lovely, and so past it.'

The early years at Bantry House were difficult, she recalls: 'Living upstairs is never easy; everything has to be carried up. For the first six years the rooms did not connect with each other, and we had two babies as well. It was so cold: there was a door up there somewhere, and when the wind blew, everything rattled. Water came in through the roof, and we ran around with buckets. Egerton was very busy, getting the business going. I remember him racing off with stacks of posters that he delivered to every hotel and B&B in the neighbourhood, driving around to Killarney and Schull, and the absolute joy when visitors went from 5,000 people in a year up to 20,000.'

When she first opened the B&B rooms, it caused quite a stir. They were modest-sized rooms, simply done, with calico curtains, not what people expected. But they have been a great success. The B&B wing nowadays has hotel-grade comfort, with silk-embroidered curtains, and underfloor heating in the bathrooms, unlike the homely family quarters. We pass from the latter to the former, through a pair of baize doors. Behind us we can see one of the unrestored rooms, exposed stonework crumbling, and daylight showing through a gap near the window frame. As we step into the luxurious B&B wing, Brigitte says, 'One thing you learn, looking after a house like this, is that it doesn't all have to happen in your lifetime.'

The perseverance and attention to detail that made her a picture restorer have been invaluable as a custodian of Bantry House's collection of antiques. She says: 'I don't know about antiques, all I know is pictures, but I do know what not to do. When you open the house, tourists come, and people will touch things; the light hits the wood, the wood gets bleached and dries up and that is painful. On the other hand, things are lived with, and seen.'

She talks of the great achievement of the Devonshires at Chatsworth House, one of England's most-visited stately homes: 'They are brilliantly clever, but they also have a lot of money in the background, and thousands of acres. We only have about 100 acres. It's impossible actually, a big house without land. If there were 1,000 acres, you would have an income, but 100 acres is nothing. Sometimes we get despondent. I get hurt or irritated by criticism. But there is a limit to what anyone can do ...'

The children from Egerton's first marriage are now in their forties, and have lives of their own in America. Egerton and Brigitte hope that the children from their marriage to each other will want to keep the house on, but the eldest, Sophie, is only in her mid-twenties, the youngest still at school. There have been offers from companies wanting to turn the house into a hotel, says Brigitte: 'It can be done, as long as it's sensitive: you would have to rebuild from the inside. It's a big job. At the moment, the house is not a money-making enterprise. The main objective was to keep it, and we have done that. Who knows what will happen in the future?'

Hollybrook House near Skibbereen is hidden from the world's gaze. Very few people know it exists at all. It is such a strange place that, if you invented it for a work of fiction, nobody would believe you. It is owned by the Chief of the O'Donovan clan, known as 'The O'Donovan', and his wife, Madame Jane, who live there full-time. Dan, as he is also called, explains in his usual self-deprecating manner, that the title is a legacy of Dev's desire to see the Gaelic tradition resuscitated. The genealogist Edward McLysaght was called in, and a list was made of about twenty people with claims to old titles who were judged acceptable in terms of historical descent. Dan reels off a list of names: 'O'Conor Don, O'Morrough, the Macgillicuddy in South Africa, an O'Neill in Portugal, another chap in Spain, O'Rourke …', and then he gets sidetracked by an anecdote about a bogus MacCarthy Mór, and we have to be rescued by his ever-sensible wife, Jane. Dan and Jane are the sort of couple who have lived at close quarters for so long that they can finish each other's sentences. They have the quiet good manners of a different age, and are known far and wide for their kindness. They love their strange old house as if it were a person, an extravagantly amusing, but also intractable, relation, who has to be humoured and carefully looked after.

Hollybrook is said to be the last large-scale country

house to be built in Ireland before the First World War. It is built in a lavish version of the Arts and Crafts style used in the UK around that time by Edward Lutyens and Norman Shaw, mingling vernacular features with classicism on a very large scale: stockbroker Tudorbethan on steroids. It is marked on the main road by a gate lodge, behind a semicircle of tall iron railings. The house itself looms up at the end of over a mile of wooded driveway, on the far side of an extensive parkland and lawn. Two three-storey wings with tall gables sit on either side of a balustraded portico, which is surmounted by a tall, central, brick chimney. It was completed in 1904 for Colonel Anthony H. Morgan and his wife, Mary. Mary was the aunt of Dan's mother, which is how he came to inherit it. Great Aunt Mary's fortune came from her first husband, a Glasgow ironmaster, and the house was designed by a Scottish architect, R. S. Balfour, who brought Scottish workmen over to build it. Aunt Mary, as she is referred to by the O'Donovans, also had an ocean-going steam yacht, in which she once travelled to Japan. She brought back two gardeners, who designed the house's once-famous Japanese gardens.

Aunt Mary had no children and the house was built for entertaining on a grand scale, not for a family. She had two other homes, one in London, and one near Cowes, as well as her yacht, in which she would sail to Castletownshend for her annual visit. She never spent a full year at the house. It was closed up from 1920 until her death in 1950, when Dan's parents took over. For this reason, its custom-built interior has had little wear and tear, and very little modernisation, making it a unique piece of domestic history.

There are drawbacks to attempting to make a family home out of what, in a more accessible location, would have been turned into a museum. They considered opening to the public, but the grants were derisory and came with impossible conditions. Peter Somerville-Large in *Cappaghglass* (Hamish Hamilton, 1985), a book consisting of thinly disguised interviews with a variety of people living in and around Bantry (the Cappaghglass of the title), paints an affectionate portrait of Dan as Lord Cappaghglass, and remarks waspishly, 'In the old days the family hardly knew where the kitchen was – now they eat in it.'

The kitchen, which has a large scullery off it, is bigger than most people's sitting room. It has a huge Aga and twin dressers that, like all the furniture in the servants' quarters, was custom-built for the house. It is uncannily like the kitchen in Queen Mary's Dolls' House (on display at Windsor Castle), as Jane remarks. I am warned that we might have to decamp from the kitchen in the course of our lunch, because the Aga man is expected. But that is no problem: we have an unusually large choice of other rooms in which to eat, including an imposing formal dining room.

The entrance to Hollybrook is through a galleried hall, known as a living hall (as opposed to a living room). Jane remarks: 'One of the many architects who've come to look at the house said the fashion for living halls only lasted ten years.' Dan adds, 'I need three days' notice to light the Jetul [stove], to get it going. In the days when we had the children here, it was great fun. We always used it at Christmas.'

Their three children are now grown up and married, and the O'Donovans have eight grandchildren, who visit regularly, along with their parents. We walk down a long service corridor to a small circular room lined with oak panelling, originally the smoking room. A door on the other side leads directly into the dining room. There is a large television, a wood-burning stove and a drinks tray. Jane says, 'For six months when we first came here I struggled to live as my mother-in-law used to live, using the library – which is at the other end of the house – as a sitting room. It was 45 paces from the kitchen when I wanted to see if the potatoes had boiled. I said to Dan, I just can't do it any more, I can't manage, and so we live in here.' Dan tots up the number of rooms they now use: 'We eat in the kitchen, we live in here, we have one bedroom upstairs and the bathroom – that's four rooms.'

The living hall is impressive in scale, but the most beautiful room in Hollybrook is the formal dining room, with its large walk-in hearth and windows on to a garden terrace. Going from the living hall into the dining room is like going into another house, so different is the architecture and décor. The twin doors from the oak-panelled hall are lined with mahogany on the dining room side, as oak would clash with the Georgian mahogany furniture. A fine portrait of King Billy (as Dan calls him) at the Battle of the Boyne hangs to one side of the table.

The drawing room, also off the living hall, is panelled from head to ceiling in marquetry, made for a Cape Cod cottage by Miss Jane Morgan, a family relation. No two panels are the same, and the borders above them are inlaid with stern texts: 'Go to the ant, thou Sluggard'. The project took Miss Morgan five years to complete. The room has windows on to the garden at one end, and a central chimney with two fireplaces. According to Jane, the room is the coldest room in a house whose coldness, in spite of Dan's best efforts with five wood-burning stoves, is legendary. Dan's parents, in order to create a room in which one could sit without being tormented by the cold (as in the living hall, and the vast double-fireplaced drawing room), built a bookcase against the Japanese paper doors, and installed a large wood-burning stove. Dan comments, 'I suppose you could say my parents mucked the place about, but they did it in order to have somewhere comfortable to sit.'

When Dan's mother died, Jane and Dan decided that Hollybrook was not a house for the twentieth century, and came down from Dublin to sell it. But they discovered that to avoid death duties they had to live in the house for three years. 'My job in Dublin had run out – I was running a building firm – so we came down here and by the time we'd lived here for three years, we rather liked it, so we stayed.'

'We've done our bit,' he says. Jane's biggest regret is that they had to let the gardens go, not being able to employ enough people to keep them up: 'The Japanese garden was already overgrown, it was let go in 1943. When we moved here in 1977, we had to let the three-acre walled garden go too. We were the generation who had to destroy it.'

Jane and Dan use bicycles to get around the estate, even to go and feed the chickens: it is a bicycle ride from the house to the stables. There are three miles of paved road on the estate. Since breaking his kneecap in what he calls 'a silly accident', Dan has taken to an adult-size tricycle. Their son Tadgh, 45, who works in London as a lawyer, has known Hollybrook all his life, first as his grandparents' home, then as his parents'. He is determined to take on the house and farm, and is currently looking into ways of making this move feasible.

Castletownshend is perhaps best known as the home of writer Edith Somerville (1858–1949). Besides being an accomplished author and artist, Edith was also Master of the local Carbery hunt and church organist at St Barrahane's for over 50 years. She is now buried in the church, with her cousin and writing partner, Violet Martin.

The village is quite remarkable in itself, however, with the greatest concentration of big houses west of Cork city. Castletownshend's main street runs down a steep hill and ends at a pier. The road is lined by large, stone-built, eighteenth- and nineteenth-century houses, most of them associated with the intermarried settler families of the village: Somervilles, Townshends, Coghills, and Chavasses. It is quite unlike anywhere else in Cork, or Ireland, come to that. 'There's a hotbed of gentry in Castletownshend,' Peter Somerville-Large (himself part of the clan) was told in 1972. Angela Eborall, an Englishwoman who has lived there since 1950, still remembers the days when Catholics were not allowed (by order of the Bishop) to attend Protestant funerals. But, as a mark of respect to the deceased, they would stand outside the church during the service.

Edith lived at Drishane House, marked on the main road by the gate lodge, on your right as you enter the village. The gravel driveway, shaded by a giant cedar of Lebanon, leads to a lawn and a glorious view of an island, framed by a headland: the grounds run down to a hidden cove. The grand entrance and vista are somewhat deceptive: Drishane is a relatively modest house, large and graceful, but compact enough to be comfortable. It is a typical Georgian 'box', with weather-slated walls. There is a wide pair of glass doors, with a distinctive semicircular fanlight, leading from the drawing room to the lawn, in addition to a conventional front door around the corner.

I visited Drishane in 1984, during the Memories of Somerville and Ross Festival. The festival, a fundraiser for the local community, was inspired by the popularity of the television series, *Adventures of an Irish R.M.*, first shown in 1983. Before it was broadcast, people still tended to dismiss Edith and Violet's stories as deriding the local population, but the TV series helped to make it clear that they wrote out of affection and admiration for their neighbours. Their novel *The Real Charlotte* (1894) is widely praised as a pioneer of Irish realism. On my visit, I found the house interior hardly touched since Edith's time, and comfortably shabby. Edith's studio, known as The Purlieu, sat swathed in dust above a wing of the stables and seemed to me to be permeated by the spirit of this remarkable woman.

Drishane was built by the merchant Tom Somerville, son of the rector Thomas Somerville, in the mid-eighteenth century. By 1811, the Somerville fortune was gone, their land and capital lost when Thomas Somerville III stood guarantor to a relative whose business had failed. Over the next hundred years, the owners of the neighbouring big houses also lost their incomes, when the Famine was followed by Gladstone's Land Acts. Such houses scraped along on pension funds from the navy or army, and the income from those who had moved into the professions as lawyers, architects, and doctors. In some cases, the women of the family also contributed to the family income. Somerville and Ross did not write for fun: they wrote because they needed the money, as a glance at their letters, with the innumerable references to shortage of funds, will prove.

Drishane passed to Edith's elder brother, Cameron, in 1898. Cameron joined the British Army, leaving Edith to manage affairs at home, and achieved the rank of colonel, retiring in 1919. Edith and Cameron were chronically short of money, Drishane's demands being far in excess of their income. In summer, Drishane was let out to visitors, while Edith retreated to a smaller house in the village. She made additional money in these years by horse dealing. Sylvia Warren of Boston came over regularly to buy young Irish horses from Edith. Edith's sister, Hildegarde, had one of the first violet farms in Ireland, and used the rail connection in Skibbereen to send the freshly picked flowers to Cork. Edith and Hildegarde bred one of the first herds of Friesian cows in Cork, owned jointly with their brother Cameron. (Both activities are commemorated in a corner of the Harry Clarke window in St Barrahane's Church).

When Cameron died in 1942, Drishane passed on to Desmond, the son of Edith and Cameron's brother, Aylmer. When he retired from the army as a brigadier in 1945, Desmond and his wife insisted that Edith should live with them, and retain her place at the head of the table. But her inability to climb the stairs forced her to move to Tally-Ho, where she died in 1949.

Until the 1950s, the houses in Castletownshend were lived in year-round, many by people with no local connection, who had retired on army or navy pensions. It was their passing that emptied the village. As you turn left down the main street, the houses on the right-hand side all share the same superb sea view that can be seen from Drishane. Tally-Ho (where Edith died), and The Cottage across the road, her sister Hildegarde's first home after her marriage, are still standing. The Red House, home of Edith's wealthy cousins, recently had a €4 million renovation. Various other large houses on Main Street are let out as holiday homes in the summer. The same people come to Castletownshend every summer, year after year, the Volvos and Range Rovers laden down with children, pets and sporting paraphernalia.

There is still a shop in the village – although the Post Office closed down in 2005 – and three pubs, the most famous being Mary Ann's. Like Glandore, Castletownshend is seething with people in July and August, and empty in the winter. One resident did a head-count, and reckoned there were 80–90 people living there year-round. The residents campaigned vigorously against a new estate across from the gates of Drishane, but it went ahead: apparently only two of a total 42 houses are lived in throughout the year. As well as blocking the view from the top of the village, it has also blocked the broadband signal for its immediate neighbours.

As to Drishane itself, when Edith died, she left only a few hundred pounds and Drishane needed roofing, rewiring, and redecorating. Desmond and his wife managed somehow, passing the house on to their son, Christopher. He used to let it out in summer via a discreet ad in the English weekly, the *Spectator*. When I asked a Castletownshend contact what sort of people rented it, he replied simply, 'very rich people'. The only famous one he could recall was the film star Richard Gere. In 2007 Christopher's son, Thomas, left England for west Cork and moved in permanently with his family – so Drishane has survived to welcome a new generation after all.

7

Are You Enjoying Your Holiday?

'Are you enjoying your holiday?' People used to ask that all the time if you didn't have a local accent. You hear it less nowadays, since the growth of tourism – from under three million a year in the early 1980s, to over eight million visitors a year in 2007. This, in addition to the increased numbers of people moving to the area, means that locals no longer automatically assume that an unfamiliar face is a holidaymaker.

Thirty years ago the only people actively marketing the region were Cork Kerry Tourism. There was no particular emphasis on west Cork. In those days the big attractions were Blarney, Cork city, Glengarriff, the Lakes of Killarney, and the Ring of Kerry. The Ring of Kerry and Killarney were far better known for scenery, and Killarney or Waterville were the places to play golf. West Cork was a minority choice, seldom on the itinerary of first-time visitors, except perhaps for a look at Glengarriff on the way to Killarney. People went to west Cork because they had family affiliations, or they accidentally stumbled on the region, and if they succumbed to its charms they came back.

What exactly are these charms? The attraction of west Cork has much to do with its smaller scale: narrow roads, lined by small fields, and attractive little farmhouses. Never mind that the latter are now probably holiday homes – they still look like city folk expect farmhouses to look. In other parts of Europe, where the roads are bigger, you whiz through the countryside at high speed, bypassing all the towns, and seldom passing habitations, which are tucked away from view. The only way you know where you are is by reading the signposts.

The mild maritime climate of west Cork fosters rich vegetative growth, with fuchsia hedges, abundant wild flowers, and easily accessible wilderness areas, all important attractions for jaded urbanites. The small scale of most development (so far) is another attractive feature. But I think the most important feature for many visitors is the comparative lack of other people, both visiting and resident. Even though there are more people in west Cork than there were in the early 1980s, there are still far fewer people than in most other parts of Europe. A research project carried out for West Cork LEADER came up with the average of 34 people per square kilometre.

Nor is there the prevalence of elderly people that can make the scenic parts of Cornwall, Devon, and Somerset feel like a giant retirement home. Older people do of course retire to west Cork, but there are also significant numbers of younger people moving to the area to commute, to downsize, or otherwise to change their lifestyle. And many locally born young couples are moving back once they have children, to live near their relatives.

The climate has saved west Cork from the kind of intensive development that has ruined much of the Mediterranean coast. It rains even more in Connemara, but it rains just enough in west Cork to put off many people. An English friend told me she knew her marriage was doomed when it rained on every single day of her ten-day Irish honeymoon. I will always remember the look of utter despair on the faces of a couple of English tourists in late middle age, who were sheltering in the door of the supermarket one summer afternoon, in rain gear, looking cold and lost. The man spoke to the woman apologetically: 'Things are working out differently than we expected,' and the woman answered, grim-faced, 'They certainly are.' Then I saw a tandem bicycle with laden saddlebags leaning against the wall, and I understood the full horror of their situation.

The fact that west Cork is relatively difficult to get to by car has saved it from the large crowds that flock to the southwest coast of England and the Brittany coast. I took a trip to Cornwall recently, specifically to gauge its difference from west Cork. In late August in St Ives, the park and ride car park (£4.20, with 1,000 places) was full to capacity by 11 a.m., and an overflow car park was being opened. People were walking six-deep along the seafront, and there were queues for everything, from food, to car parks, to toilets. It was impossible to get away from other people, even on the relatively remote cliff path to Zennor. It is perhaps paradoxical: many visitors say that what they like most about west Cork is the people: what they really mean is that they like the relative scarcity of other visitors. Because of this, the people they like, the natives, have not yet tired of talking to holidaymakers, and generally being helpful and pleasant.

Within Ireland, in the market for short breaks, west Cork has serious rivals in Dingle, the Ring of Kerry, west Clare, Connemara, the Aran Islands, Mayo, Achill Island, and Donegal, in terms of accessibility, scenery, hospitality, food and culture (traditional music, art and crafts). Not everybody rates west Cork that highly for music, for example, or Irish language and culture. And it is a much longer drive from Dublin than the west coast destinations. The long-serving TD, P. J. Sheehan, likes to remind people that when he crosses the Limerick–Cork border at Kilbehenny on his way home from Dublin, he is still two-and-a-half hours' drive from his home in Goleen.

In the early years of the twentieth century, when people spoke of west Cork, they generally referred to the valley of the

River Lee – Inchigeelagh, Ballingeary and Gougane Barra, extending through the Pass of Keimaneigh to Bantry and Glengarriff if transport was available. From the writings of Daniel Corkery and his students, Frank O'Connor and Seán Ó Faoláin, it appears that young men thought nothing of cycling from Cork city to Inchigeelagh, a distance of some 36 miles, along the valley of the River Lee. In Inchigeelagh I was told that visitors used to take their bicycles on the train to Macroom, and just cycle the last dozen or so miles. The same person also told me that there had been problems with the new signposting on Cork's City Link Road. Macroom is due west of Cork city, but if you follow the signs for 'West Cork' they lead you to the N71 for Bantry and Skibbereen, the latter a good hour's drive south of Macroom.

People did not start exploring the hilly south-western coastal area in any numbers until cars became widely affordable in the 1980s. The 1975 edition of *Ireland on $10 a Day* (Frommer), written by an energetic young American, Beth Bryant, is typical of the times. She gives Kinsale a one-page entry as a side trip from Cork city, warmly recommending The Spaniard, a pub where 'Ireland's earthiest folk group, The Dubliners are regulars'. The next destination after Cork city is Killarney, and the route she recommends goes through Macroom to Gougane Barra, through the Pass of Keimaneigh to Glengarriff, over the Healy Pass to Kenmare, and into Killarney via the famous Ladies View road. Coastal west Cork remained as yet undiscovered, even by the indefatigable Beth Bryant.

West Cork's current regional identity, emphasising the attractions of its coastal villages, its cuisine, and its marine leisure activities, is largely the work of cumulative tourism marketing initiatives undertaken by Cork Kerry Tourism, a regional division of Fáilte Ireland (previously Bord Fáilte); West Cork Tourism, a membership-based promotional and marketing organisation with an office in Skibbereen; and West Cork LEADER Co-op, which sees the promotion of local crafts, artisan food, and tourism product as interlinked. Individual businesses, which, for reasons of their own, prefer not to be affiliated with any of the above, have also had an unquantifiable input into creating the regional identity of West Cork (note the capital W).

An early LEADER slogan, 'West Cork: Our Home, Your Holiday', emphasised the way that facilities for tourists had been created within the existing infrastructure. West Cork was never a place for big hotels: the Eccles in Glengarriff was the exception. Hotels were either in the town centre, catering for commercial and business travellers arriving by rail or road – The Munster Arms, Bandon; O'Donovan's in Clonakilty; The Eldon and the West Cork in Skibbereen; Vickery's in Bantry; The Castle, Macroom – or unpretentious seaside hotels catering primarily for family holidays – Coakley's Atlantic Hotel, Garrettstown, the old Inchydoney Hotel, Owenahincha Hotel, and Barley Cove Hotel.

The introduction of reasonably priced bed and breakfast accommodation on farms and in existing homes in the 1960s helped to make west Cork an attractive destination for touring by car. It was also an ingenious way of increasing the availability of accommodation without the need for large capital investment. For the people living in the area, especially farmers, who were struggling to make a living prior to Ireland's entry to the EEC, the money was very welcome. The first group of bed and breakfast providers to organise, through their links with the Irish Countrywomen's Association, was Irish Farmhouse Holidays, set up in 1966. This consisted of twenty members, under chairwoman Nancy Fitzgerald of Knockraha in north Cork. Nancy told me that in the early days of B&B, she and her colleagues met with disapproval locally from those who believed that charging money for people to stay in your home violated the Irish tradition of offering free hospitality to travellers. But the attitude changed when it became apparent that people who came to stay expected to pay and were delighted with what they got. The

B&B providers, especially women who were isolated on the farm, enjoyed meeting and getting to know 'strangers', and many long-term friendships resulted.

Hannah Cronin was a founder member of Irish Farmhouse Holidays. I stayed with her in 1998 at her B&B on the road to Bantry, and was overwhelmed with nostalgia for the old days. Hers was a small, two-storey farmhouse, with a galvanised roof, and a style of décor that was probably considered the height of gentility in Hannah's youth: satin-covered eiderdowns, frilled curtains, giant veneered ward-robes, and woollen rugs on top of fitted carpets. Once again I experienced that particular smell of other people's toothpaste and shaving cream that used to permeate the shared bathroom. It took me back to my teenage years, when B&B cost seven shillings and sixpence a night. Hannah, a lively old lady with a wit to match, told me that this would be her last season. It was not her age that had made her decide to retire. It was because of the bathroom and the fact that she didn't have any rooms 'en suite'. She explained: 'A man came to the door, and he asked me if I was Ann Sweet. Even before he said "hallo", he asked, "Are you Ann Sweet?" I said, "No, I'm Hannah Cronin."' Next morning, as she served me breakfast on a lace tablecloth with floral-patterned china and butter curls in a glass dish, she said wistfully: 'In the old days people did bed and breakfast because they were interested in the people. Today all they're interested in is the money.'

Bord Fáilte worked hard to ensure that bed and breakfast houses conformed to certain standards, until 1996, when the various accommodation groups became self-regulatory. Tax incentives and grants from the EU encouraged the upgrading of existing facilites in the 1980s, so that a bathroom en suite became the rule rather than the exception. Since the 1990s there has been much investment in new houses designed specifically for the bed and breakfast trade. The best of these are virtually indistinguishable from small hotels, and also cost about the same. People complain about the disappearance of the traditional welcome, but frankly not all B&B owners are as much fun as Hannah Cronin, and it is often a relief at the end of a busy day, whether one is on holiday or working, to check in to an anonymous modern place with a big TV set and plenty of hot water where nobody is going to ask where you are from originally.

I cannot locate any scientific survey, but I get a strong impression that B&B has become proportionately more expensive as part of the overall touring budget, especially if the house is in an attractive or sought-after location. At the time of writing, €45 per person per night is the going rate for an ordinary room, and, if you're not sharing, this can go up to €60. Many people opt for the alternative of a tourist hostel, and west Cork has one of the best and longest-established, Rolf's Holiday Hostel in Baltimore. Rolf's, which has terrific views of Baltimore Harbour, and also a restaurant, is now being run by the children of the original German proprietor Rolf, and has a high level of repeat business. At the time of writing, B&Bs are not, in general, a strong point in west Cork, lagging behind developments in both crafts and artisan food. Both the craft and food sectors offer something different from what you get elsewhere in Ireland, whereas the majority of B&Bs (there are a few notable exceptions) seem to be much as they were twenty years ago, only more expensive.

During the 1970s and into the early 1980s, horse-drawn caravans were a feature of the roads of west Cork. Another company offered them in Wicklow, but they didn't catch on anywhere else in Ireland. While they looked traditional, their interiors were an ingenious form of modern caravan, with foldaway beds and foldaway tables rotating in use. Caravanners travelled at walking pace from one designated stopping area to the next, having been given a quick course in how to harness and unharness the horse, and feed it. By 1979 Charlie Cullinane of West Cork Travel, Clonakilty, had 36 caravans and 65 horses. In 2006 he recalled: 'There were 36 families on holiday in caravans back then, rolling into little villages like

Durrus and Courtmacsherry, buying local produce, and drinking in local pubs. It really kick-started rural tourism.'

Many people loved the enforced slower pace, but I could never see the attraction: the slowness combined with the claustrophobic living quarters, minimal cooking facilities, and the perennial damp of the Irish climate looked more like a form of penance than a holiday. I felt sorry for the horses too. By the early 1980s, there was too much traffic, even on the smaller roads, for horse-drawn caravan holidays to continue. Nevertheless, there are still signs on some roads reading 'Danger! Road unsuitable for horse-drawn caravans.'

Self-catering accommodation had always been available in the area, if you knew how to find it. Edith Somerville was not the only person glad enough of the extra income to move out of her home for a few weeks in July and August, while the tourists moved in. It was not until the late 1980s that clusters of purpose-built rental accommodation specifically designed for the tourist market started to appear. At around the same time, those in the business of promoting tourism realised that walking and cycling brought in relatively high-spending, short-break visitors, on perhaps their second or third holiday in the year, as well as attracting people to the region for their primary annual holiday. This led to the setting up of waymarked walking routes and signposted cycling trails, which also benefit the local community. Similarly, the new and upgraded hotels with swimming pools, gyms, and other indoor leisure facilities, have benefited those full-time residents who can afford to join their clubs.

Deep-sea angling was one of the first marine leisure activities to be developed. In the late 1960s there was a great vogue for hauling small sharks out of the sea and weighing them on shore, before throwing them back in again, dead. Deep-sea fishing attracted large numbers of Dutch and English visitors, usually in all-male groups. Eventually the sport focused on more palatable denizens of the deep, to the great delight of those who knew how to cook them: monkfish, ray, turbot, and ling were unknown to local tables, since they had not been caught by traditional fishermen. Salmon was highly prized by the local community, but the other queer-looking yokes were still being given away when the tourists' deep-sea fishing boats landed their catches on the quaysides of Kinsale and Courtmacsherry in the 1980s. They still are today, if you get lucky.

Increased tourism numbers have led to the development of various new enterprises designed to help the tourists amuse and educate themselves. In the 1960s the only places you had to pay to visit were Bantry House and Garinish Island, also known as Illnacullin, off Glengarriff. In fact you have to pay twice for Garinish: once for the boat trip, touted by profes-sional jarveys as you arrive in the village; and again to see the very fine array of gardens designed by Harold Peto and laid out at the turn of the century by Annan Bryce, who left them to the nation. The gardens are now in the care of the Heritage Service of the Department of Arts, Heritage, Gaeltacht and the Islands.

People from overseas, especially the European mainland, are among the most enthusiastic visitors to west Cork's megalithic sites. However, with the exception of Drombeg Stone circle (which has a signpost and a car park), locating the region's many megalithic remains is not easy. Those on waymarked walking routes, such as the Ardgroom Stone Circles, are relatively easy to locate. Some, like Bohonagh Stone Circle, near Rosscarbery, have a farmer's Duty of Care sign, discouraging visitors: travelling alone, I was reluctant to cross this farmer's land when I visited. The stone circles and standing stone you want to visit are often three or four fields or more away from the main road, on private land, with no path indicated. If the ruins are low, they will not be visible from a distance. Daphne Pochin Mould, writer, photographer and aviator, has visited most of those in west Cork and was unable to find the site at Reenascreena from the ground: she identified it first from the air, to get her bearings for a return by car.

Jack Roberts is an enthusiast who wrote and illustrated *Exploring West Cork – The Guide to Discovering the Ancient, Sacred and Historic Monuments of West Cork,* 'published' as photocopied sheets of A4 paper in plastic binding in Skibbereen in 1988. There is also a smaller volume, *Antiquities of the Beara Peninsula, A Guide.* Both are labours of love and provide a good summary of the knowledge available at the time, but lack academic rigour and professional production. (They are also out-of-print collectors' items.) They have basic maps, but these need to be used in conjunction with Ordnance Survey Maps. Jack Roberts' instructions are endearingly vague, as often happens when you are very familiar with a place. Using his book as a field guide, you come to dread the words '… can easily be found …': this is seldom the case. Looking for antiquities in west Cork, unless you are accompanied by a knowledgeable local, is a guaranteed way to get lost – not much fun on a winter evening when darkness is falling as well as rain, and you are sinking into boggy ground somewhere in the middle of nowhere, at least half an hour from the place you left your car – wherever that was.

It is surprising to find that there is no one working as a tour guide to these monuments, which could surely provide at least part-time employment. Neither is there any local museum or visitor centre (like the one at Kilfenora in the Burren, for example) providing a coherent introduction to the area, in conjunction with a properly signposted and mapped visitor trail. However, the best of the carved and ogham stones have sensibly been removed to safer places, and can be found in Cork city at the Cork Public Musuem and at UCC's recently inaugurated Stone Corridor.

Therese O'Mahony, who is also a herbalist, created Ceim Hill Museum near Union Hall in 1976 in her own home, a farmhouse that has belonged to her family for generations. It has great views over Castlehaven, and she could probably sell it for millions, but it would be a brave auctioneer who would ask her. American academics have verified that the fossils and Iron Age artefacts on display are from previous settlements on the site. Her collection ranges from Iron Age farm tools, to west Cork cloaks, lace, and memorabilia of the War of Independence. She is a larger-than-life character, a one-off, who will have even the most sceptical visitor convinced of the authenticity of everything within minutes. Long may she prosper.

Local historical societies and people with a passionate interest in the past life of their home place set up the first wave of locally created visitor attractions about 30 years ago. These pre-date the audiovisual display by at least one generation, and will be enjoyed by those who like poring over dusty glazed cabinets, gazing on original posters, and poking around in cobwebbed corners to discover artefacts in general use 50 years ago. Bandon Heritage Centre is one such treasure trove, located in Christchurch, which dates from 1610 and was deconsecrated in 1973. Among the wealth of original items on display here are the old town stocks. The West Cork Museum in a former National School at Western Road in Clonakilty is another place rich in authentic artefacts, including Michael Collins memorabilia.

The Michael Collins Centre was set up by Tim Crowley on his farm near Clonakilty, and is run entirely without grant aid. It consists of a tin-roofed cottage, which was built ten years ago on a high ridge of land with views over to Kerry. Outside is a reconstruction of the road at Béal na mBláth, as it would have looked at the time of Collins' death, complete with a Crossley tender and an armoured Rolls Royce. Tim and a rota of enthusiasts take turns to give the live presentation that forms part of every visitor's experience. I was riveted by what I heard, and very impressed by the guide, Michael O'Brien's, impartiality and his wide knowledge. Michael took early retirement from his job with Eircom to do this, while Tim still milks a herd of 60 dairy cows. The venture began in 1997, offering to guide people on tours of the Michael Collins sites in the area in their own cars, and is now taking over from the farm as Tim's main activity: tourism-agri, he calls it, rather than agri-tourism.

The Skibbereen Heritage Centre was established by a group of local volunteers in an old gasworks in the town centre, which has been turned into a small interpretative centre with a large retail area. Its twin themes, the local experience of the Famine, and the flora and fauna of Lough Hyne, sounded a bit incongruous on paper, but in fact the backlit wall of pictures of the strange marine life of this inland salt-water lake act as a kind of sedative after the more harrowing Famine material. Jeremy Irons presents and narrates the introductory film. At the entrance is a 55-pound (25 kg) bag of potatoes, the daily requirement for a family of six, an unforgettable illustration of the pre-Famine diet. Storyboards suitable for children alternate with detailed dramatisations of various tribunals for adults. (The centre also holds records of home-ownership of all the dwelling places in the area dating from the mid-nineteenth century and earlier.) The Allihies Mining Centre has a similarly wide appeal.

By far the most exciting Visitor Centre, and the one I wholeheartedly recommend when people ask me (because I work on guidebooks) what they should see, is the Mizen Head Visitor Centre at the tip of the Mizen Peninsula. Mizen Head Irish Lights Signal Station was built on a rocky island off the most south-westerly point of Ireland at the tip of the Mizen Peninsula. Mariners sailing by called the Mizen and the Fastnet the lights at the end of the world: the next lighthouse is on the other side of the Atlantic. Red sandstone cliffs rise high above the sea where currents from west and south coasts meet – a notoriously tricky spot for shipping. During the Second World War, for example, 800 boats were wrecked here in three months. One of many boats rescued thanks to the vigilance of the lighthouse-keepers, who called out the Baltimore Lifeboat on 29 September 1985, was Charles J.

Haughey's converted trawler, the *Tourima*. Chief Keeper, Richard Foran, was cited for his role in the rescue.

Whales and dolphins pass offshore at the Mizen Head; gannets, choughs, and kittiwakes dive overhead. In calm weather seals bask on the rocks under the Arched Bridge, a sturdy steel suspension bridge that is the only way on to the island, reached by walking down 99 steps from the car park. The three-storey visitor centre has a shop and café and is packed with interesting displays: a tidal clock which, as well as giving the times of high tide, also re-enacts a rescue at sea off the Fastnet on the hour; a scale model of the Fastnet Rock; replicas of the huge stones with which the lighthouse was built; a navigational aids simulator; and a replica lighthouse-keepers' kitchen and bedroom.

The existence of this visitor centre is largely the result of the determination and tenacity of one woman, Sue Hill. Sue, an Englishwoman, discovered Goleen when she married a Cork city man, Dick Hill. Dick had done his thesis in the area as a student, and they bought a house there in 1969. Her parents, Ron and Joyce Buswell, helped out with a loan, and came over to see what Dick and Sue had bought. They liked the area so much that they bought a farmhouse at Carrigacat nearby. For a while, Sue ran a B&B and did evening meals for her own and other people's guests in her parents' large holiday home. She knew there was a great demand for a restaurant in the area. But Dick's job as a producer with RTÉ took the family to Dublin, and it was not until he left RTÉ to manage Cork Opera House in 1985 that Sue bought Heron's Cove, a modern house a short walk from the village and overlooking a little cove that really does have a heronry. It was a lovely spot, but in the first winter she had a total of six people for dinner – and not all at once. However, she persevered, and the place has a good name for the freshest local fish, simply prepared, and for its excellent wine list.

In 1992 Sue's two sons had left home, and she wanted to start a business, so she set up a series of seminars, and formed the Mizen Tourism Association. In 1993, Irish Lights workers at the Mizen Head told her the lighthouse was about to be automated, and the bridge would be blown up. It was exactly the project she had been looking for. She approached Irish Lights, on behalf of the Mizen Tourism Co-operative, and they agreed to give the Co-op a 250-year lease on the land. Initially, the aim was to get back the jobs that were being lost locally because of automation. Sue consulted the artist Jules Thomas and, after much discussion, Jules produced a series of boards illustrating how the lighthouse could be turned into a visitor centre – then, as Sue says, 'I went out and sold it.'

West Cork LEADER was one of the first backers, and then Sue went public with it, encouraging local people to invest because it was for the good of the area. Stephen O'Sullivan, one of the keepers who had been made redundant, joined her in the project. ERDF/Tourism Ireland, Cork County Council, a term loan from AIB, and income from Mizen Tourism currently fund the Centre. So far there has only been one major donation, €50,000 in 2006 from a person who made a fortune in a Bluetooth company, and had a local grandfather who worked for Irish Lights. After fifteen years' hard work, all of it voluntary, the Mizen Head Visitor Centre, 29 miles from Skibbereen, and fourteen from Schull, is now averaging between 46,000 and 60,000 paying visitors a year.

There has also been an increase in the number of gardens open to the public. Lissard House near Skibbereen has a Sky Garden designed by the American artist James Turrell that is well worth a visit, even though it is a weird experience. I am told that it is best not to indulge in any consciousness-altering substances beforehand. You lie on your back on a marble plinth (like a corpse awaiting the embalmer) in a sunken garden surrounded by banks of grass, and look up at the clouds racing across the sky.

Lisselan near Clonakilty has twelve hectares of gardens planted in the Robinsonian style. The Glengarriff Bamboo Park has coastal walks through 30 different species of palm tree and bamboo. The West Cork Garden Trail promotes about fifteen gardens that open to the public, some only in June, including David and Patsy Puttnam's River House Garden.

But, in addition to creating new visitor attractions, much more could be made of the heritage buildings that already exist in the area. I would love to see a Church Trail, drawing attention to the many fine churches of different denominations and eras, some ruined, most still in use. An artist pointed out that west Cork has great potential for a stained glass trail, with several artists in the area working in that medium, and many little-visited examples of the art like the modern work in Drimoleague's Roman Catholic Church, as well as the Harry Clarke windows at Timoleague and Castletownshend, and more traditional work in several Roman Catholic Churches. Perfect rainy weather entertainment.

8

Oh what a Paradise it Seems – Incomers 1969–2007

People are very curious in west Cork. They ask a lot of questions after a very short acquaintance. Five minutes sitting beside you in a bar, for example, and they want to know your place of birth, your mother's maiden name, your marital status, and eventually they'll get around to the one that always stumps me: 'Yes, but where are you from *originally*?' In a place with roots as deep as west Cork's, where generation after generation has farmed the same patch of land, this question still has a clear answer for many people. No matter how far these lucky people travel in their lives, no matter what country they settle in or where they raise their children, they know they are from somewhere, *originally*.

The rest of us struggle to belong anywhere. For many people, west Cork, with its archetypal small farms, friendly shops, welcoming pubs, and daily life on a manageable, human scale, is the closest they've come to feeling at home anywhere. People often say they have 'fallen in love with' west Cork: it seems the best way to describe the sudden, often irrational, impulse that leads people who have had no previous contact with the area either to buy a holiday home, or to take the big step and live in the area full-time.

James Lovelock, the distinguished independent scientist, best known for his Gaia theory, was a typical 'impulse buyer'.

He uses the words 'fell in love' to describe the feelings aroused on his first visit in January 1965. He came for a winter break with his daughter, choosing southern Ireland for its mild climate, given the time of year. They stayed in the Great Southern Hotel, Kenmare (now the Park Hotel), and used this as a base for exploring. Once Lovelock found Beara, he recognised it as the place he had been looking for: 'Imagine the mountains of Wales, somehow placed within Cornwall, and all of it uninhabited but for a sprinkling of farms, small fishing villages, and towns. We fell in love with it there and then.' (*Homage to Gaia*, Oxford University Press, 2000, p.307–8). He rented a holiday cottage for the following July and returned with his wife. On that second visit he bought Ard Carrig, a cottage in Adrigole on the slopes of Hungry Hill, near the seashore.

For the next twelve years, he and his wife spent two to three months there every summer. To get to Ireland, Lovelock had to drive through parts of Wales with prominent anti-holiday-home graffiti: 'Kick the English out of Wales'. Yet even though his years in west Cork coincided with renewed IRA activity in the North and internment, he and his family were never aware of any animosity towards them for being English. He praises his neighbours, who were courteous, friendly and helpful, in particular the neighbouring farmer, Michael O'Sullivan and his wife. In 1965 the O'Sullivans were finding it hard to make a living from their farm, so Michael welcomed the offer of winter work, building a laboratory and an extra bedroom for Lovelock. Had it not been for the remoteness of the area, he would have been happy to make Adrigole his main base, instead of Wiltshire. James Lovelock describes in his autobiography, *Homage to Gaia*, how he used to enjoy walking on the wild slopes of Hungry Hill, swimming in sun-warmed peaty lakes, and sitting on a favourite slab of rock overlooking Bantry Bay and the Atlantic. Lovelock sees science as a vocation, not just a career, and it is part of his practice to work at home, prompted by materials and observations that surrounded him.

This is where he would think through the scientific problems that he faced in his work as an independent research scientist, and this is where he composed his first book, *Gaia: A New Look at Life on Earth* (Oxford University Press, 1979). It was written almost entirely in his cottage at Adrigole, below his favourite rock. The Gaia hypothesis (named after the Greek Earth goddess at the suggestion of Lovelock's friend, the novelist William Golding), proposes that the earth is made of living organisms and the material Earth, and is self-regulating in a way that promotes life overall. The Gaia hypothesis was initially criticised as being overly romantic and, while it was well received by environmentalists and climate scientists, mainstream biologists attacked it. It has since been supported by a number of experiments and in the 1980s became recognised as a theory rather than a hypothesis. Today Gaia theory is commonly referred to by the more robust term Earth System Science. Lovelock admits to a certain romanticism in the book's genesis and blames it firmly on Beara: 'As I sat in the warm sun on my ledge, high up on the sandstone slabs of Hungry Hill, it was not easy to think about the Earth in any way except romantically.'

West Cork attracts a different kind of person from those who take their holidays or invest in property on the Spanish costas, the French Riviera, or other Mediterranean destinations. They are looking for something more than a place in the sun: a place where they and their family can feel safe and welcomed (or at least accepted) by the local community. A place where the food is familiar, and pubs and restaurants are run on familiar lines. For English-speakers, there is the lack of a language barrier, or so they think, until they encounter their first toothless mountainy man.

To move full-time from a large city to a sparsely popu-lated rural area is a major socio-cultural shock, whatever your nationality. The shock is even greater if you have to work for a living. It is fine, while you are on holiday, to live amongst people who have time to exchange pleasantries about the weather, and keep saying, 'When God made time, He made plenty of it,' but when you are trying to run a business and get things done, it can become extremely frustrating. It is informally estimated (by auctioneers, who deal with house sales and resales) that up to 80 per cent of people who try to settle full-time in west Cork return to their country of origin. Holiday homes also have a natural lifespan, and are sold on according to changing patterns of family life.

There is a common pattern. For incomers, whether Irish or foreign nationals, the honeymoon phase, which can last for years, is followed by disillusion, usually brought on by rows over rights of way, water, boundaries, dumping, stubble-burning, or any of the other myriad reasons that people fall out with each other in the countryside. The third phase is either to sell up and leave, or to recognise the reality, accept that there is no such thing as paradise, and just go on being yourself. People who make it into the third phase often find that once they have stopped thinking about it, they are accepted and have friends in the local community. People often realise this when they start going to their neighbours' funerals.

But while looking at the different experiences of people who have moved to the area from other parts of Europe, whether as part-time owners of holiday homes or as a full-time residents, it is important to remember that the majority of people living in west Cork are still either local to the area, or from other parts of Ireland. A 2004 survey by Bantry-based auctioneers, Harrington Estates, showed that while 28 per cent of property buyers in the Bantry area were British-based, with 7.5 per cent from other European countries, the majority – 64 per cent – were local, or from other parts of Ireland.

In the years between the end of the Second World War and the accession of Ireland to the EEC, the government tried to attract foreign investment to disadvantaged areas by offering generous incentives to people who created local jobs. Holland and Germany were the main source of permanent immigrants attracted to west Cork by these incentives. Some went in for farming, others opened small factories, and some opened hotels or guest-houses. Many enterprises were short-lived. The initial attraction of the relative lack of officialdom and state interference was counterbalanced by the accompanying lack of infrastructure. Up until the mid-1980s, you could be waiting for three years to get a telephone installed. The roads and the signposting were terrible, flights were few and expensive, and there were no direct passenger ferry services to the continent.

Peter Somerville-Large in his book, *Cappaghglass*, spoke to a German businessman he calls Gunther Rothenburger, whose views on his adopted country are probably typical of his generation. Gunther and his wife Lise came to Ireland in 1974. They were attracted by the green, peaceful countryside, the space for living, the neighbourliness, and the lack of heavy industry. They bought an old rectory, modernised it, converted the stables to a garage, tarmacked the entrance drive, and tidied up the garden. Gunther started a small business exporting Irish goods to the Continent, an experience he quickly came to regret. The phone system didn't work. He waited two years for a Telex machine. He was so hard to reach that his German business contacts did not take him seriously. He gave up, fearing for his health. He was puzzled by the Irish way of doing things – the refusal of people selling a house to name their price, the habit of throwing washing machines and old cars into the nearest ditch when they stopped working – and concluded that the Irish were as different from the English as the Germans are from the French. The friendliness of their neighbours never developed beyond pleasantries, and he and Lise fell back on German friends, the nearest of whom lived 25 miles away.

Many Dutch and German people bought holiday homes in west Cork, attracted by the mild climate, the low price of land, and the low density of population: that magic figure of 34 souls per square kilometre. This trend started in the shadow of the Cold War, when it was pointed out that, because of the prevailing winds, south-west Ireland was one of the few places that would escape nuclear fall-out in the event of an atom bomb exploding on the European mainland.

Otto Kunze's move to Ireland in 1976 was a carefully planned career change. Otto was a social worker in Berlin and studied climate charts when planning his move to Ireland, since he intended to grow organic vegetables and open his own restaurant. He identified a small strip between Galley Head and the Old Head of Kinsale as having the highest annual temperature and the lowest annual rainfall. He bought a stone-built cottage in this area, at Dunworley on the Seven Heads. The only disadvantage was the site's exposure to salt-laden winds, so a shelter-belt had to be planted. While this was growing, Otto learnt his trade by working with Gerry Galvin, at the Vintage Restaurant in Kinsale. The original Dunworley Cottage Restaurant opened on 1 June 1984, and quickly acquired an enthusiastic clientele, in spite of being a half hour's drive from the nearest town. Otto met his Dutch wife, Hilde, in 1987, and in 1990 they moved down the road to a larger site. While the shelter-belts grew up and the soft fruit plants and tunnel got established, Otto and Hilde renovated the ruined cottages and built their own new house and restaurant.

To finance this venture, Otto moved back into social work, supervising the fostering of troubled children from city centres in Germany with Irish families, mostly within the farming community. Otto comments: 'It worked really well, rather to our surprise. These were kids that they couldn't keep anywhere in a locked-up situation in Germany, even with three social workers to one child, while here, after a while we got them in to mainstream secondary education, doing Junior Certs and even Leaving Certs. It worked partly because of the culture shock. One of the girls is still living here, with an Irishman, and they have two children.'

Otto's Creative Catering combined a seasonal restaurant with outside party catering. Pigs, a Saddleback–Tamworth cross, were added to the homestead, and used in charcuterie as well as roasted. 'This is our paradise,' said Hilde, when I visited them in June 2004, to celebrate the twentieth anniversary of the opening of Dunworley Cottage. It was a clear sunny day, with the cliffs carpeted in sea pinks, larks singing overhead, the blue sea stretching to the far horizon, a garden overflowing with organic fruit and vegetables, and a family of porkers snuffling in their pen.

But the hard work of running a five-acre organic garden, two tunnels, and rearing pigs, as well as the restaurant and four guest bedrooms, began to take its toll. In June 2007, Otto was diagnosed with heart trouble and, by September, Otto and Hilde had put their house and restaurant on the market and retired.

The marriage of German Otto and Dutch Hilde is, they believe, unique in the annals of modern-day west Cork. The Dutch and the Germans do not mix, even in west Cork. Otto explains: 'The German soldiers behaved very badly in Holland when they were retreating, running out of petrol and diesel, and the last thing they did was to confiscate all the bicycles for their retreat.' When Hilde met Otto, the first thing she said was, 'Can I have my bicycle back?'

You used to be able to tell a Dutch- or German-owned house renovation because of the meticulous detail and great expense with which they had been restored, using local stone and wood, and creating gardens that need minimal maintenance. Now such features are commonplace among Irish and UK holiday-home owners too. But alas, many of these houses lie empty for eleven months of the year. The film–maker and writer Maurice O'Callaghan owns two once-ruined properties near Kilcoe, which he has restored in traditional style. But, he pointed out a little uneasily, there were probably famine deaths on the hearths of all the houses near where he lives.

A small number of people from England and Dublin with dreams of self-sufficiency moved to west Cork between the late 1960s and early 1980s, when land could be bought or rented very cheaply. Quintessential blow-ins, they were usually travelling, often with a van or a caravan, and stopped when they found what they were, unconsciously perhaps, looking for. Many have, as predicted, blown away again, while those who stayed have raised families, become part of the community (but are still not regarded as locals), and now have grandchildren living in the area. They got by somehow, not just by signing on for the dole, but also by working at any available job, preferably an outdoor one: fishing, working on the roads, forestry. Those who stayed tend to be well educated (Oxford University and Trinity College, Dublin, feature largely), and from the middle to upper class, so much so that the younger people call this generation 'the upper crusties'.

Brian Lalor, writer, artist, archaeologist, editor, and currently director of the Graphic Studio, Dublin lived in west Cork from 1974 to 1989, in order to concentrate on his art. He also ran a gallery in Schull, one of the first to exhibit the work of the many artists living in the area. A record of his time there can be found in *West of West – An Artist's Encounter with West Cork* (Brandon Books 1990), a collection of writings and etchings. His acutely observed, often acerbic, essays constitute the best available account of the blow-in experience, and his etchings are an important record of a disappearing west Cork. He can rightly claim to have moved to 'a remote area of west Cork which no stranger had ever penetrated'. This place no longer exists: today everywhere has been penetrated by strangers.

It is not surprising that people who had grown up in the rapidly developing cities of post-war Europe should find the wild scenery and romantically tumbledown buildings of west Cork attractive. What was more surprising was the warmth of the welcome given to these strange-looking, impecunious incomers by the local population. Annie Goulding, who moved to Allihies in 1971, thinks it was because her elderly neighbours had little contact with young people, and did not see her and her long-haired husband, Tim, as in any way different. Jenny Richardson, a Scottish artist, was living near Allihies at the time, and had experienced hostility from the locals in rural Scotland. She ran away when an elderly Allihies neighbour, whose speech she could not understand, approached her. It turned out her was offering her free milk from his cow.

What really puzzled the locals was why these well-mannered, well-educated young people should want to live in run-down houses with no electricity or running water. They themselves had only recently acquired both facilities, and it seemed a retrograde step.

The only academic study to be made so far of in-migration to west Cork is an unpublished MA thesis, written in the Department of Geography (UCC) by Heather Hegarty in 1994: *A Geographical Analysis of the Socio-cultural Interface Between the Locals and the Incomers in West Cork*. This is a lively, well-researched piece of work, but it also highlights how much the scene has changed since 1994. The incomers that Hegarty interviewed shared attitudes that she describes as 'counterurban and countercultural'. They came to west Cork to 'be their own person' and 'do their own thing'. No wonder 80 per cent of them returned to their countries of origin.

❖

Stephen O'Keeffe, of Schull auctioneers James Lyon O'Keeffe, is in his late thirties. He has noticed that many people his age who enjoyed childhood holidays in the area, now find themselves returning on holiday with their own children, whether they have local connections or not. These people often end up buying a holiday home. Stephen's company manages about 80 holiday homes, mostly around Schull. He calculates that the letting season lasts for 22 weeks in summer, with another two weeks at Christmas and two mid-term breaks. 'Some houses may get only three occupied months, others will get the full 26 weeks,' he says. Many were built under tax-incentive schemes, and they have been sold on as holiday homes.

Fred Astaire's daughter, Adele, and her husband, were among the first to buy and restore an old farmhouse near Schull. In the late 1970s and early 1980s, people could buy a coastal site with a ruin for a four-figure sum, and then get planning permission for a new or renovated house. Those days are gone, at least around the Mizen area, according to Stephen. He reckons that coastal frontage or good sea views add about €200,000 to the value of a property, but says that more modest, low-maintenance property within walking distance of the town is also much sought-after. 'There will be always be great value when there is a shortage of supply, and there's a shortage of supply in Schull,' he says. The same is true of the whole fashionable coastline, from Rosscarbery to Crookhaven.

For Londoners, it is quicker and easier to fly to Cork Airport and drive to your place in west Cork that it is to sit in the Friday evening traffic on the M4 attempting to reach your place in the West Country. Increased competition has led to cheaper fares, and more direct flights to more destinations in Europe and the UK than anyone could have imagined. The

Monday morning Heathrow flight from Cork carries about twenty regular commuters from Kinsale and points west, who return as soon as they can during the week, to rejoin their spouse and family.

More and more people are finding, like David Puttnam, that gradually the so-called holiday home is becoming the main residence. Puttnam originally began looking for a holiday home in western Scotland. He says, 'It started in 1982, with me going off to do a movie called *Local Hero*. I went off literally two weeks after winning the Oscar [for *Chariots of Fire*] … it was the most amazing respite to go to the west coast of Scotland for eight weeks. It was one of the happiest times of my life. But we couldn't find what we wanted there – it was either too big or too expensive.'

The Puttnams came to west Cork in 1988 on the first leg of a driving holiday, and stayed with friends near Union Hall. Out on a walk the next morning, Puttnam met an architect who told them about the place that would become their home. The old farmhouse was half-ruined, but it had a wonderful unspoilt view of the River Ilen. He asked the vendor to hold it for him for one week, while he and Patsy thought it over. A week later they bought the ruin and fourteen acres. The house they have built looks old and is spacious and comfortable, without being ostentatious. Accessibility to London, where they had another house, was not a factor, since they had been thinking of Scotland.

They had a country house in Wiltshire too, says David. 'What happened was just fascinating. Every single opportunity, when I could go to one or the other, I found myself coming here. So in 1996 we sold Wiltshire, after fourteen years. It was a much bigger, more elaborate place. I retired from the film industry in 1997, and by a process of osmosis, between 1997 and 2002 we found ourselves living here. Property in London was going crazy, and we owned quite a big house, which made me nervous. So two years ago, I decided to sell it, give myself a pension, and here we are.'

The London house was replaced with a small flat, and David goes over about once a week, Patsy once a fortnight and, until the end of his presidency in 2008, they will also be travelling a lot for UNICEF.

Their west Cork home is relatively modest – by film producer standards. They bought it as a tumbledown farmhouse. David insists that they would not be able to afford it if it came on the market today. They added a gate lodge, and the house is now approached along a driveway, running parallel to the river and high above it. A tall stone wall with arches leads to a large gravel patio behind the house, with geraniums in pots and informal plantings of nasturtium. The front of the house has the river view and two large bow windows, an idea which David borrowed from a house he'd seen in the west of Ireland. The windows have shutters, giving a homely Provençal look. In front of the house is a wide grass terrace, inspired by the one in Monet's garden at Giverny. The wildflower meadows sweep down to the river, bordered by mature trees that the Puttnams planted when they bought the ruined farmhouse. David says 'The view was the original reason we came here, but our friends in the local community are very important now.'

One of west Cork's most articulate enthusiasts is Rabbi Julia Neuberger, a quintessential Londoner. She and her husband Anthony have owned an old fortified house at Leamcon near Schull since 1984: 'We were going to a wedding in Dublin, and our friends, who have a house outside Schull, said if you're coming to Ireland you must come and see us. We didn't realise how far it was. We seemed to be driving forever through sheeting rain. When we got as far as Skibbereen the rain stopped, and we had that amazing light that you can get after rain, and we had three wonderful days.' They came back several times while their two children were small, renting every time, and one summer it poured with rain and the house they were in had no reading lamps. That was the tipping point for Julia: 'It was a nightmare. So I said we'll just have to buy a house. Anthony thought I was mad, but he humoured me, and it gave us something to do in the rain: we went and looked at a lot of houses and found this one.' Julia has written all or part of all her books in the house, finding the peace of the countryside conducive to work. 'I like the people hugely, the warmth and openness, and slight dottiness … then there is this bizarre thing of an embryonic Jewish community in the area. A whole group of us quite often get together on a Friday night, for the Sabbath.'

Glandore's most famous resident, Tony O'Reilly (net worth estimated at \$1.1 billion by Forbes Magazine), chief executive of Independent News and Media, bought a waterside hotel in Glandore about 30 years ago and turned it into a private house. He has recently consolidated four houses on the seaward side of the main road as a closed compound. He is reportedly not a frequent visitor, but then he has four other homes – a 1,000-acre stud farm in Kildare, a *château* near Deauville, an island retreat in the Bahamas, and a town house in Fitzwilliam Square, Dublin.

While Dublin politicians and businessmen favour Schull and the Mizen Peninsula in August, Londoners prefer Glandore. One year there were so many regular contributors in residence that *Any Questions* was actually broadcast by BBC Radio Four from the community hall in Glandore. Greg Dyke, former Director General of the BBC, is a close neighbour of David Puttnam near Skibbereen. Carol Vorderman, the TV show host, made a neat profit when she sold her house in Glandore for €1 million in 2006. And so on, and so forth … the list is long. But the great thing is that nobody really cares: celebrities, major and minor, go about their daily business largely unrecognised, and unacknowledged. Nuala O'Faolain was once famously asked, 'Are you Somebody?', giving her a great title for her memoir. In west Cork, they don't even bother to ask: we are *all* somebody is the underlying assumption, and to hell with you if you think you're more important than me. Two of the highest terms of praise given to strangers are 'genuine' and 'down-to-earth'. These qualities matter more than fame or fortune.

Victoria Glendinning, biographer and literary critic, calls the prevalence of the London 'chattering classes' in west Cork its 'Chiantishire' aspect, a reference to the similar cluster in Tuscany. She said: 'That was not the reason I came, rather the reverse. It was quite shocking when an awful lot of English media people discovered west Cork and wrote all these articles about it.'

In 1989 Victoria was living in London with her husband, Terence de Vere White, man of letters and a former books editor of *The Irish Times*, and had inherited just enough money to buy a house in Ireland. Coolnaclehy, which they bought in 1989, was an old house, tucked away off a back road, approached by driving across a bog and opening and shutting a galvanised gate. It was on a bend in the River Ilen and had a sylvan charm. It was big enough for her four sons from her first marriage and Terence's grown-up children to visit. The interior was comfortably Bohemian. A Persian guest had left some beautiful writing in Arabic script on the kitchen beams. Terence painted one of his favourite mantras, 'Nothing is forever' over an alcove in the dining room. Terence died at Coolnaclehy in 1994, after a long illness. Victoria kept the house for another ten years, using it as a place to unwind, rather than for writing. She enjoyed the informal social life, entertaining her sons and their friends, and walking. She spent much of her time hacking back brambles and worrying about loose roof slates and rotting woodwork. When she remarried, she finally decided to sell Coolnaclehy. When I asked her what west Cork had meant to her, she paused only briefly before giving a one-word answer: 'happiness'.

The legislation introduced by Charles J. Haughey in 1969 exempting writers and artists from paying tax on income from their creative work, has had a small but significant impact on the permanent population of the area. It is in the nature of tax-motivated short-term residents to gravitate to the Dublin area, but some who were in it for the longer term settled in west Cork. The screenwriter and director Wolf Mankovitz settled near Kilcrohane, and advised Patrick Skene Catling to move to Ireland, where writers were held in respect and exempt from tax on literary earnings. Skene Catling is author of one of the most successful-ever children's books, *The Chocolate Touch*, (1952) as well as an accomplished journalist, and sometime novelist and screenwriter. He recounts in his autobiography, *Better Than Working* (Secker & Warburg, 2004), that he quickly learnt the value of the advice about Ireland given to him by an Irish colleague: 'Behave as if you were going to live in a foreign country – because you are.' In the early 1970s, Skene Catling went house-hunting in Ahakista, renting a cottage and fourteen acres for £5 a week, a bargain even then. He is still in the area, now an octogenarian, reviewing for *The Irish Times*, writing fiction and playing golf.

The graphic artist Tomi Ungerer and his wife Yvonne flew into Shannon in 1975 and rented a car, discovering west Cork by accident. The couple had originally met in New York, where both became disillusioned with city life, moving to a smallholding on a remote peninsula in Nova Scotia, an adventure that Tomi described and pictured in his book, *Far Out Isn't Far Enough* (Grove Press, 1984). When they decided to leave Nova Scotia, where the harsh climate meant that they had to slaughter all their livestock every autumn, a number of friends suggested Ireland.

'It was like a sign,' says Yvonne, whose family emigrated from Galway some generations back. 'Everyone kept saying, why don't you go to Ireland?' They met P. J. Sheehan, the South-west Cork TD, by chance in a hotel in Castletownbere. When he heard what they were looking for, he said he knew exactly the right place for them, and he did. The new base meant that Tomi, who maintains close links to his native

Strasbourg, no longer had a transatlantic commute. Their three children were born in Bantry and went to the local school. Yvonne was for many years a well-respected commercial sheep farmer and this, plus having children and attending Sunday Mass, meant that she integrated easily into the local community. Her sons have taken over the farm, which is no longer run commercially. Because his family is now settled in County Cork and he regards it as his second home, in 2007 Tomi made a generous gift of work from his archive to UCC.

Writer, explorer, film-maker and lecturer Tim Severin moved to Courtmacsherry in 1974, and it has been his base ever since. That such a well-travelled person has chosen west Cork as his home says a lot. The tax exemption for writers was not a major factor, he says. Severin is best known for *The Brendan Voyage* (Hutchinson, 1978), which proved, by repeating the feat, that it was possible for the sixth-century Saint Brendan to have sailed to America in a leather boat. The book was translated into 27 languages. He has since made a career from travelling and writing about other 'replica voyages' in the Mediterreanean and Asia.

Now in his sixties, weary of uncomfortable travel, Severin has reinvented himself as a novelist. Severin remains every inch an Oxford-educated Englishman. He came to Cork because it was the only place he could afford to buy property. He decided he could live anywhere within an hour's drive of the airport and chose Courtmacsherry, swapping his rented garret in London for a terraced house on the water's edge. He is generous with his time, opening festivals and exhibitions. Home is now a new house beside the Argideen River, built in 1993 when he converted an old mill to self-catering accommodation, to provide an economic safety net, in view of the unpredictability of his chosen profession. Severin has never thought of moving: 'It's just such a lovely place to live. Everything is so easy, and there's still a very strong sense of community. And because there is such a long tradition around here of people going away and coming back – perhaps emigrating or going to sea – people find my travelling quite normal. It's very international in a rather curious way, and I'm very comfortable with that.'

People move to west Cork nowadays for positive reasons: it is no longer seen as dropping out of society, nor is it a rejection of urban living, nor a rejection of the dominant culture. For most people, it is simply a matter of choosing to live in a cleaner, more pleasant environment, where jobs and business opportunities can be found or created. People are commuting to Cork city and Limerick from Clonakilty and further west in order to be able to afford a nice house in pleasant surroundings.

The Soho Solo project was launched in 2003 as an EU-funded pilot project identifying people who have migrated to a rural region – Cork and Kerry in Ireland, Beira Interior in Portugal, Cadiz in Spain, the Canary Islands, and Le Gers in Gascony – bringing with them their own business and clients, to work mainly from home. It promotes the Atlantic regions as a place to live and work, thereby encouraging rural sustainability and regeneration. A successful pilot project led to local funding from the Cork Business Innovation Centre and the County and City Enterprise Boards in Cork and Kerry for a Soho Solo helpdesk in south-west Ireland. The aim is to identify exisiting Small Office Home Office workers (Soho workers), to offer support to these entrepreneurs, and to promote the concept of Soho working. The networking aspect of Soho Solo's existence is one of the most important: it helps to overcome the isolation many home workers experience, and it has also led to partnerships between enterprises, and to people using the services offered by other Soho Solos.

The significance of this concept for geographically remote regions like west Cork is enormous: it means that new people are moving to the area, usually with their families, and bringing their own jobs with them. These range from telecoms start-ups, to management consultancies, marketing enterprises, and arts and crafts enterprises. Often, but not always, much of the work is done by using the Internet, and is described as 'independent of physical location'. About half of the 350 companies currently in the Soho Solo directory are based in west Cork. By moving to the area, these people contribute to their local community: purchasing goods and services there; increasing the numbers of children in local schools; and very often making a voluntary contribution to the local community (coaching soccer, for example, or joining a community service organisation like the Lions Club, or becoming active in the local church), as this is a good way for a home worker to mingle and make friends. The great thing is that all the social benefits accrue to the community, without the incomers competing with locals in the market for existing jobs.

Pat O'Flaherty appreciates the networking opportunities offered by Soho Solo. He moved from Dublin to a coastal property in Glengarriff with his wife and three small children in 2003. He has a corporate background in Information Technology and now runs a web-based telecoms enterprise, FoneValue. Although he is from west Galway, Pat chose west Cork because he liked its cosmopolitan mix of residents: 'We looked at other places, but we didn't find this scene with people of different nationalities living in the area that you get around here. It was the best day's work we ever did. When we rang the headmistress of the local school and we told her we were coming with three kids, you could almost hear her dancing a jig. The kids do horse-riding, ballet, drama, and karate. The quality of life here is amazing.' Pat reckons that anyone making the move from urban to rural should bring enough money with them to live for between three and five years, in addition to the price of their house.

Mike Regan, another Soho Solo, was born in London in 1959 to Irish parents and has numerous relations in west

Cork. Changes in his life, including a divorce and a new partner who was also keen to live in west Cork, led him to leave London, where he had his own IT company. He now runs an Internet business, itzoom.com, providing email and other services for a global market of IT professionals.

He is still adjusting to the drastic difference between a north London suburb and Scrahanaleary, midway between Durrus and Ballydehob: 'I'm living in a beautiful rural location on top of a hill, two and a half miles from the nearest shop. But the downside is that you end up getting a bit of cabin fever. I spent the last six years in London putting data networks in for large corporate companies, a job where I was out meeting people all the time. I miss the interaction with people. But the aim is to survive and thrive in west Cork, by developing a business strategy that will provide a reasonable income, without creating the same pressures we have left behind.'

In 2004, I wrote a piece for the *Irish Examiner* about the West Cork Technology Park. This is a high-tech business park in a pleasant, campus-like environment. John Fleming, managing director of Fleming Construction, who was born at the Seven Heads, bought the land and developed the buildings in a bid to give a boost to his local area. The West Cork Technology Task Force, a voluntary body consisting of high-powered local business people, academics, and teachers – including former Minister Joe Walsh, the CEOs of SWS, West Cork LEADER, Carbery (Milk Products), Fleming Construction, and Bandon Co-op – meet regularly to monitor the project. Its chairman, Dan MacSweeney, CEO of Carbery, said: 'Speaking as a local businessman and as a parent, I see people coming out of school and wonder why we have to send them to Dublin, London, or Los Angeles to work. We have excellent, quality graduates in west Cork, and we would like to keep them here.'

The West Cork Technology Park intends to reap the benefits of the new telecoms-based economy for the residents of west Cork. For example, the SWS Group offices at the West Cork Technology Park handle the back-office operations of large Dublin-based companies: the bulk of the accounts department of the Independent Newspaper Group is no longer housed in Dublin's Middle Abbey Street, where office space is at a premium; its pay cheque operations are now carried out at the West Cork Technology Park. There are currently around 350 jobs on site, and the intention is to increase this to around 1,000. Certainly, people are keen to move to the Clonakilty area: the Department of the Marine and Bord Iascaigh Mhara (BIM) are about to relocate there and, by all reports, the civil servants involved are largely happy with the new location.

In order to spice up the piece I was writing about the Park, I added a vignette of happy young workers leaving the West Cork Technology Park by car, with a surfboard on the roof, heading for the beach for a few hours' surfing before going home for tea. I assumed it would be cut, as wildly over the top: in fact, it has become the everyday reality for many people.

9

A Very Expensive Hobby

I, the poet, William Yeats,
With old mill boards and sea-green slates,
And smithy work from the Gort forge,
Restored this tower for my wife George;
And may these characters remain
When all is ruin once again.

To be Carved on a Stone at Thoor Ballylee
William Butler Yeats

Ireland has always been rich in ruins, a legacy of its troubled history. Ruins, large and small, were always part of the landscape, and many felt, like the poet W. B. Yeats, that any effort to restore them was a short-term, shoring-up operation against the inevitable. Ruins were the way things were meant to be, the norm to which, as Yeats assumed, everything would revert. But times are changing, castle restoration is now big business, and these restorations are being built to last.

The knowledge and expertise to restore castles has grown apace in the past ten years. West Cork's most famous castle-restorer, the actor Jeremy Irons, has done a magnificent job on Kilcoe Castle, one of the biggest tower houses on Roaringwater Bay, a fifteenth-century building with walls up to eight feet thick. He is highly knowledgeable, and speaks of what he ironically calls 'a very expensive hobby' with real passion. He spends long months away, filming on location, partly in order to pay for the work done on Kilcoe and is understandably offended when people make fun of his efforts, assuming that a glamorous film star knows nothing about stone and mortar. Women, who are always assumed to be ignorant of such matters, will identify immediately. In fact, Jeremy worked as his own project manager throughout the long restoration process, and is held in high esteem by tradesmen and craftsmen alike.

Jeremy Irons is patron of the West Cork Craft Guild, and is known for being generous with his time in promoting and launching the work of local craftspeople. I was talking to him once after the launch of a wooden game for Murray Heasman, a craftsman who specialises in Celtic design and who had also carved an intricate door for Kilcoe. A television journalist, who had recently made a series about west Cork, confidently came up and introduced himself. In an instant, the warm, friendly man I had been speaking to became icily hostile, and repelled the invader with a venomous hiss: 'You're the idiot who said on television that I painted my castle pink!' Then he swivelled on his heels, neatly turning his back on the television man, before turning back to me and reverting to Mister Nice with a dismissive flick of the eyebrow. It was such a consummate display of the actor's art that I almost applauded.

Kilcoe Castle is not pink, and it is not painted. Before beginning his restoration, Jeremy travelled extensively around both Ireland and Scotland, looking at castles that had been restored and learning from the experts. One of these experts was Tim Meek, who worked largely for the Scottish National Trust. Jeremy was so impressed with the beautiful stonework displayed at Kilcoe that he did not want to render the exterior. He believed that cleaning the stones of the castle and repointing them with lime mortar – a process that took twelve people nine months, working in all weathers – would make it weatherproof. But, as he wrote in a piece in *The Irish*

Times in May 2001, during the first winter '... water poured through the walls by the bucketful.' He consulted Tim Meek, who advised him to render the castle and to cover the render with ten coats of limewash.

Limewash is naturally white, and that would have been the traditional finish – hence all those tower houses known as 'White Castle'. But Jeremy was rightly concerned about the starkness of white against the landscape and the effect of weathering over twenty years. He preferred to choose a colour that worked with the surrounding countryside, and looked as good when it was wet and dark as in sunlight. The decision was taken to add ferrous sulphate (or Copperass) to the lime. This is not a pigment so much as a process: it actually rusts when you paint it on. This turned the castle the same colour as the iron traces that leach out of the rock around the castle and the same colour as the seaweed at its base. Most commentators did not understand what had happened, and were critical of the colour. As Jeremy wrote: 'For a while in its long history it [Kilcoe Castle] had turned the colour of fresh rust, or as those who have been so vociferous in print before coming to see for themselves would call it, peach.' Six years later, people have come to like the area's new landmark, and point it out with pride.

The next time I met Jeremy he was in Kinsale, once again doing a good deed: opening Kinsale Arts Week. Unlike many other celebrities, he did not just turn up for the opening ceremony, make a speech, and leave as soon as politely possible. He stayed the night and was hanging around on the waterfront the next day, with his two graceful black dogs on leads, waiting for an open-air concert. He knew I wanted to visit Kilcoe for this book, and took the time to brief me while we waited, sitting on a wall in the sun.

Once he started work on Kilcoe, he told me, word got around and people came calling. He described a team of young Germans, with top hats and little waistcoats, travelling around Europe, doing apprenticeships. The stripes on their waistcoats indicated their trade. A couple of journeymen from a French guild of stonemasons turned up, in high-waisted cord trousers and braces. They did not expect much money, but expected to learn while working, and to get their board and lodging. He said, 'I always ask tradesmen if they play an instrument, and if they do, they are usually right for us. I say to them, what we are doing is a jazz riff on the medieval. We don't want theme-park authenticity. For example, in medieval times they didn't have furniture, as we understand it. But I was lucky to be able to source some suitable pieces on my travels – Chinese pieces, Indian pieces. We let the castle speak to us and it told us what to do. We were lucky in that way.'

Meanwhile, he was going straight from Kinsale to the airport, and would be gone for the month of August. I was to get back to him in September, to arrange a visit to Kilcoe. Before coming to Kilcoe, he said, I must go and talk to Richard Good-Stephenson at Cor Castle about concrete and lime mortar. 'Richard's castle is not as old as mine, but he's done it up beautifully.'

It is impossible to write about the castles of County Cork without giving credit to James N. Healy, whose book *The Castles of County Cork*, was published in 1988 (Mercier Press), with 72 line drawings and ten maps by the author. James N., as he was known, was an enthusiast for all things relating to his native county, Cork. A graduate of UCC (B.Comm, 1947), he was equally well known as an actor and singer as he was as writer and broadcaster. He spent all his spare time for seven years visiting the site of every castle in the county, and finding out as much as he could about their history. I am told that his book has errors, but his informal way of turning up and talking to people, adding their anecdotal evidence to the library research, makes for an unusually enjoyable work of reference. Those who buy castles in order to restore them, as opposed to those who inherit them, tend to be colourful, larger-than-life people, who think big.

In 1981, when James N. Healy was researching the book, Cor Castle was a ruin. Richard Good-Stephenson was then a teenager, living with his family in a modern bungalow on the far side of the ruins. Healy reports: 'Young Richard Good-Stephenson told me it was his ambition to rebuild the castle; at current costs it would be a massive project, but it would be nice to think that it could be accomplished.'

I had wanted an excuse to visit Cor Castle for years, ever since I saw its restoration slowly taking place. It stands high up on the south side of the Bandon River at Innishannon and I had caught a distant glimpse of the work in progress from the village itself. As the scaffolding was removed, a beautiful building was revealed, with stone towers at either end, linked by a turreted section rendered in a mellow ochre.

The Castle was originally built by the Croker family, who came to the area from Somerset around 1711, but it is highly likely that an earlier building stood on the site, since it overlooks such an important river crossing, which was probably a ford before the bridge was built. In about 1811, Chambre Croker (Richard's ancestor) built the 'new' castle: old photographs show a fortified house, rather than a castle, with the pleasing proportions of a substantial Georgian manor. It was this building that the Republicans burnt down in 1921, giving the commanding position it occupied as the reason for its destruction. Working from the old photographs of the exterior, Richard and his team were able to recreate the building that stands there today in all its glory.

Richard is a tall, slim man, in his early forties, neatly turned out, with short, dark hair, serious and reserved. After ushering me into the large, elegant drawing room, the first thing that he shows me are photographs of the castle as it was in his childhood: an overgrown, roofless ruin with a sycamore tree growing up through the earth floor. There is now a coffee table on the exact spot. We both look from the coffee table to the photograph of the tree and back again. It is an eerie moment.

Richard went to school in Bandon, and then to Wesley College, he explains: 'I went straight from there to America. My first passion was flying aircraft, so I went from boarding school to America to learn to fly, and I was out of the country for about fifteen years. I'm an airline pilot by profession. I ended up with British Airways, and I was a captain at Gatwick on 737s. I still keep my licence up; last week we flew to the Isle of Man for the weekend. I fly for fun and business now, as opposed to flying for a living.'

Richard and his English wife have two sons, now aged nine and ten, and they moved back to Ireland so that the elder could start school. The restoration at Cor was already well under way: 'I started the business whilst I was flying, and then it took off, and I couldn't fly and do business together, so I chose the business. And I ended up back here.' The business he refers to is a specialised branch of property development: the purchase, restoration, and resale of historic buildings. He commutes to England every week, where he is working on the restoration of an 11,500-square-foot, nineteenth-century building, which had been institutionalised for the last 50 years.

His business now has two strands to it. One is the buying and restoration of historic buildings, and the ancillary one is the manufacture and sale of lime mortar and lime renderings through a company called Lochplace, with offices in Inni-shannon at an old forge below the castle. Lime mortar is what I have come to talk about, and I could not have been sent to a better man.

Richard explains that lime mortar, also known as lime putty, has been used all over the world since Roman times. It was rediscovered in this part of the world in the 1970s and 1980s, when English Heritage were puzzled as to why a lot of the buildings they were working on were deteriorating faster after they had been done up than before. So they spent a lot of money on research, and they realised was that this was happening because they were using cement. They solved it by using lime mortar and banning cement on their properties. Nowadays most people – builders, conservation architects, the Office of Public Works – understand the importance of using lime on old buildings. Richard adds wryly: 'Whereas when we started restoring Cor ten years ago, people thought we were cracked.'

Because of his background in restoring old buildings, Richard was aware that they were going to have to use lime as opposed to cement at Cor: 'It was early days for the re-emergence of lime, so we decided to set up our own lime manufacture before we started, with the intention of making enough to utilise it on this particular building. We use a modern technology that produces lime with a hydraulic set, in other words, it has the ability to set under water. We soon found there was a huge demand for it, so there is now an ancillary business supplying lime products.'

Its advantages over cement are breathability and flexibility. Richard explains: 'It might only be millimetres, but what happens when you repair an old building with cement is that the building will continue to flex, and as a result of that you'll get little cracks in the cement. Water gets into those cracks, and then it gets into the walls, and it can't get back out again because cement doesn't breathe. You get a build-up of moisture in the wall, which ends up as internal dampness. What happens with lime is that on a wet day the moisture will get absorbed into the wall, and on a nice fine day like today, it will go out again. It's breathing, in and out. One of the reasons why they built old masonry walls so thick, two foot or two foot six, is because the moisture never got all the way in, before going out again. If you have an old building, use the technology that the building was built with; you don't try to change it. Cement is fine for a modern construction, although we find that more and more people are using lime for a modern construction because it is more eco-friendly, it's healthier for the environment, and it's more pleasing, aesthetically.'

Lime washes, like the lovely ochre colours used at Cor and at Kilcoe, contain natural pigments, which give a decorative finish to the lime plaster. They also provide the final layer of protection. Limewashes have been used by Lochplace on some newly built houses on Kinsale Harbour, giving them a soft, weathered look, so that they blend in more easily with their eighteenth-century neighbours.

Richard then took me on a tour of the ground floor of his house. Every room has a different plaster ceiling, copied (with permission) from existing historic homes, including Birr Castle. All the ceiling ornamentation – swags, grapes, leaves, and stems – were created 'from the bag', by craftsmen working under an English master-plasterer. He trained a local team – one young man, who is still in the area, did his entire apprenticeship working on Cor Castle. The windows were made in Northern Ireland, drawn up by an architect to get the proportions exactly right, including the slender glazing bars. The doors were handmade from an oak that came down on the farm. It is furnished in period, in a restrained, classical style, and it is quite honestly one of the most beautiful houses I have ever seen.

Richard is rightly proud of it. He compares it to Kilcoe: 'Jeremy's castle is a different period from this; his is medieval, so he has done it up as a medieval building. Obviously, in medieval times, defence was the most important thing, and comfort was secondary. In the nineteenth century, when Cor was built, things had moved on, and so comfort was the most important thing. But Jeremy knew from the beginning that he should be using lime putty.'

I leave Cor Castle, driving down its sloping avenue between giant bushes of blue and white hydrangeas, enveloped by a warm, ochre glow. Hidden away behind its plantation is an architectural jewel, even better close-to than from a distance.

Thoroughly briefed on lime mortar, thanks to Richard, I finally made my visit to Kilcoe, in the company of Bena Stutchbury, Jeremy Irons' architectural adviser and site manager during the resoration. Kilcoe was built around 1430 by the MacCarthy clan on a two-acre island at the head of Roaringwater Bay. It has a commanding view of the sea and surrounding countryside and was the scene of the last stand by the MacCarthy clan in 1603, before the local clans were finally subdued. It is unusual in that it consists of two towers.

The slender northern one, referred to by Bena as the 'turret', has seven storeys, while the larger southern tower has five storeys. The turret and southern tower are not interlinked until about twenty feet up, and Bena thinks the turret might have been added in order to make Kilcoe bigger than Rincolisky Castle, an O'Driscoll tower house that can be seen some miles to the east. Both tower and turret have a wall thickness of about eight foot at the bottom, tapering to about four foot six inches at the top. The tower is about 70 foot tall, the turret about 90 foot − 100 if you count the flagpole. Access to the island, which is popular with local walkers, has been maintained, while a sign outside the castle giving its history asks visitors to respect that it is now a private home. Jeremy usually manages to spend about four months of the year there; he also owns a farm nearby.

The large wooden doors to the castle's forecourt open with a loud mechanical creak worthy of a Hammer horror film. The caretaker's cottage in the courtyard was excavated and the first three feet, from the foundations up, are original. Bena reckons this is the oldest part of the castle, probably where people lived while the main tower was being built. This is where they discovered one of the original ogee carvings, later used for the tops of the slit windows, and a strong design feature of the finished building. We enter through the tradesman's entrance, which leads to a workshop with a sign on the wall, 'Danger: Erection in Progress', a souvenir of the 35 months when the castle was scaffolded. Work started on the castle in 1997, and much of the wood used is green oak, brought down in the big storm of 1996. It came from Liam Hegarty's Baltimore boatyard, and the boatbuilder was a great help throughout the long process of restoration. Bena was involved from the start, leaving in 2003: 'Work will never really be finished.' She has the highest praise for Jeremy as a natural architect, and an ingenious lateral thinker: 'The same imagination that makes him such a good actor makes him a great designer.'

There were up to 30 people working on the castle at any one time. Locals and travelling craftsmen would come looking for work. The names and contact numbers of those employed were put on a list. This was circulated, and the team was encouraged to work in a cross-disciplinary way, sharing knowledge and expertise. The stone steps were in good repair, but anything carved had been taken or recycled – for example, as gravestones in the churchyard next door. Almost everything was handmade on site, from the wooden toilet seats to the wickerwork ceilings. (Vaulted ceilings were originally made of wicker supported by timber; the stonework was built over this frame.) Bena says the restoration process generated continual high drama: 'It was like *The Picture of Dorian Gray*: the more arguments and drama that occurred, the more beautiful the castle became. It was like a love affair with a building, and it's the same with other castle-owners. They become totally in love with their castle, and totally obsessed by it.'

The result is an exquisite home of great charm and beauty. Its owner liked the verdict of the visitor who described it as 'dark and quirky, a bit like Jeremy.' What I liked was the imagination, ingenuity, wit and attention to detail: from the bedside lamp with its chain-mail fringe; to the full-size, carved wooden horse in the castle's main room (either from a saddlery, or used by an artist for posing equestrian portraits; the metal cartwheel used for hanging kitchen utensils in the kitchen; to the massive bath in the main bedroom positioned beside the window with the best view. While the castle looks very big from the outside and has five levels with three large rooms and three mezzanines in the main tower, there are several smaller, oddly shaped rooms, linked by narrow passageways. These and other problematic spaces have been successfully made comfortable by using the kind of ingenious lateral thinking found in boat interiors – a natural solution, given Jeremy's love of boats. It is exactly as Jeremy says: 'We let the castle speak to us, and it told us what to do.'

It was a fine sunny day in late December, and Bena and I went out on to the roof of the turret for a break from the two-hour tour to revel in the long views, our reward for climbing all those stone stairs. There is a jacuzzi here, just below the perch beside the flagpole, where Jeremy likes to sit with a drink on a fine summer evening. It is a tremendous achievement, and all done without a single grant or tax concession from the government. Kilcoe reminds me of a giant version of those puzzles where every single piece of differently shaped wood has to be put in the right place in order for them all to fit back into the box. The range of beautiful craftsmanship contained in one building is remarkable – and all the product of age-old skills. The fact that it is put together with a kind of edgy wit – one man's vision of how it had to be – makes the whole an outstanding work of art, a true original.

There is a smaller tower house across Roaringwater Bay, visible from Kilcoe, called Rincolisky, which is being converted by Stefanie Jaax, reluctantly and very expensively: in spite of several applications, she could not get planning permission for a new building on the site, not even one designed by an architect to look like a ruin. The project, which Bena Stutchbury has also worked on, must be overseen at every stage by heritage architects, and is costing far more than it would to build a new house: it is also far slower. First the stonework had to be cleaned by removing the ivy and scraping the cavities. Then it had to be pointed by filling the cavities with lime mortar. Eight years after initially applying for planning permission, it is still not habitable, although Stefanie does have the top room complete, with a solar roof, designed in such a way that the castle still looks like a ruin. Eventually she will have an inner concrete shell, containing an uncluttered, contemporary interior, the opposite approach to the one taken at Kilcoe.

It took Skibbereen solicitor Patrick McCarthy and his wife Bernie eight years to restore Dún na Séad, the O'Driscoll castle in the centre of Baltimore, ruined since 1650. Like Egerton Shelswell-White, Lord of the Manor at Bantry House, Bernie herself is often taking money at the entrance from June to September, when the castle is open to visitors. 'It's a cosy place to live in, because it's not huge,' she says of her castle home. 'The thick walls make it warm, and there's a nice contrast with the village being very quiet in winter and busy in summer.' When they began work on Dún na Séad in 1997, the lime mortar was, of course, sourced from Richard Good-Stephenson's company, Lochplace.

The castle is right in the middle of the village, built on a huge rock that dominates the harbour, and, having known it as a ruin for so many years, it is strange to see it roofed and glazed, with a flag flying from its corner. It was built in 1215, and became the chief residence of the O'Driscoll clan, and the centre of administration for their trading activities. The O'Driscolls made their money from charging visiting boats for fishing rights and supplying them with water. In 1649 the castle became a garrison for Cromwellian troops, after which it fell into ruin.

Today it is approached from the rear by steps up to a rectangular grassy area, once the bawn, or defended courtyard. A sunken barbecue pit in one corner reminds you that this is now a home. The McCarthys have done a good job of making a tourist attraction out of it, by installing informative storyboards covering the castle's history and displaying archaeological finds from the restoration. The main hall on the first floor is open to the public, with stairs up to the gallery and battlements. A parrot in a cage recalls the piratical reputation of the O'Driscolls. You can walk out on to the battlements, view the leaded roof, and appreciate the commanding view enjoyed by the O'Driscolls of Baltimore Harbour and the islands.

Patrick McCarthy's mother was an O'Driscoll, originally from Sherkin Island and Hollyhill, near Ballydehob. Patrick was prompted to restore the castle by his belief that if someone did not do something, it would fall down. He says: 'There was ivy that must have been over 100 years old growing right through it, with stones lodged inside.' Before he started work, he took courses in lime mortar and went to Kildare to learn about dry stone walling. He travelled around Ireland looking at other ruins. 'You'd often see ruins in fields with a big crack running down the gable end. But because this is built on solid rock, there wasn't one crack in the property.' Before work could start an archaeologist was employed, and the results of test trenches and digs were analysed by UCC: 'We got a complete history from the pottery pieces we found, dating back to 1300, from all over Europe. The castle was lived in by quite well-off people who did a lot of trade with Europe.' The restoration was more expensive than predicted: at one point a crane had to be brought into the village, along its one narrow entrance road, with a camera hanging from it to create a photographic record of the castle's stones.

In 2003, when the project was complete, Patrick chose to

avail of the tax breaks available to those who open historic buildings to the public for at least 60 days a year: 'It's fantastic the people you meet, including architects and archaeologists. There isn't a lot to do in Baltimore on a wet day and, when the ferry arrives back from Cape Clear, we get an influx of people who have seen the castle from the sea.' Patrick and Bernie enjoy the visitors so much that the castle is now open for four months, from June to September.

Once you've seen one restored tower house, you start seeing them everywhere. I notice while driving past that Timoleague Castle, one of the three destroyed by the IRA at the same time as Cor, has been done up again. I contact the owner, Robert Travers, and he explains that it is not really a restoration, but that the ruin has been roofed to halt further deterioration. Damage had been done to the east side when the IRA had attempted to blow it up in the 1920s. In the 1930s the five-storey tower house was taken down to two storeys, owing to fears that it was about to fall on one of the infrequent trains that rattled by on the branch line to Courtmacsherry. Says Robert: 'The walls coming down were thrown into the interior until they met the rubble coming up. The event was gleefully photographed by the *Cork Examiner* and raised not a murmur of protest. The walls, which are twelve to fifteen foot wide, were left uncapped, so the west Cork rain did its worst, and the lime mortar leached out. A tree started to grow in the walls and in 50 years the east side, which abuts the existing house (rebuilt in 1926), was in danger of collapse. So we had a problem: either to secure it and cap the walls, or watch it fall.'

As with all castle restoration, nothing could be done before a full survey was carried out and planning permission secured. That process took about two years. The Office of Public Works stated that no attempt should be made to rebuild the structure to its original height, and that there should be a clear distinction between the medieval structure and modern interventions. The solution to stop the walls collapsing outwards has been to put a square steel frame on top of the walls, supporting the new slate roof, and to cap the walls. Virtually nothing has been done to the original structure underneath, although at some future date floors can be put in and the structure brought into use as a dwelling, and the interior and exterior of the walls repointed with appropriate lime mortar. The full story of the castle from Norman times to the 1970s can be found in James N. Healy's book.

Dunboy House, also known locally as 'the Puxley Mansion', has been brought back from ruin in a truly spectacular feat of reconstruction. The house started life in 1783 as a large farmhouse, belonging to the Puxley family, who had come to Berehaven from Galway some 50 years earlier. They built it slightly inland from the original dún and castle belonging to Donal Cam O'Sullivan Beare that was blown up in the aftermath of the Battle of Kinsale. The Puxley family added a tower to their house in 1838. They reopened the copper mines at Allihies and, since they became wealthier, they commissioned an architect, John Christopher, to build an imposing Tudor–Gothic mansion, topped with turrets and Tudor-style chimneys. In fact it was never finished, as Puxley lost interest in it after the death of his wife. The main house never had a staircase and many of the statues and other ornaments imported from Italy were never unpacked.

The family used the older part of the house when they came over from Cornwall for holidays until it was burnt down in 1921: apparently the local IRA unit thought that the British garrison on Bere Island might find it a good strategic move to occupy the house, which commands views over a wide arc of the bay. The butler, Albert Thomas, who had taken refuge at the garrison on Bere Island before the attack, wrote an account of this event in his autobiography, *Wait and See* (Michael Joseph, 1944).

The roofless ruin, with a Scots pine growing inside a split mullion, used to be grazed by cattle. Many visitors have remarked on the beauty of its waterside site, with the Slieve Miskish Mountains rising behind. A local consortium, Dunboy Castle Ltd, decided that something should be done with this important heritage property. At the moment there are only two small hotels on the Beara peninsula (not counting Glengarriff), both in Castletownbere, and neither of them belong to the Irish Hotels Federation. A team of 140 workers, led by supervising engineer, Christopher Southgate, have combined in a project with a budget of €60 million, to recreate the original house and link it with 82 luxury hotel suites, the whole to be known as the Capella Dunboy Hotel. Southgate comments that the great hall at Dunboy is more like the entrance to a Gothic cathedral than to a home. But the local community's hopes that the hotel would bring more visitors to the rest of Beara were dashed before the hotel had even opened, when the developers began advertising heli-golf excursions to Waterville on the neigh-bouring Iveragh Peninsula (the Ring of Kerry).

10

The Murder of Sophie Toscan du Plantier

Two old men in pyjamas were sitting on the side of a bed in a top-floor ward of Cork University Hospital, looking at the lights of the city by night, spread out beneath them. They were remembering the good old days. One of them summed it up: 'Long ago, there were no murders in Cork, and you could park your car in Patrick Street.'

Sweet dreams. The murder of Sophie Toscan du Plantier on 22 December 1996, one of the most talked-about murders in recent times, is also just another statistic in Ireland's growing murder rate. In 1965 there were seven murders in the Irish Republic in a population of just under three million. This figure is rising steadily: to 54 murders in 2005, in a population of just under four and a quarter million. So, while the population increased by roughly half, the murder rate increased almost seven-fold.

There have been other terrible murders in west Cork before and since: matricide, fratricide, and murder by arson have featured in recent years among the local community. Such terrible domestic tragedies speak volumes about the misery people endure in their everyday lives and seldom make the national headlines. But the unsolved murder of a beautiful, wealthy Frenchwoman, in which the prime suspect was an Englishman, has gripped the imagination of the Irish public since 1996. The beauty of the victim and her glamorous life-style contrasted harshly with the terrible violence of her end, battered to death in the laneway of her holiday home at Toormore, near Schull – an apparently motiveless attack that involved neither robbery nor sexual assault. People who had always felt safe in their homes were suddenly afraid. Sales of bolts and deadlocks surged, as doors that had been left on the latch for years were secured against the possibility of a violent intruder. The murder of Sophie (she is usually referred to only by her Christian name) marks the beginning of west Cork's loss of innocence, contradicting the old belief that west Cork is different: a safe, friendly place where bad things like this do not happen. There was a sense of outrage in the local community, spreading far beyond the Mizen area, and anger that the laws of hospitality should be abused: that a woman who was a guest in the territory and had trusted in her safety, should be killed so brutally.

Sophie's murder investigation is a story of multiple mis-managements: mismanagement of the State Pathologist who, because of the government's insistence at the time that one person could cover the whole country, arrived 24 hours after the event; alleged mismanagement by the local Gardaí, unused to serious crime scenes and murder enquiries; and finally the widespread speculation about both victim and suspect, which went unchecked by the law. These unsubstantiated rumours arose largely because the victim and chief suspect were outsiders, and neither had a network of family and friends in the area to stand up for their good name. Looking back, it becomes clear that the press canonisation of the victim and their demon-isation of the suspect was not, as some claimed, trial by journalism but was simply about selling newspapers.

Sophie Toscan du Plantier née Sophie Bouniol, was a 39-year-old French film-maker, with homes in Paris and the French countryside, as well as a farmhouse at Toormore, about five miles west of Schull. She was married to a well-connected film producer, Daniel Toscan du Plantier, (the Minister for

Culture, Jack Lang, was among their circle of friends), and she had a son from a previous marriage. She came to Cork alone, for a pre-Christmas break, and was murdered in the dead of night, a few yards from her front door. The murder weapon has never been found, but it is believed she was attacked with an axe and then bludgeoned to death with a concrete block. When the story broke – bringing an unprecedented eruption of violence into the warm glow of the run-up to Christmas – I hoped, like many people, that the murderer was not a local, and that it was a private matter, a jealous lover perhaps, nothing to do with people living in the area. But this soon started to look unlikely, even though there were rumours of a marital rift. One of the earliest theories about the murder, apparently based on romantic cliché rather than any specific knowledge of the characters involved, alleged that the husband had taken out a contract on his wife, in revenge for being cuckolded, and had employed a professional hit man.

The obsession with the murder is due in a large part to the fact that, although it remains unsolved, many people believe that they know who did it. The man who has publicly referred to himself as 'the prime suspect', Ian Bailey, an English journalist, is alleged to have confessed to at least four reliable witnesses. He has been reported as boasting in local bars of having committed the perfect crime, and people name him freely. Some refer to him openly as 'the murderer'. Women in particular seem to relish describing their encounters with this diabolical character: how he fixed them with a basilisk stare, and frightened them half to death.

While an increasing number of people in the Mizen area prefer to change the subject, and get annoyed when it is introduced, the murder is still discussed in Schull with a passion, eleven years later. Everyone has a theory. In August 2007 a Frenchman, who has lived in west Cork for over 30 years, told me confidently that 'the Toscan du Plantier murder' had nothing to do with west Cork: he alleged it had all the hallmarks of a hit job by the Marseilles mafia, and assured me that Sophie was involved in money-laundering, 'big time'. This theory seems about as likely as the idea that a werewolf was responsible, a tale that presumably gained currency due to the full moon on the fateful night.

Bill Hogan, an American cheesemaker, poet, raconteur, long-term resident of Schull, and an admiring acquaintance of Sophie, says: 'You don't think about the murder in summer, when everything is buzzing. It's in the winter, when you come back to the bare bones of it, that's when you think about it. It comes up every winter.' Giana Ferguson of Gubben Cheese near Schull had to prohibit the murder as a topic of conversation among her workers, such was the intensity of debate. Giana believes the murder has damaged the community, polarising opinions and encouraging wild speculation.

To understand the enduring obsession with the case, it is necessary to look closely at Schull itself. While much of west Cork goes into hibernation from November to Easter, the tiny village of Schull (permanent population around 400) always seems busy. In mid-December business in the centre continues briskly: there's a bank, a pharmacy, two small supermarkets, a tempting array of specialist food and craft shops, at least half a dozen places to eat (one of them offering a choice of eighteen house wines by the glass), and the inevitable traffic jam. But everything still closes down for lunch. Schull manages to combine a degree of urban glitz with the old-fashioned rural friendliness and much sought-after slower pace of life. Within days of your arrival, off-season, the shopkeepers will be calling you by name. It is often chosen by wealthy people relocating to the area to downsize or to run a business from home – Cork Airport is less than two hours' drive. These people can sense the presence of like-minded souls, year-round, and see evidence of an open, welcoming community where spouse and children are safe.

Whether or not they can afford to live in Schull itself, many people with school-age children move to the area specifically to be within the catchment area of Schull Community College (SCC). This non-denominational, co-educational college – a state-run school, not a fee-paying one – opened in 1983 after concerned parents living on the Mizen had lobbied for a new secondary school in the area. Children from Crookhaven, for example, were facing a 54-mile round trip to attend secondary school in Skibbereen. That first term, 70 children were enrolled, and the school was expecting a maximum of 180 students. By 2004, the school had 450 pupils. The catchment area includes Crookhaven, Goleen, Schull, Durrus, and Ballydehob.

The school has an attractive waterside site on the western side of Schull Harbour. The Fastnet Marine and Outdoor Education Centre opened on the school grounds in 1997, to give every pupil to the opportunity to learn to sail. SCC is the only school in Ireland to have sailing on the curriculum, and its students constantly do well in national and international competitions. A planetarium was developed in 1989, and a new observatory with a powerful telescope opened in 2004. The school is known for its tolerant, cosmopolitan atmosphere, something which parents from different ethnic and religious backgrounds find reassuring. Fifteen or even ten years ago this was a more important consideration than it is now, in a more culturally diverse Ireland. Children from fourteen different nationalities were represented among the school's population when it celebrated its twenty-first birthday in 2004.

Bill Hogan has lived in Schull for over twenty years. I asked how the murder had affected people: 'The presumption is that it has had a negative effect, but I remember that the community pulled together, just after it happened. People trusted the Guards to do their job, and kept an eye out for each other. It's made people less innocent and more aware. The local community here is quite smart, and it's a very loving community. There's a lot of nice people around, even though it's a bit mixed socially. There's a lot of wealthy people, a lot of artists, the local farming community, the local fishermen. In summer there are some really good parties. Then there are people right on the coast, still farming and living in poverty. Often they are elderly. They're still living with open hearths, no central heating or double-glazing, but they all seem to get on. Very few people knew Sophie, but if she had been around for longer she would have fitted in perfectly.' Sophie would occasionally ring Bill and ask to come over and buy some cheese. She always introduced herself on the phone as 'Madame Bouniol', and only once came unaccompanied. Bill was impressed by her lively intelligence, her interest in human rights, environmental and cultural matters, as well as her beauty and elegance. She spoke English with a Foxrock accent, having been an exchange student in Dublin as a teenager.

Toormore is in an especially rocky section of a notoriously rocky coast. The house was behind a gate, kept closed because of grazing sheep. It was on high ground, and Sophie had an especially tall bed built so that she could see the light of the Fastnet Rock from her bedroom.

On Friday 20 December 1996, Sophie flew from Paris, via Dublin, to Cork Airport, and picked up a hired car at about 2.30 p.m. Her final two days passed in an unremarkable round of talks with her caretaker, visits to familiar bars, and walks.

Sophie rang her husband at 11 p.m. on 22 December, and had what he later described as a long and congenial conversation. Outside, it was a clear, frosty night, with a full moon. The pubs in Schull were busy, with people coming home for Christmas, and others celebrating the long Christmas break with a convivial night out. But out at Toormore all was silent, although a few people were woken in the early hours by what they took to be screams of pain from a trapped animal. At 10.30 the next morning, a neighbour found Sophie's body in the lane leading to her house. She was wearing a nightshirt, white leggings, and brown lace-up boots. She had been attacked with a sharp weapon, probably a hatchet, and bludgeoned by a large stone or concrete block. She was clutching a clump of hair and had blood under her fingernails. She had opened her back door to somebody, and then fled in terror with this person in pursuit. It was apparently a random, motiveless killing; with no witnesses and no murder weapon.

A fuller account of these events and their aftermath can be found in Michael Sheridan's book, *Death in December* (O'Brien Press, 2002). This is a superb exercise in real-life crime writing, a vivid yet sensitive description of the crime, its location and the victim's life. One of Sheridan's most valuable contributions is his demolition of the rumours that have persisted since the murder, rumours that in turn have fuelled theories and speculation. There was, for instance, a persistent rumour that she knew her killer and was having a relationship with him. This was backed up by 'clues' uncovered by the investigating team, including two wine glasses on the sink in the kitchen, indicating that Sophie knew the killer well enough to invite him in. There were no wine glasses. Similarly, two kitchen chairs found close together were indications of a late-night conversation. Sophie's mother has explained that it was her daughter's habit when reading to pull two chairs together and rest her legs on one of them.

Another theory was based on the assumption that Sophie was planning to divorce Daniel and had come to Ireland to think it over. Fearing that a divorce would give Sophie a claim to half his estate, this theory surmises, he had commissioned an assassin and asked him to make it look like the random act of a madman. The Gardaí have scotched this rumour: and since du Plantier had already divorced two wives without murdering them, it would seem an uncharacteristic course of action on his part. Experts quoted by Sheridan claim that the manner of Sophie's murder was the act of a man out of control, not the cold, carefully planned *modus operandi* of a professional killer.

Sheridan's profile of Sophie highlights her beauty – 'she lit up the room' – and her innocence. While he mentions that she could be a difficult character, he leaves out the fact that she had a lover in 1994 and took him to Toormore with her. He also fails to mention a story reported in *Paris Match*, claiming that an ex-lover of Sophie's had attempted to strangle her on the Métro. Daniel told another reporter that Sophie was 'fearless', and regularly drank coffee in establishments frequented by drug dealers and other low-life in the area of Paris near their office.

The least convincing part of *Death in December* is its final section, 'Profile of a Killer'. This does not actually name the 'prime suspect' as Ian Bailey, even though the profile seems to be an uncanny match for aspects of this man's personality. Bailey, an Englishman who had been in the area for about five years, was a trained journalist and the local stringer for the *Cork Examiner* (now the *Irish Examiner*). When the *Examiner*'s west Cork correspondent, Eddie Cassidy, heard about a body in Schull, he thought it might have been a hit-and-run accident, certainly not a murder. He asked Bailey to supply him with information. Once it was clear that this was a murder case, Bailey also made contact with other media organisations, including the *Irish Daily Star*, the *Sunday Tribune*, and *Paris Match*. I remember seeing the 'Eoin Bailey' by-line in the *Irish Examiner* at the time, and thinking what a windfall the terrible crime must have been for a low-earning local stringer.

Bailey is a striking figure, a black-haired man well over six foot tall, who had become disillusioned with journalism, and had come to west Cork to reinvent himself as a poet and musician. He had an offbeat, sarcastic sense of humour, and could be arrogant. He was known to be 'fond of a drink', and was regarded as something of an eccentric and a loner. He had moved to west Cork in 1991, after a five-year marriage ended in divorce, and he met Jules Thomas while working at the fish factory in Schull – a job at the fish factory was a rite of passage for many impecunious blow-ins – where she was a customer. He changed the spelling of his name to Eoin, and on occasion even spelt Bailey, Ó Baille. Apart from the fish-factory job, he had a gardening sideline and literary ambitions. He also made contact with the *Irish Examiner* and *The Southern Star*.

His partner, Jules Thomas, was an artist and had come to the area from Wales some twenty years earlier. She lived with Bailey and her three teenage daughters in an old farmhouse outside town at Lissacaha, about halfway between the village of Schull and Toormore. In May 1996 Jules Thomas had spent three weeks in hospital recovering from a brutal beating administered by Ian Bailey, who had been drinking whiskey. They had split up temporarily, but by December they were back together again.

Bailey and Thomas had been drinking in Schull on the night of 22 December, and had returned home at around 1 a.m. Bailey stayed up in the kitchen, writing, while Thomas went to sleep. People noticed he had scratches on his face the next day, 23 December, which he said were from killing a turkey, and he was seen having a bonfire on 26 December, although he maintains that he did not. Several people said they had noticed that he and his partner seemed to know more about the case than anyone else, and to know it sooner. But that was his job. A witness claimed to have seen a man of Bailey's build washing his boots in a stream near Sophie's house in the early hours of 23 December. (Seven years later she retracted this statement and claimed she had been pressured to make it by the Gardaí.)

Ian Bailey and Jules Thomas were arrested on 10 February 1997, seven weeks after the event, for questioning in connection with the murder. They were released without charge. Bailey was arrested again in in 1998, and again released without charge. Against his solicitor's advice, he gave several radio interviews after he had been released from police questioning. It seemed apparent initially that he enjoyed the publicity. As time went on, Bailey became obsessed with the case, keeping clippings, and talking of little else. He was drinking heavily, and showing signs of paranoia, according to one of the people who employed him as a gardener. He is reported to have confessed his own involvement to a number of witnesses. But confessing to a murder is not the same as doing it. He was behaving irrationally and very stupidly. But was that enough for people to take it upon themselves to decide that he was guilty of murder?

One person (who has never given evidence under oath) told me the unlikely story that Bailey came to his house about ten days after the murder and said that he couldn't remember what had happened that night, but that the cops thought he had done it. This person claims to have kicked Bailey out of the house and phoned the Gardaí, telling them that the reporter would agree to plead guilty but insane. This person also claims that the Gardaí agreed that Bailey was probably guilty, but that they wanted to be sure they had enough evidence to send him down for a good long time, not the year or so that he would serve on an insanity plea. When I hear this story, recounted ten years later with breathless excitement as if it had happened yesterday, I wonder how much it has been coloured by the hysteria that seems to have possessed certain inhabitants of the village of Schull in the aftermath of the murder. This is the opening sentence from an article on False Confession Syndrome in the *Journal of the American Academy of Psychiatry and the Law*: 'There are many reasons that criminal suspects give false or unreliable confessions, covering a broad range of scenarios – coercion by police, mental illness or retardation, and publicity-seeking, for example.'

The poet John Montague was a part-time resident of Ballydehob and Bailey had worked in his garden, hoping that in return Montague would help him to further his own career as a poet. In January 2000, Montague published a piece in *The New Yorker*, entitled 'A Devil in These Hills: A Murder in a remote Irish village unsettles the new Europe.' (The devil comes from an interview Daniel Toscan du Plantier gave to *Le Figaro*: 'There is a devil somewhere in the hills of southern Ireland.') This piece was a major contribution to the demon-isation of Ian Bailey. In fairness to John Montague, it must be said that he was not to blame for the 'gruesome drawing' of Bailey featured in *The New Yorker*, which he says he objected to: this was a caricature of Bailey with an array of dangerous-looking garden implements, and Sophie's house in the background. The article was reprinted in *The Observer* in March 2000, this time as a photo spread. Montague quotes Bailey summing up the case in these words: 'No witnesses, no murder weapon, no forensic evidence, no motive. It will take a long time.' Montague pointed to the possibility of Bailey's innocence, and put forward the theory that Bailey could have been made a scapegoat by the local community because he had never fitted in there.

The piece angered many locals by the publicity it gave Bailey, and the way that it introduced the region to an international readership by describing an unusual random act of violence, the only murder to have taken place on the Mizen since records have been kept. People objected to Montague's picture of life in the area, whose inhabitants he characterised as either very rich or dole-scrounging hippies (both minorities, in a hard-working, overwhelmingly traditional, rural popula-tion), his knowing, gossipy tone, and his claim that the case had engendered widespread mistrust of outsiders in the area. However, the piece does paint a convincing picture of Bailey as a difficult character, a misfit, and a dreamer with more ambition than talent and application, who had gone badly adrift in his efforts to start a new life. Montague asked the Gardaí to put a tap on his phone after he reported receiving a number of threatening phone calls.

In August 2001, Ian Bailey was arrested for another assault on Jules Thomas, hitting her with his plaster-encased leg and crutch while laid up by a torn Achilles tendon. He blamed the combination of alcohol and painkillers. He pleaded guilty, was fined and given a three-month suspended sentence. There followed a rearrest at Cork Airport where he was about to take a flight to England and, because he could not pay the fine, he spent a number of weeks on remand in Cork prison. Many people believed that at this point Jules Thomas would withdraw her alibi and reveal the truth about the night of the murder. The press seemed convinced that this time the case would be cracked open.

However, once again, the couple was reunited, and continued to live in the house near Schull, but hopes of resuming a normal life were fading. A gregarious ex-local recalls, 'The only negative thing about living in Schull was Ian Bailey. I never went to the market because he was always there, selling carvings and other stuff. Nobody knows what to do with him. There's a sense of unease lurking there because of him, and he seems to enjoy it. He turned up to join the choir in Skibbereen, and the choirmaster said, "I'm sorry, we're full up". And he was at the launch of *The Fish Anthology* at West Cork Literary Festival: in he walked and just sat there. I had to leave, even though there was free drink.'

In 2003 Bailey took the unusual step of suing eight Irish and British newspapers in the Cork Circuit Court, claiming that his life, career, and reputation had been ruined by their coverage of the 1996 murder. Excitement ran high, as it was apparent that, in the course of the libel hearings, details of the domestic violence and of Bailey's confessions to the murder would emerge. I attended the trial on 16 December 2003, the day that several other local witnesses gave their testimony. Jules Thomas was at Bailey's side every day during the trial, but showing signs of strain by day seven of the ten-day process. The judge was careful to caution that the trial should not become an enquiry into the death of Sophie Toscan du Plantier, stating that Bailey '… is not an accused. He is entitled to bring a case for defamation.'

Bailey himself, who took the stand for two days and remained calm under pressure, described his shock at how he had been portrayed in the press after his first arrest, and the impact the articles had had on his life. He said: 'I am still to some degree untouchable. I was stripped of my presumption of innocence. I used to go out when I wanted to. I'd go to Bantry or Skibbereen. I don't do that any more. Life has been a struggle. It feels like I am being eaten alive ...' The detailed descriptions of the injuries received by Jules Thomas that emerged on subsequent days left few people with any sympathy for Bailey.

On the day that I attended, fourteen neighbours and one-time friends of Bailey and Thomas gave evidence. What was most remarkable, in a cumulative process, was how frightened these people seemed. Some were more articulate and confident than others. Malachi Reed, then 21 years old, recalled an incident with Bailey seven years previously with impressive self-confidence. But it was obvious that all these people had felt real fear at the closeness to them of an evil event, and its unfortunate aftermath. They were, by and large, people who had chosen to live a quiet, low-key life, away from the hustle and stress of modern urban life, and had had this enormity thrust upon them. This seemed to me to be a community traumatised by its collective experience, convinced indeed that there was a devil living in its midst.

In his ruling after the Christmas break, Judge Patrick J. Moran struck out the defamation claims taken against the *Sunday Independent*, the *Independent on Sunday*, the *Daily Telegraph*, *The Times* (London), *The Sunday Times* and *The Star*, saying, 'The defendants were perfectly justified in describing him as violent towards women – he has not been defamed by that.' Neither had the eight newspapers defamed him by referring to him as the prime suspect in the murder investigation, and they had also reported his assertions that he had nothing to do with the murder. However, he ruled that Bailey had been defamed by the *Irish Mirror* and the *Irish Sun*, both of which alleged that Bailey had been violent in his relationship with his ex-wife. The judge also commented on the coolness of Ian Bailey in the witness box, and the fact that he never got annoyed during cross-examination. Then he pointed out that Bailey appeared to be fond of notoriety and had courted publicity after his first arrest. Bailey was sub-sequently awarded €8,000 against the *Irish Mirror* and the *Irish Sun*, and landed with €200,000 legal costs. He has no way of paying these costs, according to a statement made by Jules Thomas.

In October 2005 Schull businesswoman Marie Farrell withdrew statements placing Ian Bailey at the scene of the murder and made complaints against the Gardaí, claiming intimidation. In April 2006 Sophie's family dropped its civil action against Ian Bailey. Bailey appealed the Circuit Court decisions but in February 2007 in the High Court, he unex-pectedly withdrew his libel claims against five newspaper groups. The newspaper groups agreed to contribute €70,000 towards Bailey's costs, and to waive costs awarded to them in his 2003 Circuit Court action. They also agreed to his Counsel reading out a statement, which read (in part): 'Mr. Bailey withdraws all claims against the defendants. The defendants confirm that nothing in any of these articles was ever intended to suggest that Ian Bailey murdered Sophie Toscan du Plantier. The defendants are not saying now, nor did they ever say, he was a murderer.' A Garda inquiry into the handling of the original investigation is continuing, although its conclusions have been expected for some time now.

Why will the Gardaí not bring a case? Presumably they do not have enough evidence for a conviction – in Irish law you cannot be tried for the same crime twice. In December 2007, for the first time, Sophie's parents did not make the pilgrimage to west Cork for a memorial mass. Meanwhile, Ian Bailey is studying for a law degree at UCC.

11

Mozart in the Cow Byre – Successful Enterprises in the Arts

Francis Humphrys hates the image foisted on him by journalists, who love to repeat the 'dairy farmer to international music impresario' story. But the fact is that in 1992 he was a dairy farmer, and today he has retired from farming and is the Director of West Cork Music. The annual West Cork Chamber Music Festival attracts the best of international talent, and has a budget in excess of half a million euro.

In fact, the cliché fails to do justice to an extraordinary man, whose character combines an appealing humility with total self-confidence in equal measures. He is one of those rare people who are incapable of dissimulation: he could not tell a lie to save his life. This has probably made him as many enemies as friends, but his friends are fiercely loyal. Educated at Oxford, with distinguished military and diplomatic traditions in his family, he would probably have ended up in the Foreign Office. But after Oxford, where he read politics, philosophy and economics, he moved to west Cork. 'It's a tangled tale,' he says. 'I'm not sure how I came to Ireland. I came here on holiday and fell in love with the place, and all I could afford to buy was a little house on an island, Long

Island. And the miracle was being able to sell it at the other end and buy this little farm, both for sums that make people turn purple and explode nowadays. It was the only good investment I made in my life, buying this farm.'

He was the archetypal hippie, with long hair down to his waist. The 45-acre farm near Durrus is a difficult farm on rocky land, which would nowadays be considered unviable. A man of passionate enthusiasms, Francis' great interest, when I first met him in 1982, was chess. But gradually music started to take over his life. He rigged up some speakers in his milking shed, and made the interesting discovery that Mozart increased the organic herd's milk yield. But the nearest place to hear live music was Cork city, over an hour's drive away. The Vanbrugh Quartet was in residence at UCC, and the National Symphony Orchestra came down a couple of times a year. But the concert-goers' schedule does not suit dairy farmers, who are used to early nights and early mornings. Francis was constantly afraid of falling asleep at the wheel as he drove home.

At about the same time, Egerton Shelswell-White at Bantry House started putting on classical music concerts. Francis was among the four or five people in the audience for the first ones, and he decided they would have to do better than that. In 1992 the Rector of St James', Durrus, asked Francis to write a booklet celebrating the 200th anniversary of the church's building. Along with some other parishioners, Francis organised five concerts in the church – including a *Messiah* – to mark the occasion. This gave him a taste for the role of music impresario. Bantry House's library was a beautiful venue with precisely the intimate surroundings in which chamber music was first played, and Egerton was happy to hand over the running of the concerts to Francis.

Francis made contact with the Vanbrugh Quartet and, on the advice of Niall Doyle, then at Music Network, set up West Cork Music. All of the work, including manning the box office, ushering, and selling wine in the intervals, was voluntary until 1997. Francis himself writes most of the programme notes and edits the souvenir programme. The Vanbrugh was keen to get involved with a festival, and cellist Christopher Marwood became artistic director. He shared Francis' commitment to producing a serious event that would involve first-rate musicians and make people sit up and notice. The first week-long festival took place in 1996, coinciding with the bicentenary celebrations of Wolfe Tone's attempt to land a French force in Bantry Bay. The Parisi Quartet, Barry Douglas, and cellist Robert Cohen were among the musicians assembled. Seamus Heaney read from 'Station Island', while Cohen played a Bach cello suite. Subsequent festivals have included the Borodin String Quartet, Irina Schnittke, John Tavener, Ian Bostridge, Catherine Leonard, Hugh Tinney, and Joanna McGregor. West Cork Music also administers the Masters of Tradition concerts, put together by Martin Hayes, presenting the cream of Irish traditional music players. There are about a dozen classical concerts throughout the year, all featuring leading Irish and international names, and once- or twice-yearly special cycles of concerts, designed to attract a visiting audience. In 2000, for example, the Borodin String Quartet played the entire cycle of Shostakovich string quartets over six evenings. Before West Cork Music came along, you would have had to travel to a major European city to hear chamber music of this quality: it is a boon and a privilege to have it available so close to home.

The commissioning and premiering of new music has always been a strength of the Chamber Music Festival. So too is the commitment by visiting musicians to giving master classes during the event, culminating in performances by young musicians on the final Sunday. The festival also creates much-needed performance opportunities in Bantry town for young musicians. A year-round education programme in local schools has the long-term aim of creating a local audience for chamber music. It has not been easy, building an international festival from scratch. Francis' family and his wife Corrie have been stalwart supporters. For several years the deeds of Francis' farm sat at the bank to cover the growing deficit. In spite of grant aid from the Arts Council, RTÉ, and Cork County Council among others, it is a constant struggle to keep going. In 2008, RTÉ will begin the phasing-out of their funding over a three-year period (while remaining committed to the Festival broadcasts) and there are long-term concerns over the availability of Bantry House as a venue. Francis Humphrys is a permanently worried man.

But all this is forgotten during festival week, when Bantry House is closed to visitors, and entirely taken over by musicians for nine days. About 70 musicians take part in over 50 concerts. Many of the concert-goers are regular attenders, the lucky ones having bought a ticket for the whole week. People soon know each other by sight, and conversations are often struck up and friendships formed, while leaning on the balustrade enjoying the view over the lawns to the sea. A courtesy car comes and goes from Cork Airport, delivering musicians and their instruments to the door of the stately home. Morning coffee concerts are held in the Rose Room, lined by tapestries woven for Marie Antoinette, its large windows looking west over Bantry Bay, the view reflected in a mirrored background behind the musicians. The afternoon, main evening, and late night concerts are all held in the main venue, Bantry House's library. In the library the musicians play in front of the enormous French windows that open on to the Italian gardens, rising in terraces linked by the Hundred Steps. Many of the 'local' audience will have driven an hour or more for the experience. They are, professional musicians apart, mostly an ageing audience, with good strong faces and an individual way of dressing that indicates an artistic or intellectual background. The words 'sublime' and 'apotheosis' are frequently overheard.

❖

Clem Cairns, a Dubliner, moved to west Cork to farm in 1987, and lives near Dunbeacon on Dunmanus Bay. Clem had one of the first registered organic dairy farms in Ireland, but gave it up in 1994 and went fishing on a trawler. He hated it, but he needed the money. It was while he was fishing that Clem had the idea of running a short-story competition, charging a reasonable entry fee, and publishing the winners in a book. *The Fish Anthology*, which now charges €20 per entry or €45 if you also want a critique of your story, has appeared every year since 1995. The competition attracts around 2,000 entries a year, from all over the English-speaking world, and has so far published some 200 writers. From 2008, entries are accepted only online, further simplifying the administrative side. Judges have included Pat McCabe, Roddy Doyle, Joseph O'Connor, and Carlo Gébler.

The year of the first Chamber Music Festival, 1995, was also the first year of the publication of the short story anthology. In 1997, the launch of *The Fish Anthology* took place during the Chamber Music Festival, and was the centrepiece of a 'Fringe' literary festival. By 2006, the West Cork Literary Festival had become so successful and grown so big that it now takes place in the week following the Chamber Music Festival. The Literary Festival is still administered by West Cork Music, and Clem now shares the running of it with artist Lorraine Bacchus, receiving funding from Cork County Council Library and Arts Services, the Arts Council, and Fáilte Ireland. Once again, Bantry is packed out for a whole week, as book lovers gather for free lunchtime readings in the library, as well as a variety of workshops, book launches, and evening readings, each with an entrance fee. In 2007, 250 people gathered in St Brendan's Church to hear the English novelist Jeanette Winterson talk about her upbringing in a strange religious sect, described in her first novel, *Oranges Are Not the Only Fruit* (Pandora Press, 1985). Over 2,000 people attended the Literary Festival's events that year. The audience is mainly Irish, with some from the UK and the USA. Most of the big

names on the Irish literary scene, and an increasing number
from the UK and further afield, have read at Bantry. The
smallness of the town means that you are likely to run into the
writers in bars and restaurants, and the event creates a
considerable buzz.

Sue Boothe-Forbes, an editor, emigrated from Boston to
Eyeries on Beara in 1997. She runs a residential artists' and
writers' retreat, Anam Cara, in her home, a spacious bungalow
overlooking Coulagh Bay. She originally had the idea for the
centre on a post-divorce trip to Connemara. Then a friend of
hers came to Eyeries to watch the filming of Deirdre Purcell's
novel, *Falling for a Dancer* (Pan, 1994), and spotted the
bungalow for sale. As soon as Sue saw it, she knew her search
for a home and retreat centre was over. People usually find her
via the Internet and come to stay for a minimum of one
week. Some stay as long as six months. In summer there are
guided workshop retreats for both writers and artists. Sue
takes all the domestic worries away from her guests, who each
have an en suite bedroom–study. They eat a buffet lunch when
it suits them, and can socialise or hibernate in the evenings.
The poet Nessa O'Mahony was a regular visitor when she
was starting out, and Sue did much to encourage her
neighbour, Leanne O'Sullivan, who is now one of the better-
known young Irish poets. The chef Gerry Galvin, who is
working on a novel, is another regular visitor.

The house and its extensive garden are full of quiet spots
to sit and read. The food is home-cooked and home-baked,
with eggs from a flock of hens and ducks. The setting is so
idyllic that it would be all too easy to spend days on end
watching the view as clouds scud across the sky above the sea.
But, according to Sue, most people are highly motivated:
'People tend to come here when they are considering a
change of career or embarking on a big new project. The

unwinding period is part of the whole experience, especially if they have arrived jet-lagged. One room is known as the postcard room, because the view is so lovely – I always warn people that it may take a few days to settle in to work.'

Interaction with the local community has always been a priority, and Sue's guests were responsible for the colourful murals that decorate the outside of Eyeries National School. In winter she has a musical and literary open house on the last Friday of each month, partly because she needs something to look forward to at that time of year. The proceeds of these events are donated to a charity of the performers' choice. Last year they raised over €5,000 for a local charity. The only blot on Sue's horizon in 2007 was the continued lack of broadband: 'Don't even talk to me about it,' she snarls with uncharacteristic rage.

Deirdre Purcell, who was an actor, an RTÉ presenter, and a journalist before becoming a best-selling novelist, describes her house in Kilcatherine as 'a haven': 'The Beara Peninsula is one of the most beautiful places on earth. There is something quite mystical about this part of the world. We have the Atlantic on three sides. It is a great place to work. I get more work done here in a week than I would in two months at home in Meath.'

Deirdre's third novel (she has written eleven so far), *Falling for a Dancer*, was made into a mini-series by RTÉ and the BBC in 1997. It was set in Beara, and was also filmed there, an experience she describes as one of the highlights of her life: 'The first morning of shooting I got up about 5.30 a.m. and went off to have a look. The filming was over at Cod's Head. I came round a corner and saw this field absolutely covered with catering trucks, cars, buses, and vintage cars that were being used in the film. I had to stop the car because I got very emotional. I realised that something that had started with one image in my head had caused all this – and helped to create employment on the Beara Peninsula. It was a fantastic feeling.'

Arts Festivals come and go, usually depending on the availability of a committee of volunteers, not just during the festival, but all year round. 'Art in Schull' in early July is generally a lively event, highlighting local crafts and artists. Rosscarbery has a weekend Arts Festival in mid-May that is pleasantly low-key and different. For many years this was masterminded by Cal Hyland, an erudite rare-books dealer who moved to Rosscarbery in 1991. Cal intended to retire and run Pilgrim Books as a mail order company. Instead, he and his wife Joan opened a café–bookshop, Pilgrim's Rest, which ran from 1998–2003, and was famed far and wide for Joan's home baking. (It is still open, under new management.) Their daughter, Grainne, and her young child moved to Rosscarbery to help, and they have stayed. From 2008 Grainne will be chairperson of the Ross-carbery Arts Festival.

The Beara Community Arts Society was active in the 1990s, and held some excellent group shows, featuring the many artists resident on Beara. One of its most successful projects was a peninsula-wide patchwork quilt that involved many women who had not had any contact with the arts before. But the Society is currently in suspended animation, owing to a shortage of volunteers. Says Penny Durell, a former chairperson: 'It sort of fizzled out. The ones involved put a lot into it, and you get burnt out. Then with the improvement in the economic situation, everybody has jobs: before that, half the people were on the dole, and they had time to get involved. It's hard nowadays to get volunteers: people are working very hard to earn a living, and juggling their lives.'

Margaret Thomas Warren (1912–2004), known to her friends as Tommy, moved to Castletownshend with her husband, Bayard, in 1979. Bayard Warren was from a family of Boston Brahmins, and his aunt, Sylvia Warren, had been a keen huntswoman and a good friend of Edith Somerville, often buying horses from her to ship back to the USA. When Bayard and Tommy came to Castletownshend, they bought one half of the house in which Edith Somerville had died, as well as a derelict boathouse with its own pier down at the water's edge. Bayard was a keen yachtsman, so he brought his boat with him and spent much of his last years restoring the stone-built boathouse, travelling up and down the hill in a little electric buggy. Tommy was devastated by his death in 1982, and decided, in his memory, to make use of the boathouse to further her interest in art. She loved to quote Edith Somerville: 'I would put in a plea that the Parish of Castlehaven may be kept as a national reserve for idlers and artists and idealists.'

Margaret Warren was born in Texas. Her passion for flying grew from the first time she saw an airplane. As she recounts in her autobiography, *Taking Off* (Images Publishing [Malvern] Ltd, 1993), her first job was as a barn-storming stunt flyer, walking on the wings of a monoplane. At seventeen, she was one of the first women to gain a commercial pilot's licence and was a member of The Ninety-Nines, the club for women pilots founded by Amelia Earhart. She was a courageous woman with a steel-willed determination and a great sense of fun, which made you forget her age. She could be formidable too: it was advisable to call her Mrs Warren until instructed otherwise.

Tommy took up painting, and in winter she invited friends to share lessons at the boathouse. Local artists taught there, including Terry Searle and Vicki Helps. In 1988 Fergus and Patricia O'Mahony bought Mary Ann's pub, and became good friends of Tommy's. When Tommy decided to start holding summer exhibitions in the boathouse, Fergus' cooperation was a key element. It is not inappropriate to mention the catering before the art: Tommy was well aware that most people who came to her openings were there for the social aspect, rather than the artistic one, and she didn't care. She enjoyed the company and the glass of wine on the grassy quay outside the boathouse as much as anyone. The exhibitions were held on the second-floor room, with its half-oriel windows looking out on to the sea.

The Boathouse Gallery shows, 1990–2001, were done properly: from the printed invitation to the production of a catalogue, the hanging of the paintings, and the employment of a PR company. Each show cost between €3,000 and €10,000 and Tommy took no commission. Her belief was that Arts Council and business sponsorhip were fine, but there should also be room for a personal input – for someone like her, who could afford it, to do something different. Some of the artists she showed were friends, other were recommended to her by art professionals. Artists who showed at the Boathouse Gallery ranged from senior figures such as Tony O'Malley, Anne Madden, and Louis le Brocquy, to younger artists like Felim Egan, Alice Maher, Dorothy Cross, Martin Gale, Dermot Seymour, and Hector McDonnell, as well as less-widely known local artists including Sally Fitzgerald and Ann Chambers.

For the last few years of her life, Tommy was blind, and found the boathouse increasingly inaccessible. But her blindness did not deter her: she could still see colours, so she took up painting again, with remarkable results. Attempts were made to secure the boathouse's future as a gallery and community hall (the hall had also been used for small-scale theatrical performances), but it was too complicated. Tommy consulted her son and daughter, Michael and Mary, and they agreed that she should make a gift of the boathouse to the Castletownshend Rowing Club. The club won the AIB All Ireland Rowing Club of the Day Championship for the third year in a row on Sunday 22 August 2004. Margaret Warren passed away in Bantry Hospital, aged 92, at around the same time.

The West Cork Arts Centre (WCAC) was set up in 1985 on North Street, Skibbereen, in a building that had been a bank and then a school, as a multi-disciplinary arts centre with the emphasis on contemporary visual art. Artists living locally and members of the business community, as well as those involved in education and community initiatives, recognised the need for a place to hold regular exhibitions, while building an audience for art by holding classes and workshops for children and adults. At the time there was not a single arts centre or professionally run gallery west of Cork city. The WCAC continues to be the only publicly funded art gallery between Cork and Tralee, where the visual arts gallery of Siamsa Tire is based. The WCAC serves both Skibbereen and Bantry rural and urban areas, as far as the Beara peninsula. There is a thriving film club, a busy youth programme, and a growing community arts sector. The annual landscape group show, held every summer, was a highlight of the year, as was the Christmas Craft Fair. The latter is still running, but such is the explosion in numbers of artists living in the area, that the landscape show has been replaced in the all-important July–August slot by a 'Celebration' of west Cork artists, taking place simultaneously at other art venues in west Cork.

The WCAC has a small shop, and has always been very supportive of the area's craft-makers. For the first three years the Arts Centre managed with FÁS grants, until 1988 when Jack O'Connell was appointed its first full-time paid director. Today the director is Ann Davoren. The premises consist of two small galleries, with the shop and offices on the ground floor. The rest of the building is owned by the local Vocational Education Committee of County Cork, and the WCAC needs more space. Plans have been made and almost €3 million of funding secured for a move to new, larger premises on the site of Wolfe's Bakery in Townshend Street, where there will be improved performance and film club facilities, bigger and better galleries, and studio space for artists.

The art dealer, Angela Flowers, owner of the Angela Flowers Gallery in London's Cork Street and Flowers East in Hoxton, has been showing a selection of her artists at her holiday home in Rosscarbery every August since 1984. The L-shaped gallery at Downeen has introduced people to some of the finest contemporary artists. With so many new galleries opening today, it is hard to believe that for many years this was the sum of west Cork's art scene: the West Cork Arts Centre, two week-long shows at the Warren's Boathouse Gallery, and a small show at Angela Flowers' house.

Jim Donovan, an Australian with Irish roots, opened The Private Collector Gallery in Innishannon in 1999, on a prime site on the main N71 west Cork road. It has 6,000 square feet of space, and sells a range of work, from sought-after early twentieth-century artists, including Markey Robinson, Louis le Brocquy, and Patrick Hennessy, to established mid-career artists. Others, such as Tim Goulding, Ian Wright, and Majella O'Neill Collins, are actually resident in west Cork. Several artists have been able to give up the day job, thanks to sales at The Private Collector.

The Catherine Hammond Gallery is at the other extreme of the N71, in Glengarriff. The village was chosen for three reasons: its beauty, its location on the scenic route to Beara, Kerry, and Killarney, and the availability of plenty of parking. It's a modern space with a high ceiling, and is especially suited to showing contemporary paintings. It came as a pleasant surprise when it opened in 2000, surrounded as it was by leprechaun-selling craft shops, but it was in fact the forerunner of the revival of this part of Glengarriff, which now has a couple of good contemporary café–restaurants and a new hotel complex.

Catherine Hammond came to Ireland from Boston specifically to open a gallery. She trained as a curator at the Smithsonian Institute, and spent eighteen years at the Boston Institute of Contemporary Art. She came to Ireland in 2001 and, like many before, 'fell in love with the place'. *Drawing Texts*, a show curated by Jim Savage that she saw at the Crawford Gallery in Cork, alerted her to the number of good artists working in Ireland, and she became aware of the potential for a good gallery outside Dublin. She says: 'I think it is important not to give in to the centrifuge created by a city like Dublin. People living outside Dublin should be able to have the same experience of going to a gallery and seeing good work. Good art demands good space. It's a form of disrespect to show good art in inadequate conditions.' While Catherine has introduced some American artists to Ireland, most of her shows have featured leading Irish artists including Bernadette Kiely, Eilís O'Connell, and west Cork residents Tim Goulding, John Kingerlee, Jacqueline Stanley, sculptor Linda Cohu, and photographer John Minihan.

The Doswell Gallery opened in July 2007 in Rosscarbery. Chris Doswell, the owner, had a print gallery and framing business in Limerick for many years, but was frustrated by the pressures of working in the centre of the city – she had relocated to King John's Island – and by the growth of the framing business. After looking around, she and her partner bought a corner shop on Rosscarbery's main square. Visitors with an eye for oddities may remember it for its sign that read 'Electrical Footwear' – not, in fact, an amazing new invention, but an advertisement for the shop's combination of electrical goods and footwear. The shop needed gutting, and it took Chris four years to get to the point of opening. In July 2007, the show was the second venue in the WCAC's annual summer show, which helped to bring it to people's notice, while in September the same year Angela Flowers' daughter, Rachel Heller, had a show there. Angela has been a great supporter of Chris, and welcomes another gallery in the area. Chris still has clients for her framing business from the Limerick days, which is just as well. The main square at Rosscarbery is off the main road and it can be quiet, says Chris. Luckily she lives on the premises: 'Some days we've only had two people in, and one of them is usually an artist looking for a show.'

When Fergus O'Mahony and his wife, Patricia, moved out of the rooms above the pub at Mary Ann's in 2003, Fergus converted his old sitting room and conservatory into a gallery. He named it The Warren Gallery, in homage to Margaret Warren, with her permission. It's not a great space, but his enthusiasm makes up for its imperfections. He overcomes the disadvantage of its location, remote from the majority of his clients, by holding regular shows in Dublin, two- or three-day events at the Gresham Hotel. Fergus is enormously astute, but his passion for art is genuine, and infectious. He is as keen on introducing talented newcomers to the market as he is on representing established figures, chiefly Matt Lamb.

Matt Lamb is a phenomenon. Whatever you think about his art or his philosophy, you have to admire his energy and his commitment. Before becoming an artist, Matt Lamb, a native of Chicago, ran a chain of 36 undertakers, and was a Papal Knight twice over. His organisation was known as the 'MacDonalds' of undertaking. At the age of 51, Lamb was told he had an incurable disease and would be dead within five years. He immediately sold his businesses to paint full-time.

Some twenty-five years later, at the age of 76, he is an internationally recognised self-taught artist, dividing his year between studio homes in west Cork, Florida, Paris, Chicago and Wisconsin. A slim, bearded man with long, grey hair and faraway eyes, wearing a black Harley Davidson T-shirt and jeans, he looks more like a retired rocker than a retired undertaker. He is represented by major galleries in Chicago, Nantucket, Miami, Palm Beach, Zurich, Argentina, Spain, and Germany. And, since 1998, by Fergus O'Mahony and the Warren Gallery, Castletownshend. He produces so much work that he employs a full-time curator to keep track of it all. He was presumably a rich man before he started painting: however, unlike most artists, his artistic activity has added to his fortune. It probably helps that, since Matt Lamb took up art, his style – outsider art, untutored art, *art brut* or naive art, as it is variously called – has quite coincidentally become a major international craze. Matt Lamb is the genuine thing: he cannot draw anything beyond stick figures, but he has a strong natural sense of colour and composition. In 2007 people would happily pay his going rate of €2.32 per square centimetre, which works out at €8,500 for a 60 cm x 60 cm oil painting. In October 2007 Fergus sold €370,000-worth of Matt Lamb's work in three days at the Gresham.

Matt Lamb's west Cork base is on top of a cliff, hidden away at the end of a steep driveway near Union Hall. It is home for three months of the year – June, July and August. His wife Rose's grandparents were from Rosscarbery, while his own were from Mayo and Kerry. He carries both American and Irish passports, the Irish one making him a European, and thus easing the red tape involved in shipping paintings to and fro. The unpretentious two-storey house is chiefly remarkable for its semicircular bay windows over-looking a millionaire's panorama of sea and farmland, and for the fact that every available inch of wall space is occupied by a Matt Lamb painting.

His tour of the house is not, in fact, a tour of the house. It is a tour of his work in progress: this heap of canvases are dry and ready for shipping, those are the crates they will go into. He says: 'Between all my studios, I probably work on 400–500 pieces at a time. They are left, and then I go back to them.' The energy and focus that once made him the Midwest's most successful undertaker have been redirected into his artistic activity. He works all day every day, from 6.30 or 7 a.m., until bedtime. 'Every day?' I ask: 'Every day. Yep. I'm driven. This is what I do. I do art.'

There are many artists living and working in west Cork, full-time or part-time, and there are also many other galleries: the Mill Cove Gallery, Castletownbere; The Gate Gallery, Skibbereen; Digress Studios and Gallery, Skibbereen; Cunnamore Gallery, operating mainly online; and the Sarah Walker Gallery, Castletownbere, which, like many of the smaller galleries, opens only in the summer. In addition, many bars, cafés, and restaurants have paintings for sale on the walls, and many community halls have summer group shows.

Artists tend to cluster around the Schull–Ballydehob area, on Sherkin Island, and around Eyeries and Allihies on the Beara peninsula. West Cork has taken to art in a big way. There are a lot of mediocre artists out there, but there are also some very good ones. The artist William Crozier, Scottish-born of Irish parents, has had a studio at Kilcoe since 1983 (he also has one in Hampshire), and responds to the local landscape in glowingly colourful, strongly structured paintings. The critic Dorothy Walker compared the impact of his work to Roderic O'Conor's Breton landscapes at the turn of the century. Jacqueline Stanley, who also works in Dublin, moved her studio from Wicklow to west Cork in 1996, and has captured the distinctive landscape around Mount Gabriel in her cheerfully impressionistic style.

Down on Beara, on the Ring of Eyeries, you might see a man in a kaftan praying to Mecca on the seashore: this is John Kingerlee, who moved from London, to Cornwall, to Ireland, and converted to Islam. He has been enormously successful in the past few years with his strange blend of abstract and landscape works, which are deeply influenced by the rocky landscape around him. Some artists, including Louis le Brocquy and Anne Madden, whose studio is not far from John Kingerlee's, are regular visitors to west Cork, but do not respond directly to the landscape in their work.

Charles Tyrrell, known for his rigorous abstract paintings, has lived near Allihies since 1984, and well understands the pull of landscape: 'When I first came down here from Dublin I probably embraced the landscape to some conscious degree, and then I stopped doing anything conscious with it. It doesn't suit me, that sort of direct connection. I'm driven to make certain sort of paintings: they are about themselves primarily, internal, formal affairs. I start at a very clear empty place and work towards reality. I don't start with reality, and abstract *from*, I'm not of the 'abstracting from' school. So, when landscape comes in, it comes a guest, and appears in varying degrees. But there's a bit of me that wants to shoo everything out. I don't know if it's over-rigorous, but I don't want to wallow in the landscape, or in nature ... I find it a little bit limiting.'

Tim Goulding has pretty much painted his way into the landscape at Allihies and out of it again in the past 30-plus years. His work nowadays is more about an internal life of the mind, than the world around him. Cormac Boydell has lived and worked in Allihies for so long that it is as if he has absorbed its essence, and this gives an unusual strength to his rough-edged, brightly decorated ceramic works. He says: 'It's not directly to do with the landscape. It's a more intuitive thing. A place like this seeps into you, and informs what you do, even when you aren't aware of it. I don't set out to copy or recapture the scenery around me – there are plenty of others who can do that.'

12

On Cool Mountain – Craft Enterprises

As coastal property became more expensive, impecunious good-lifers gravitated inland, to the Trawlebane area behind Bantry, to Drinagh, Rossmore, and to the hills to the west and north of Dunmanway – the Shehy Mountains, the Maughanaclea Hills, Cool Mountain, Coppeen, and Shanlaragh. Some of these had been following a well-trodden path that leads from London, west to Totnes and surrounding areas in Devon, or to west Wales: many people have told me that they found Devon becoming increasingly suburbanised and crowded, in comparison with west Cork, and moved in search of a more rural, more isolated, location.

The introduction of anti–traveller legislation by Margaret Thatcher's government and the availability of the dole led to a large influx of crusties: barefoot yurt dwellers with dirty dreadlocks and the inevitable dog on a string. While some of these were every bit as awful as they looked, a number of them turned out to be talented art school graduates (or dropouts), and have integrated into the local community, where their children are swelling school numbers.

Some are involved in crafts, or have set up small organic farms or herb and plant nurseries on land they either bought, or rent cheaply, from mountain farmers glad of the cash. The traditional Friday market in Bantry is often the outlet for their produce. The market is also a useful gauge of the numbers and nature of the area's transient population. The bad apples, often in fact people in need of psychiatric help, or people with drug or alcohol addictions, tend to move on. There seems to be an informal network, with other centres of population in Birdhill, County Tipperary, and west Waterford.

I first covered the Cool Mountain story back in the mid-1980s, when the first wave of crusties arrived in the Dunmanway and Bantry area.

I was trying to get back into journalism after some years out of circulation, writing books. I thought a good strong feature on this new wave of incomers would help. I started by making enquiries among some long-term residents of the hills to the west of Dunmanway. A friend of a friend said she would introduce me to some tepee dwellers. We drove through teeming rain up ever-smaller boreens, and parked on the side of the road. We then walked across a couple of muddy fields of scrub, to a place where two large, sodden tepees were pitched. Beside them was a ruined building with a makeshift roof. I was received by a man with a long ponytail. Everyone seemed to defer to him. He sat on a chair beside a small, circular table, while the women and children sat on the floor, on rugs and cushions. It was very smoky, from a smouldering fire. I was seated in the only other chair, opposite the man. I was nervous, suddenly feeling a very long way from civilisation.

In an attempt to establish my credibility I used the word 'hippies', pointing out how it had come to be used locally in an indiscriminate way to describe anyone who looked a bit unconventional. The man objected strongly to the use of the term, and got to his feet, pointing his finger at the door: if I thought they were hippies I could leave right now. I looked down at the table and saw a revolver there. I don't know how or when it had appeared, or if it had been there all the time. It was a chunky, silver and black gun, like you'd see in westerns. I very much hoped it was a replica, but I didn't hang around to find out. I made my way back across the muddy fields alone, walking as fast as I could without actually running. I have no idea whether that particular crowd stayed or left, nor indeed exactly who they were. I once tried to find the place again, but couldn't be sure. Most likely they were just passing through, as so many people did in those years. Dole tourists, they were called, among other things. All over the world, remote rural areas attract weirdos, transient or permanent.

When someone suggested in November 2002 that I should write about the Coolmountain Craft Co-op, a group of people who were reviving traditional craft-making skills, I was naturally wary. Like many, I had heard lurid reports of wild goings-on at the Coolmountain commune. So I went to consult Mike Collard at Future Forests, the tree nursery that he and his family run in the hills near Kealkil.

Mike, as a senior blow-in, was one of the few people open-minded enough to employ some of these weird-looking newcomers and his employees all have the greatest affection and respect for him, treating him like a guru because of his tremendous knowledge of plants which 'do' in west Cork. Mike introduced me to master-thatcher Simon Cracknell, and his partner, Jane Florence, who live in a round, hobbit-like house on Cool (sometimes spelt Coole) Mountain. Both are middle-class art school dropouts, with a growing family, and have been here nearly twenty years now. Jane organised my first visit to Cool as a journalist, if a little reluctantly.

When I went to Cool in 2002, Coolmountain Craft Co-op consisted of people who had been in the area for about fifteen years. Nobody wanted to talk about why the original commune failed. Coolmountain commune centred on a thatched house known as The Dome. The original communards were looking for a simpler way of life, more environmentally aware, and less in thrall to consumer society. At one time about 80 people were living on Cool. No one looking for a place to park their van or pitch their tepee or yurt was turned away. The accepted story is that the kindness of the original members led to the commune being exploited and brought into disrepute. There were problems with drugs and paranoia. In the longer term, the more sensible characters prevailed, and the others moved on.

People were able to buy land cheaply from a local landowner more interested in cash than farming, and built their own homes from recycled materials and whatever was close at hand – stone, wood, reed-thatch. They generated small amounts of electricity from the mountain's stream until a mains supply was laid on. Some of the houses are decorated with handmade details like hand-carved front doors and mosaic walls; others are just cobbled together from recycled materials. In 2007 about 25 people were living in Cool West, the site of the original commune on the side of a hill. You can see the settlement from the distance, but only if you know it is there. The prettier houses are thatched, with a rounded shape that seems to have grown out of the hillside. There is always smoke from the wood fires, and there are thriving vegetable plots, polytunnels, and exuberant flower gardens. Cars are parked at central points, and the houses are reached by footpaths, with heavy goods carried in by tractor. But it is no paradise. Like all villages, some people keep a tidier plot than others, and some continue to live in old caravans and buses. I never visit Cool unless I have an invitation. These people value their privacy, and are wary of strangers.

The alternative-lifestyle people currently living on Cool Mountain and scattered about the area, all the way west to Bantry and east to Crookstown, are now an accepted part of the local community. The key factor in the process of integration has been their children. Many live as they do in order to bring up their children in a safe environment, where they can enjoy relative freedom. Coolmountain is very child-friendly: in 2002 the old community hall was being used by the kids as an indoor skateboarding venue. About 70 per cent of the children at Togher National School in 2002 came from what Kathleen McCarthy, who was responsible for home-school liaison, tactfully called 'alternative backgrounds'. She said: 'They have made a huge difference to us and the parents are more than generous with their talents. It would be a very different place without them. We all learned when their children started coming to school; we all had to broaden our minds.' Thanks to the newcomers, the school had enough pupils to need a second teacher. One of the alternative lifestylers, John Crawford, who runs the forge, also used to drive the school bus.

Coolmountain Craft Co-op is no more, but some of the individuals involved are still in the area. There are talented stonemasons, who often work on landscaping projects for Mike Collard. Katrin Schwart from Germany is a skilled basket-maker, and one of Coolmountain's longest-term residents. She has been making baskets for nearly 25 years, having chosen the trade as something she could do from home while her three children were growing up. She makes a traditional range of shopping baskets, log baskets, and cradles. She calls herself a willow maniac. One of her biggest projects to date was the design and manufacuture of wickerwork ceilings for Jeremy Irons at Kilcoe Castle. About 50 per cent of the willow she uses is grown at Cool, the rest is imported from England. It has to be boiled, and the tannin that results gives it the distinctive colour. She says this process died out in Ireland during the Second World War. Most of her imported willow comes from the Somerset levels, where the tradition is still alive.

John Crawford, a large amiable Englishman also known as Big John, still runs the hot metal forge. His workload varies from what he calls 'fancy stuff' – mosaic tables, mirrors, and wall sconces – to practical work, making parts for tractors or frames for generators. Tinsmith Andy Harris, also English, and his wife, Nicole, live about ten miles from Cool, near Coppeen. Andy works in recycled copper, using cylinders that were once hot-water tanks. It's an old system of sheet metal working, cutting out the shape on the flat, then making a bucket or a coal hod, or whatever, by folding the seams. Andy learnt the trade when the couple were travelling: 'We'd meet men who'd done tin-smithing all their lives – the tinkers, as they were known, who went around repairing pots and pans. It's very simple really, you don't need many tools: snips, a hammer, and a pair of pliers. They'd watch me work, and show me a simpler way.' Andy cannot survive on this trade alone: he also works as a builder.

Jane Florence, also English, did one year at art school, but did not go back after she had the first of her four children. Almost every inch of her home is decorated with something she has made – from felt curtains to mosaic window lintels, willow sculptures, wood carvings, and cast-clay gargoyle heads she sells as patio ornaments. She has received grants from the Department of the Environment and Cork County Council for her art projects with young people. She made a 22-foot Willow Woman with Bandon Youth Reach, and organised a county-wide recycled sculpture competition. She is currently involved on a voluntary basis with running a youth club for teenagers and young adults 'on the mountain', as she puts it.

Simon Cracknell, a bearded Englishman with long, blond dreadlocks and a warm smile, is Jane's partner. He started to learn thatching in order to get a roof on his own house, as it was the cheapest way to do the job. A thatcher friend from Dorset came over and gave Simon a crash course. He is now a recognised expert on Irish thatching traditions. Work by Simon and his thatching partner, Mike Curtis, can be seen at The Mills, Ballyvourney, the Bandon Garden Centre, John Quaid photographers in Ovens, and at Dunworley. He says: 'When you're out and about thatching, it draws people; and among them are old thatchers in their eighties and nineties. They stare at you intently for hours, and at the end they come up and interrogate you. I've been cross-examined by two old boys with walking sticks, wanting to know who's this young upstart working in their area, even though they're long retired. I would love to go around with a tape recorder and talk to these old boys. There is so much expertise out there, just dying out.' Simon is a thatch-enthusiast. He had just come back from Dublin, where he'd been looking at the new housing estates: 'If only they'd put thatch on the roofs, they'd look gorgeous from a distance, but at the moment they're just an eyesore.'

He told me how, in the pre-fireplace days, when people had a central fire of turf and no chimney, the thatch would get blackened with tar and last two or three times as long: 'Some old thatched houses have up to ten layers of thatch – you don't remove it, you just keep lashing it on. I've been on roofs that are so high you can't reach the rafters from the outside. Basically, you stood where your house was and you looked around and used what you had. You'd cut the top sod off the bog, the "scraw", and lay that face down on the roof, and pin material like heather into it. Then, as that dies, it tightens on to the fixings. Often, in countryside like this, there's no reed – because there's no arable land – so people used heather. On a boggy hillside, with a few sally trees growing, that's what you use. Whereas in arable areas, they'd use straw.' Simon is also known for his stonework. As a stonemason too, he is self-taught. 'It's all in the eye,' says Jane. 'Simon has the most amazing eye.'

My first visit to Jane and Simon was on a Saturday in November. When we'd finished talking about thatching, Simon, who had been working up in Dublin all week, retired to the sitting room where he lay on the floor in front of an open fire to watch the rugby on TV. I sat and drank Earl Grey tea with Jane in the conservatory, while she waited for her children to get back from an outing to the skateboard park in Cork. Hippy commune? This was Saturday afternoon suburbia anywhere in Ireland.

❖

Mike Collard of Future Forests is probably the closest thing west Cork has to a real hippy. He dropped out of Oxford to work as a gardener, in the early 1970s. 'I was eighteen months in college before I decided I didn't want that sort of life, I wanted to work with my hands,' he says. 'I got a job as a gardener in Oxford, in a walled garden with an acre of vegetables and fruit. There was one other gardener, an old man who had been there since he was fourteen. I learnt more in six months working with him than I had in eighteen months in college.'

After a spell as a farm labourer, learning to plough with horses, Mike and his wife, Cathy, came to Ireland, in his words, 'to find real people living real lives'. They arrived in Kealkil when there were still itinerant workers doing timber extraction with horses. He started as a forestry worker, thinning Maulavanig Wood, the 40 acres of forest above their site, using horses. He eventually took on contract planting and woodland management for Coillte, Ireland's largest forestry company. Douglas fir thinnings were used to make rustic sheds and picnic tables. Says Mike: 'The main principle that we've worked with, ever since the beginning, is that there are livings to be made and creative things to be done with timber that other people would condemn as firewood.'

Future Forests has a maze of winding paths, with bridges over streams, bogwood sculptures, and thousands of plants. It is a place of pilgrimage for gardeners in search of some special tree or shrub. The main building, which is ingeniously crafted from odd-shaped wooden off-cuts and bog timber, started life as a sawmill. It has a sod roof, and incorporates a spiral tree-trunk staircase, woven panels, and stained glass. In the summer, it has displays of work by local crafts people; in autumn, the busy season for dispatching mail-order bare-root plants for trees and hedging, it is the pack-and-dispatch HQ. Behind the buildings a network of paths climbs the hillside, each path bordered by alphabetically arranged trees and shrubs. The nursery stocks one of the largest ranges of trees in

Ireland, as well as a rich selection of native hedging (much of it sold by mail order), over 100 varieties of apple, and over 250 perennials. Behind the exuberant creativity is a formidable amount of organisational talent, much of it belonging to Louise Amery, who also left Oxford in the 1970s for west Cork, and is part of the family. (The one thing you won't find at Future Forests is a toilet: when I asked, after several cups of tea, if I could use the facilities, I was directed to the upper slopes of the tree nursery.)

Mike and Cathy had six children. Cathy died of cancer, with only about three months' warning, in 2000. Mike took semi-retirement, to look after his younger children. His daughter, Maria, works full-time in the nursery with Louise, while his 26-year-old son Christy, also a drummer, works there on and off, between time spent with his baby girl, Saira, and other projects – for instance masterminding the funky Chill Stage for the Body and Soul area at the Electric Picnic in 2007. Seán, a computer scientist working in Cork city, also helps out at weekends. The Collards' eldest daughter, Aideen is a barrister in Dublin, while his two youngest are still studying. Says Christy: 'Dad's had enough and wants to write, so we are evolving into a new era.'

After 30 years quietly working away in the backwoods, Mike and Christy were thrust into the limelight when they became the contractors for Mary Reynolds' gold medal award-winning garden, Celtic Sanctuary, at Chelsea in 2002. The garden, loosely inspired by a stone circle, was simply a typical corner of west Cork wilderness, transferred to the world's most competitive garden show. Christy did much of the stonework. Most of the ferns and mosses used in the Chelsea garden were ethically sourced near the nursery on wasteland that was about to disappear under a building site or be paved in road widening. The elite of the horticultural world was in raptures of delight over ferns, mosses, and humble plants that, in their native habitat, are generally dismissed as weeds. Mike says: 'Celtic Sanctuary drew attention to the need to protect threatened environments. The abundance of diversity of the country roadside has vanished from most of rural England, and is rapidly being eroded here. Gardening without weed-killers and using clever planting of native plants is part of the future for motorways and other county council spaces.' A small children's play garden in Ballingeary was designed and built by Future Forests and illustrates this approach.

Mary Reynolds met Mike and Christy at a garden festival, and when she was offered the chance to design a garden for the Chelsea Flower Show, she knew that nobody else would be capable of translating her vision to reality. The story of Future Forests, Mary Reynolds, and the Celtic Sanctuary garden, has been turned into a film script, and is currently in development in London. It falls into the category of 'romantic drama'. Christy says they were horrified when the first draft was presented by the scriptwriter: it cast the Future Forest people as a band of lost, mad hippies. They would not sign the waivers to let it go ahead. A second visit from a London film producer was more reassuring. After meeting Mary for the first time, Christy went travelling through Ethiopia on a bicycle ('Looking for real people, living real lives, just like me and Cathy,' says Mike, nostalgically). The film version has a determined Mary flying out to Africa to convince him to come back and work on her project. Inevitably, a romance between the two talented, good-looking, young people ensues. Meanwhile, there are mad dashes from Kealkil to London with a fifteen-foot hawthorn tree on a low-loader, and several lorryloads of wild plants and rocks. A small army of colourfully attired Future Forest workers set up camp in a little flat in Marble Arch, sallying forth to Chelsea every morning, led by Christy in blond dreadlocks, to realise Mary's enchanted vision of an Irish wild flower garden that eventually wins the Gold Medal at the Chelsea Flower Show. Cue schmaltzy diddly-i music and credits ...

❖

The growth in the number of people in the west Cork region making a living from the manufacture of handmade goods, now referred to as crafts, appears to date from about 1970. Among the forerunners of this generation were Philip and Lucy Pearce, who revived the tradition of pottery-making in east Cork in 1953, when they founded Shanagarry Pottery, now run by their son, Stephen Pearce.

Today there are over 100 professional craft workers in the west Cork area, professional being the key word. If craft-making is going to be your chief source of income, you have to have high standards, not only of craftsmanship, but also of business practice. An excellent product is admirable, but unless it is produced consistently, efficiently delivered and effectively marketed, it will not make you a living. Many people with high ideals have learnt tough lessons when the dream of moving to a scenic area to make a living out of doing what they loved to do failed to put any bread on the table. These days, however, people are more realistic in their expectations, and there is more support for people working in crafts, while the craft-makers themselves have realised the value of collective promotion.

The national body is the Crafts Council of Ireland. The CCOI encourages high standards of contemporary design, and encourages people to produce expensive, one-off items for the collectors' market at home, in the UK, and the USA. The West Cork Enterprise Board (WCEB) is helpful to people starting up or wishing to expand a business, offering capital grants and training supports, including a year-long programme for craft-makers that encompasses business prac-tice, marketing, and product development. The WCEB has almost 100 enterprises listed on its register of craft producers. Cork County Council also supports the development of the crafts sector across the county through its Office of Community and Enterprise, by helping to raise the sector's profile and strengthening networking. In 2005 the Cork County Development Board produced a 72-page colour booklet with a map, introducing 67 craft enterprises throughout the county.

West Cork Craft and Design Guild is a self-selecting group of the more artistically inclined west Cork craft-makers. Founded in 1997, its patron is Jeremy Irons. Guild members share a website, publish promotional material, and hold group shows. Its members have the highest artistic standards, producing beautifully designed objects in wood, ceramic, glass, and textiles that could compete with any other European country. Alison Ospina, a qualified woodwork teacher who moved to the Skibbereen area in 1996, makes one-off sculptural chairs from coppiced hazel, runs courses for people with no experience of woodworking to do the same, and is spokesperson for the Guild. She says their procedure for recruiting new members is strict but, she hopes, fair, with a jury meeting of fifteen to twenty members looking for work that is of a high standard of craft, but also shows innovation in its design.

For most craft-workers the year falls into a seasonal pattern, with a busy summer season followed by a lull before Christmas craft fairs which are held locally, in Cork, and in Dublin. January to Easter is generally quiet, and for many people is the time to make work, and build up stock. In summer there are various craft fairs, often connected with arts festivals, 'family fun days', or old-time threshings; in fact, anywhere people meet. Schull's Sunday Farmers' Market has a significant number of craft-makers in the summer.

Ivan McCutcheon, who has looked after the crafts sector for West Cork LEADER Co-op since 2005, sees the link between place and product as an important one for craft-makers, just like the way the production of artisan food is associated with the place from which it comes. Fuchsia Branding, which has been important in the establishing of the region's artisan food sector, is also an important part of craft marketing strategy, the use of the symbol leading customers to expect a high quality product closely associated with the region in which it is produced. Craft outlets, whether studio-galleries or craft shops, enhance tourists' encounter with the area, providing a leisurely shopping experience that differs from the urban one. Because handmade items are relatively expensive, people like to take their time over a purchase. As in the food scene, the existence of a number of craft producers creates a cluster in which, rather than competing, people are enhancing each other's work by creating a bigger pool of good quality, handmade items.

By 2007, 30 craft enterprises, most of them single-person operations, opted to become involved with the Fuchsia Branding programme of West Cork LEADER. As a development agency, raising the profile of the craft sector by including it in this programme seemed the most effective strategy. These craft-makers are primarily sole traders, some of them new to the craft sector, and they find the networking aspect of LEADER to be the most important one. Others speak well of the short training courses it has offered. Making things all day long on your own can be a strange experience for those accustomed to a traditional workplace. One craft-maker, who had recently moved from hobbyist to professional, told me that a marketing course run by LEADER, which reminded craft-makers of the simple fact that when attending a craft fair you should smile at potential customers and engage them in conversation, has made a huge difference to her sales.

Ivan also points out that very few craft-workers make a full-time living from selling their work: they are likely to have a mixed portfolio of teaching the craft to adults or children in a local institution, running studio workshops, or having a part-time job as an art teacher in a post-Leaving Cert college or secondary school.

Ben Russell, woodcarver and a member of the West Cork Craft Guild, is typical of the mixed-portfolio craft worker. Primarily an architectural woodworker and woodcarver, most of his work is commissioned directly, and has included altars for two Cork city churches, hand-carved inscriptions, and occasional sculptural pieces. Ben is originally from the south of England, and his wife, Joyce, is from the Yorkshire Dales, but home is now a two-acre holding in the Shehy Mountains near the Pass of Keimaneigh. Says Ben: 'We started off here in 1978, and spent three years with no electricity, and five years without a phone. We've kept goats and hens for 26 years. We've gone from cutting the turf off the bog and bringing it home in a donkey and cart, to having seven computers in the house, and being very IT-orientated.' Owing to their mountain location, in 2007 they were still waiting for broadband.

Ben sets time aside each year to run three-day wood-carving courses in his studio. Several people he calls 'west Cork celebrities' have taken his course, including Jeremy Irons and Ian Bailey. He gets quite a few sculptors and cabinet-makers seeking to broaden their expertise, and anyone from a Rolls Royce bench-joiner to a jewellery-maker from Holland. Ben is also a photographer, and has written and illustrated over 100 articles for specialist magazines. Joyce is a gardener and also writes articles about gardening, for which he takes the photographs. In the past few years he has started teaching digital photography, first at VEC evening classes in Bantry, where he learnt what the demand was, and then on one-day photography workshops, held at Gougane Barra Hotel and Bantry House. Ben enjoys the variety of teaching photography in pleasant locations.

Rory Conner, cutler, is a member of the West Cork Craft Guild, and the only full-time knife-maker in Ireland. His father was the Church of Ireland rector in Bantry, and Rory now lives in Ballylickey: 'I went really, really, wrong – instead of going into the church, I ended up in a shed in the garden making knives!' For a man who spends all day at this occupation, he sounds incredibly cheerful. He has two ranges: custom-made knives, and a low-volume cutlery range, sold in craft shops and delis. While known for his beautiful cutlery, his knives (greatly sought-after by chefs) cover the range from kitchen work and outdoor pursuits to specialist knives for various crafts. Rory spent some time in California working for a custom knife-maker, learning the trade, before coming home to set up in business. When I ask if he's making a living, he laughs again and says. 'I drive a 1990 VW Golf. Some weeks are not so good, I'd be scraping along. It's low paid, and I put in long hours, but I'm doing what I want, and I have ambitions to do better. The job itself is isolating in some ways, but I have family around, customers visiting me, and I do some shows.' His lifeline, he says, is audio-books. He gets through two a week from the library.

The first wave of craft-workers to move to Cork were primarily potters, as all makers of ceramics used to be called, and most hoped to make a living selling their work from the studio. Jim Turner, who set up Rossmore Country Pottery in 1982, was for many years chairman of the Cork Potters. The group ranged from makers of practical tableware to ceramic artists, such as Pat Connor, Ian Wright, and Cormac Boydell. In the early days nearly everybody had a range of tableware. The organisation produced a simple mimeographed map, which was distributed by the Crawford Gallery in Cork, the West Cork Arts Centre, and the Cork Craftsmen's Guild, a shop in the Savoy Centre, Cork, managed by Christine McDonald. The Cork Craftsmen's Guild originally opened in 1973 in a tiny shop in Paul Street, to provide an urban outlet for the county's increasing number of craft-makers. In 1992 a Bantry-based couple, Englishman David Rose and Tanya Touwen from Holland, set up a national agency, Ceramic Art Ireland, to market the skills of Irish ceramic artists at home and abroad, but it failed.

Jim Turner is amused that, in 2007, politicians are taking exactly the same line as they did 25 years ago: 'Basically, what they want is for us to open factories and export all over Europe. They have no interest in the product, they just want us to expand and employ lots of people.' The biggest change in the last twenty years, according to Jim, is that Irish-made tableware has become too expensive in comparison to imports, and in any case is not in vogue any more. Most potteries are one- or two-people businesses. The trend is away from practical pieces towards one-off individual work, which would look as at home in an art gallery as in a craft shop. In fact, some ceramic artists are being encouraged by art galleries to work in bronze. It is easier to sell a small bronze for around €4,000, than a fine art ceramic for around €400.

The way to survive is to produce less, and diversify. Jim's own case is typical: he runs Rossmore Country Pottery with ceramic artist Etain Hickey. Jim, who graduated from Camberwell School of Art in the late 1970s, teaches at Rossa College, Skibbereen, and also runs short courses. Etain has a retail outlet in Clonakilty, the Etain Hickey Collection, but only 15 per cent of its turnover is from Rossmore. Etain, who studied at Dun Laoghaire School of Art and Design is one of Ireland's leading ceramic artists. But she is not producing a lot of work at the moment, because she is in the shop most of the time. She enjoys it, but is finding it too expensive to stock only craft-makers from west Cork.

Today the business plan is probably more important than artistic talent when it comes to succeeding in the craft sector. Adrian Wistreich is chairman of Cork Art and Design (producers of the County Cork Craft Guide), chairman of Hands-On Craft Teaching Network, and chairman of the tourism website, West Cork Calling (a 2007 start-up). He was also a key figure in the revival of Kinsale Arts Week in 2005: three years later it has a full-time salaried director and an annual budget of €350,000. In 2000, after 22 years as a market research analyst and publisher in London and seven years as managing director of his own company, employing over 40 people, Adrian sold his share to the Daily Mail Group, and moved to Ireland with his Irish wife and ten-year-old daughter. He set up Kinsale Pottery and Art School in some attractive farm outbuildings. The school caters for adults and children studying ceramics, arts, and other crafts throughout the year, and is always busy. While Adrian specialises in sculptural ceramics and smoke-fired pottery, 90 per cent of Kinsale Pottery's income comes from running art classes and workshops. Adrian teaches for fifteen to eighteen hours a week, and employs ten craft-makers in a part-time capacity to teach other courses, representing 25 per cent of his income. He says: 'When I left London, it was because of my frustration with business life. Ireland represented an escape, and also an opportunity to fulfil a long-held dream of being an artist. In the event, I have come to realise that I will never be an artist in the traditional sense. I have accepted that I am funda-mentally business-driven, and that art is now my business.'

13

The Allihies Postman – Artists and the GAA

There used to be a bar in Allihies run by a woman with a strong northern accent. She was from Ballymena, and had married into the pub, and went on running it after her husband died. This was where I met the Allihies postman one sunny afternoon. It was one of those rare afternoon sessions in a rural pub where everything seems to gel. The postman was already a very old man, in his nineties, terribly dignified, tall and straight, and thin as a rake. He attributed his health to the round he used to walk with his postbag: fifteen hilly miles a day. Could it have been fifteen miles? There was some lively company. We were all talking about different places we had seen – Galveston, New York, Toronto, Vanuato Islands, Perth, London – you name it, someone had been there.

'And what about you?' I asked the postman, thinking he might have worked on trawlers or transatlantic liners in his youth.

He paused for effect, and then said proudly, 'I've been to Goleen. Twice.'

I don't think he intended to be funny, but we laughed aloud at the oddness of the claim, and he joined in. Was he serious, or was he trying to put us in our place as braggarts? None of us thought to ask.

Goleen is a small village on the Mizen Head – and, if you think about it, it is a long way from Allihies by road. Since it is on the opposite peninsula, if you go to Goleen by road you have to go up to Glengarriff, through Bantry, around the back of Mount Gabriel and down the Mizen Peninsula. It's closer by sea: perhaps before he was a postman he had spent time on the fishing boats? I met him around 1987, so he would have been in his prime in the 1920s, and could have been one of the local men who made a living fishing for cod and mackerel, which was then salted and exported in barrels to America.

It wasn't until hours later, in the middle of the night, that I wondered why it had not occurred to anyone to ask the postman *why* he had been to Goleen. Why on earth would anyone go to Goleen if they lived in Allihies? Then it dawned on me: perhaps it was a GAA match. Why would a man travel from Allihies to Goleen? Twice? I decided to find out more about the Allihies postman.

Being a peninsula, Beara has many of the characteristics of an island – its own microclimate, fiercely independent people, a sense of remoteness far greater than its geographical position merits, and a coastline and landscape of powerful, raw beauty. Beara inspires fierce loyalty. As Synge wrote of the Great Blasket after his 1907 sojourn: 'I have a jealousy for that Island like the jealousy of men in love' (*In Wicklow, West Kerry and Connemara*, 1910). These island-like characteristics of Beara are to be found at their most concentrated at its extreme tip, in an area known as Allihies.

Going to Allihies is like going to the end of the world. These days it is more difficult to get to than an island, now that the ferry services have improved so greatly: it certainly takes longer. There are three possible approaches: the coast road through Cahermore; the short cut inland off the coast road; or the road from Eyeries, on the north side of the peninsula, through Caherkeem and Reentrisk to Cummeen. This last is the road that I drove the first time I went to Allihies. I will never forget the feeling of sheer delight as the switchback road twisted and dipped between heathery slopes, overshadowed by mountain sides of solid rock, until suddenly, cresting a hill, the sea was ahead, and the road meandered past a series of small, rocky coves. It was like a dream landscape, or something from a children's picture book.

I find a liberating sense of exhilaration in the glacial landscape of Allihies, but for other people it is a more serious business. A landscape created by the passage of the ice sheets, dropping large boulders as they melted and inundating the valleys below, leads to an expanse of sea, surrounded by a curve of rocky promontories, with a clear horizon in its centre. It is a strong place, an extreme place. It makes me think of the end of the world. This is where we will hop off when the time comes, making an easy transition to the other world, just out of view, beyond the horizon. When the lights went out on 31 December 1999, a giant candle was ceremonially extinguished in Allihies and officially declared to be the last light of the millennium in western Europe.

The poet John O'Leary, a long-time resident, has written, 'I think of the bay and the ring of the mountains of Allihies as a scoop of light, groined out of the earth as by a giant hand. It may be that the roaring light and the broken lightning configuration of the coast has something to do with an enlargement of mind and heart …' (*Shelters 1*, The Wilderness Sanctuary Artists' Retreat Centre, 1999).

When the locals talk about Allihies they are not referring to the village itself, which is called Cluin, a straggling line of brightly painted houses at the base of the rocky mountain, but to the rural area that covers the whole of the extremity of the

Beara Peninsula, from Reenmore Point in the north, to Cahermore in the south, and Garinish in the west, the last settlement before the Dursey Sound. The area is surrounded on three sides by the Slieve Miskish Mountains, slopes of sheer rock on which nothing grows but heather and patches of rough grass. The third side is the rocky, indented coastline of the Atlantic Sea. I've mentioned rocky indented coastlines before, but this one is the rockiest of all, and the coves are the smallest. You cannot over-emphasise the rockiness of Allihies. There are many small lakes in the hills and two of these, Coom Lake and the Black Lake, supply the reservoir for the village. A river flows from the mountains down through Kealogue to Ballydonegan Strand. The twelve acres of white sand look like the ultimate natural bounty, but are in fact the waste product of copper mining. The distinctive chimney of the North Engine can be seen standing on a hill a mile away from Ballydonegan, on the opposite far side of the village of Cluin.

I hadn't visited Allihies for some years, and I had forgotten what a small community it is. This was brought home when setting up appointments: I misdialled a phone number and the person who answered knew the person I was looking for and gave me the correct number. Within half an hour of arriving in Allihies, I knew that the postman's name was Con O'Sullivan. He did not walk his fifteen-mile round; he rode it on horseback. The house he had lived in was now owned by Cormac Boydell and his wife, Rachel Parry. They use the horse's stable as an office. Con O'Sullivan died aged 95 (21 June 1900 – 6 June 1995). His son was the fisherman-turned-artist, Nealie O'Sullivan, who still lives in Cluin, with his wife, Veronica. His granddaughter, Maria O'Sullivan, born and brought up in England, had recently returned to Castletown-bere, where she is practising as a solicitor. But nobody could tell me why he had gone to Goleen. It was unlikely to have been for a GAA match: his generation were not greatly interested in GAA, and besides, his district of Allihies was not known for its GAA players, but for its oarsmen.

When I first went to Allihies in 1977 it had the quality of a ghost town: you felt that there were people there, looking at you, but you didn't see anyone. Some coastal places have in fact died, that is to say, are now empty of people. Cleanagh, for example, on the north coast near Reenmore Point, was a fishing community up until the 1930s. No one lives there now. They say that the sun never comes out in Cleanagh in the winter. When I look at it on the map, I see it faces north, which may explain that impression. Cod's Head was a thriving fishing community in the 1930s, salting and exporting its catch of cod to America. But when the Depression era was succeeded by relative prosperity and people could afford to eat things other than salted cod, the cod fishery collapsed and the settlement died.

The copper mines just outside the village of Cluin employed over 1,000 people in the mid-nineteenth century – the village houses were built as homes for the miners and the Protestant church dates from the same era. Employment figures started to fall as the ore became more inaccessible and therefore more expensive to extract, and the mines finally closed down in the mid-1930s. The miners' skills were in demand in the copper mines of Butte, Montana, and many of them emigrated. Others left for London, Cork, and Dublin in seach of work. The alternative was a hard life in which subsistence farming was supplemented by the profits from fishing in small open boats for mackerel, herring, lobster, and salmon for five or six months of the year.

The original Allihies blow-ins were a colourful group, who made their move west at the height of the psychedelic era: real 'flower children'. I was shown a photograph of a smiling young Cormac Boydell with curly, blond hair, standing next to a sunflower as tall as he was. His friend, Tim Goulding, with long black hair and blue eyes, was in a psychedelic folk-rock group called Dr. Strangely Strange. He drove between Allihies and Notting Hill in a dark blue Transit van, believing that the world's problems could be solved by good vibes, colourful clothes, trippy music, free love, and organic gardening. The first time I met Cormac, he told me that Allihies was on a ley line, which is why it was such a strong place to live. I encountered the poet John O'Leary outside one of the Allihies pubs, and he talked about the pleasures of living in a place where you had to invent your own entertainment, and how much he enjoyed the solitude of the long winters.

But I do not want to make Allihies sound like a cliquey place full of hippie oddballs. Cormac and Tim are both serious artists, and have worked long and hard at their practice. Both are now members of Aosdána, as is the artist Charles Tyrrell, one of several other artists living in Allihies. The raw power of the Allihies land and seascape attracts artists; they settle in the area (and in other parts of Beara) because they find it conducive to their work. Others come on working visits, staying for as long as they can afford. The earliest incomers knew each other because there were so few of them, but this is no longer the case. Proportionate to the overall population, there are an awful lot of artists in the area, both resident and transient.

The influx of blow-ins began when Hugh Brody, a social anthropologist from Queen's University, Belfast, chose to study Allihies in the late 1960s, along with another village in County Clare, to illustrate his thesis on the decline of the west of Ireland. He lived in what is now Jimmy's Pub, and produced a thinly disguised portrait of the village in his book, *Inishkillane* (Penguin, 1974). He described Allihies as '... a dying community, which clings tenaciously to life ...' and predicted a particularly gloomy future for the young fisherman Nealie

O'Sullivan. A local character called Herby used to say that if Hugh Brody ever came back to the village he should be thrown down a mineshaft. Brody himself was amazed that the locals had bothered to read a work of social anthropology that was primarily of academic interest. To his credit, Brody came back to the village, and he met Herby, and was not thrown down a mineshaft, but lived to be awarded a Canada Research chair in Aboriginal Studies at the University College of the Fraser Valley in British Columbia.

Norman Steele, then a lecturer in philosophy at Trinity College, Dublin, knew Hugh Brody and came to visit him in Allihies. He eventually settled on a farm near Eyeries, Coom, where he still lives with his wife, the cheesemaker, Veronica Steele. Norman was at the vanguard of a small influx of Trinity graduates, among them the erstwhile flower child of the photograph, Cormac Boydell. Cormac is a Trinity geology graduate who impulsively bought an old farmhouse while re-visiting the Ireland he remembered from childhood holidays: the farmhouse that had once belonged to Con the Post. Cormac's blue-eyed Dr. Strangely Strange friend, Tim Goulding, visited Norman also – and came to stay for good in 1971 with his wife Annie, having bought an old schoolhouse for £200.

Annie still lives in the old schoolhouse and speaks warmly of the elderly neighbours who welcomed her into the community when she moved there in 1971. What she remembers most about the old days was how easily the generations mixed, young and old attending the same functions, and treating each other as equals. Do people find the winters very long? Is there much depression? Annie answers by telling a story about an elderly man who ran a pub in the village: 'He was giving out after a spate of suicides among young people, and he gave this big lecture: sure what's wrong with them at all, sure everyone's depressed, the old granny sitting by the fire, she was depressed, the old granddad, he was depressed too, we were all depressed, but sure what did we do about it? We just got on with it! We wouldn't think of hanging ourselves in the shed. What's wrong with them? You get used to being depressed.'

I have always been struck by the way that the incomers living in and around Allihies got involved with the local community. *Discover Allihies* was a booklet produced in 1975 by eight 14-year-old schoolgirls, as part of Bishop Eamonn Casey's Diocesan Youth Involvement Scheme. (Eamonn Casey was then Bishop of Kerry – although Allihies is in County Cork, it falls into the Diocese of Kerry.) It is an excellent compilation of local history and topography, with a great map giving local place-names and locating standing stones, ring forts, a dolmen, a Celtic church, holy wells, and a mass rock. On its cover is an early painting by Tim Goulding, and five other artists are credited with help for the project, which also involved members of the Beara Community Action Project.

Discover Dursey by Penny Durell (Ballinacarriga Books, 1996) is a classic of local history, recording the history of this rocky island, its place names (over 200), the myths and legends associated with Dursey, and the memories of old people interviewed by the author. It was a labour of love, and took five years, intermittently, to write. Penny Durell lives in the last house on Beara, across the sound from the island. She kept thinking someone should write a book about that place, and gradually realised that she was going to be that 'someone'. Though she looks and talks like the sensible, practical Englishwoman that she is, her story is highly romantic. On holiday in Ireland, she saw a postcard of Tim Goulding's painting of Reentrisk.

'I just had to find that place,' she says. She came to Allihies, and asked the woman in whose house she was staying if she could help. 'She asked me to step outside the door, and she showed me the road: it was just across the bay. So I went up the road, and an elderly lady invited me in for tea, and then this fellow walks in carrying two buckets of water, helping her out because she had no mod cons, not even water. I knew, the minute I saw his boots, that this man was going to be part of my life. I told him about the postcard, and he said that's strange because the original of that picture is actually in the house where I'm living – he lived next door to the old lady.' Two years later, Penny married the fellow with the buckets, David Durell, and left her career in publishing to come and live on Beara. She says: 'I loved it in Reentrisk, even having lived in America, where we had en suite bathrooms and central heating and all. In Reentrisk, it was a bucket out in the shed, no running water, no electricity.'

Their new house is more weatherproof, has all mod cons, and they have planted a shelter-belt so that they can garden on its two and a half acres. David grows vegetables, and does some gardening work for other people. Penny did not learn to drive until 1989, and since then has been a key figure in both the Beara Historical Society and the Beara Community Arts Society. Penny admits that she is a bit isolated. The round-trip to Bantry takes three hours. But they have satellite TV, and manage a couple of trips away every year. 'There's a film on in Bantry that I'd love to see,' she says. 'But it's just too far to go to see a film.'

Michael Sheehan was born in 1912 at Caherkeem near Eyeries and emigrated as a young man. He lived in London, Australia, and New York, where he was President of the Beara Club. He was widely read, had met George Bernard Shaw and Maude Gonne McBride, and wrote for *The Irish World* in New York. In 1989 he returned to a cottage in his original townland, where he began to paint from memory the rural Ireland of his childhood – before emigration had decimated the population – and also acquired fame as a seanchaí, repeating stories his mother had told him about her native place, Dursey Island. Among the neighbours who looked after him in his old age were Charles Tyrrell and Tony Lowes, who recognised and appreciated the quality of his work. As well as painting on canvas, he also used wooden crates, boxes and chunks of driftwood. Thanks to Tony's efforts, Michael Sheehan's work was shown in Beara Memories at the Crawford Gallery, Cork, in 1995. Tony also loaned several works by Sheehan to Irish Originals, a show I put together for the Crawford Gallery in 2003.

It was the presence of artists in the community that encouraged Nealie O'Sullivan, the son of Con the Post, to take up painting and driftwood art. He has now given up fishing for art. His work can be seen at his wife Veronica's tea shop and B&B in the village.

The Allihies Mining Centre was the result of ten years' work by a committee of nine people, including the artist Charlie Tyrrell. As well as being a member of Aosdána, and one of Ireland's finest abstract artists, Tyrrell is also chairman of the Allihies Parish Co-operative Society. The mining centre is located in a former Methodist church that was built by the Cornish miners who came to Allihies in the mid-nineteenth century. The building passed to the Church of Ireland, and was attended by those serving in the Coastguard, the Royal Irish Constabulary, and the descendants of Cornish miners. It closed in the 1940s. It had been a roofless shell for years, known as the Protestant Church, admired by many visitors for its Gothic windows and its hauntingly beautiful location, midway between the sea and the mountains. The architect, Larry Fewer of Boyd, Barrett, Murphy and O'Connor (Cork) has kept the conversion simple, linking the new extension to the old by a glass arch, with the windows on the new west gable echoing the Gothic shape of those of the old church.

There is a gallery space in a loft at the west gable end and beneath it is the Copper Café (run by Annie Goulding in the high season), which boasts the most westerly espresso machine in Europe. The Centre serves as a meeting space for community groups in winter. A committee member, Theo Dahlke, of the Beara-based graphic design firm Sandmount Studios, won the tender for the internal design and exhibition. With its combinaton of storyboards, working models and original artefacts, the display is first-class: engaging, informative, and evocative of the tough reality of the mining life.

The mining heritage fraternity in Cornwall have been generous supporters, and are the source of some extraordinary nineteenth-century photographs, shot underground and lit by burning lime (hence 'in the limelight'). The project cost €700,000, and had a €100,000 shortfall. Fund-raising began in 1999 with an €88,000 grant from the Millennium Fund. The remainder came from the Department of Arts, Sports and Tourism, Cork County Council, FÁS, West Cork LEADER, Ireland Funds, and individual private contributions. The Centre was opened by President Mary McAleese in September 2007. Her speech drew on a visit she had made in May 2006 to Butte, Montana: 'In Butte they talk of Beara as if it was down the street. They talk of Ireland as home. Those brave emigrants were true pioneers and this museum captures an important part of their story, the start of their story.'

From the gable end window of the museum Charlie Tyrrell points out the house of the brothers Tommy and Willie Hodges, on whose farmland the church is sited. Without their generosity in allowing the assocation to acquire the site for a nominal sum, there would have been no museum: 'Cornish by name, but west Cork through and through. They worked in the mines briefly in the 1950s when a Canadian company was doing exploratory work. Otherwise they are Protestant farmers, they farm really well, and they are very old-fashioned people.' They are pictured in the museum display as young men in miner's gear.

Charlie Tyrrell is originally from Meath, and was living in the heart of derelict Georgian Dublin. He was friendly with the sculptor Danny Osborne, who was living in Allihies at that time:' I came down here visiting, and slowly but surely it took me over. Somehow it was an easy move from Mountjoy Square, where I was living, to here; both were extreme places. Mountjoy Square was extreme in an urban setting, and this was extreme in a rural setting. I bought a roofless ruin, with Sandy, my wife at the time, in 1984. It was just an experiment, we said we'd try this out, and here I am.' When I ask if he is away much of the time, he answers 'I'd be out a fair bit', speaking of Allihies the way islanders speak of their island. He shows in Dublin and Cork, and believes that practising artists should spend some time teaching, which he does. Allihies has become much more prosperous in the time he has been here: 'It's always been very busy in July and August, but there's a hell of a lot more houses gone up to cater for the summer thing, second homes and rental stuff. You can tip the balance, and have too many empty houses, which affects the heart of a place. I would like to think Allihies has reached its capacity for that sort of development.'

The subject of empty houses came up with Annie Goulding too. Most of her neighbours are now part-timers, with jobs and other homes in the city, who have bought a place in Allihies because they have family connections, but also, one assumes, because it is so beautiful. Rachel Parry Boydell also mentions the proliferation of holiday homes, and says most of the houses in the centre of the village of Allihies are not lived in for most of the year. On the plus side, there is now a small supermarket and delicatessen, where once you'd be lucky to find an orange in the shop. 'But,' says Rachel, 'there's also the lack of something. The village has this funny empty feeling. On the rare times you go in the pub, you don't know anyone. The people there are the part-time visitors who have holiday homes, and they know each other, but we don't know them.'

Rachel and Cormac Boydell have made a nice home out of the house that once belonged to the Allihies postman. The traditional small farmhouse tucked away behind a hill only a short walk from the seashore is a real gem. Cormac met Rachel, an English artist who trained at Goldsmith's, at a Transcendental Meditation course in England. Their daughter Molly was home-schooled, and now lives in Dublin. Molly had just had her first daughter. 'A grandchild! It's awesome,' says Rachel, 'I can't take it in.' She has recently returned from visiting Molly in Dublin, a six-hour drive. Cormac was just leaving for the Buddhist Centre, Dzogchen Beara, where he is an Instructor. The practice of Buddhism is increasingly important in his life.

Rachel has put much of her energy over the last ten years into various projects undertaken by the Beara Community Arts Society. She also initiated an ambitious project, the Wilderness Sanctuary, which has created two artists' retreats on the nearby coast. The brief was that they should be big enough for a table and a bed, and be built on site from materials found there. Inevitably, this was mainly stone, and the resulting buildings recall the beehive huts of the Dingle Peninsula and the monastic settlement on the Skelligs.

Rachel calls herself 'an oldcomer', as opposed to a newcomer. She says: 'While the older generation would be self-employed artists, a lot of the younger generation have come here because of the Buddhist centre, either to work there or practise there. They live regular lives, with jobs and families. It's not a monastic thing, but the teachings encourage you to have the support of the people that you practise with, so it's part of your life to feel you're part of the community.'

She pauses for thought, then adds: 'And of course some of

us are dying. We are definitely the oldcomers, now that we're at the stage of dying here.'

Peter and Harriet Cornish moved to Ireland in 1974 to establish the retreat centre that has become Dzogchen Beara. They bought an old farmhouse with 150 acres at Garranes, on Black Ball Head, whose land offered spectacular views over the Atlantic Ocean. In 1992, the centre became a registered charity under the spiritual guidance of Tibetan Lama, Sogyal Rinpoche, author of *The Tibetan Book of Living and Dying* (Rider Books, 1994). Sogyal Rinpoche is also the founder and social director of Rigpa, a thriving international network of 106 Buddhist meditation centres, with groups of followers in 23 countries around the world. Rigpa, under the guidance and patronage of the Dalai Lama, aims to present the Buddhist tradition of Tibet in a way that is both authentic and relevant to the lives and needs of modern men and women.

In June 1993, Harriet Cornish died of cancer at the age of 44. She died in Marymount Hospice in Cork, in an environment created by her husband and friends to resemble her room at home, complete with paintings of Tibetan deities. Her final days were accompanied by the constant presence of friends, incense, and chanting. Her peaceful acceptance of the inevitable was an inspiration to her friends, her carers, and to medical professionals. Her husband and friends vowed to use what they had learnt from Harriet's death to create a residential Spiritual Care Centre for people with chronic or terminal illness on a site at Dzogchen Beara. Julie Christie is one of its patrons; the other is Dr Balfour Mount, the Canadian oncology surgeon who coined the term 'palliative care' and pioneered the hospice movement in North America. President McAleese visited the site of the new Centre on her 2007 visit to Beara and unveiled a bronze plaque in memory of Harriet Cornish. The Rigpa community has already raised

€2,400,000, and is confident of raising another €800,000, to enable the first phase of the centre to open in October 2008.

Matt Padwick, from Wales, is the manager of the existing retreat centre. He moved here in 1998 and is one of five full-time staff, three of whom live on site. There is a guided meditation every morning in the shrine room, which is built on a high cliff looking south to a wide stretch of open sea. In summer between 30 and 40 people meditate each day, while in winter it falls back to a resident core of ten to twenty. Matt is unsure how many people have moved to the area permanently because of the centre; some come for three or six months, as their circumstances permit, while others have made a more permanent move. Weekend and seven-day retreats are well subscribed, while the cottages and the twenty-bed hostel on site are booked up well in advance. Many people stay locally in B&Bs or rented accommodation. As the fame of the retreat's extraordinary location spread, the number of casual visitors dropping by in the summer has grown to such an extent that there is now a café during high season, and volunteers open the shop most of the year. Visitors can join the guided meditations, also enjoy various meditation gardens, or just sit on a bench and look out to sea.

It had been a long day, starting at home in Kinsale. I had been to the end of the world, and to its spiritual heart, and I wanted to come back to reality. So I headed for Castletownbere. Castletownbere was the setting for my first novel, *A Joke Goes a Long Way in the Country* (Hamish Hamilton, 1982). The local people were kind enough to enjoy the attention, and I still get a warm welcome. It is probably the only place in Ireland where I am known, even slightly, as a novelist, so not surprisingly I love the place – and I have my regular ports of call, including MacCarthy's Bar, where the late Pete McCarthy got such a warm reception.

Adrienne MacCarthy left a nursing career in London, as the family was unable to find a suitable manager for the family business, which includes the famous pub. She was relatively new to the job when I first met her in 1978, still very English in manner, and there were doubts about whether she would last the course. In fact she has made a great success of it by changing nothing. The front of the bar is still a grocer's shop and provisioner to trawlers. As Pete put it: 'MacCarthy's is an effortless compromise. The front half is a grocer's shop with seats for drinkers; the back half, a bar with groceries.'

I went in for a livener. The only thing new was a poster of the dust jacket of *McCarthy's Bar*, in which Pete is posed in the doorway of the bar, with a pint-drinking nun sitting on a bench to his left. It was just before seven in the evening; too late for the 'quick drink after work' crowd, and too early for the serious evening drinkers. There were a couple of German tourists, looking bemused, and a pair of locals rather the worse for wear, teetering on bar stools. Dole day, perhaps.

After the ritual drink in MacCarthy's, I am on my way back to the car when I experience a strange moment of hesitation. Do I go to the anonymous hotel, where I can have an indifferent meal without having to talk to anyone and crash into bed? Or do I go to a comfortable modern B&B, where I can have a hot bath, en suite, and watch TV for the rest of the evening? Or will I do what I always do, and stay above Titch Murphy's Restaurant (recommended by the Cyclists Touring Club), in one of the simple, impeccably clean rooms with no TV, no en suite, and no double-glazing? Have I got too grand for a room above Murphy's Restaurant? When I say grand, do I mean old? Of course not! I will stay at Murphy's Restaurant, where I have been staying since Titch's mother's time.

The hug he gives me when I come in the door, after an absence of several years, confirms that I've made the right choice. Titch hugs a lot of his customers, who are also his friends. You may wonder why he is called Titch, a strong-looking man in his early fifties, who is neither very tall nor very small. John's nickname was inherited from his father, a six-footer and one of two Donal Murphys in the town. His wife, Joan, is known as Joan Titch. Allihies is also rife with nicknames, as was Kinsale, before it grew bigger.

John has been secretary of Beara GAA for 27 years. He does the Monday morning 'Beara Report' for the local radio station, County Sound. When he's finished cooking for the evening, I ask him to explain what GAA means to a Beara supporter: no better man. Beara has six teams: Adrigole, Glengarriff, Urhan (Eyeries, Ardgroom), Garinish (out Allihies way), Bere Island, and Castletownbere. Beara is the only division in the county that doesn't play hurling: 'We've a very closed tradition of Gaelic football here on the Beara peninsula,' says John, 'We've no hurlers down here. We're the smallest division in Cork County, drawn from the smallest population – about 4,000 – but we've produced some very good footballers. Our input to the county is fairly serious.'

What does GAA mean to him? 'It's a big part of who you are. You really know how important it is, when there's a GAA funeral. A GAA funeral is always massive; it's like the mafia, the whole extended family come. I always say to Joan, when my time comes, you'll give one last look into the coffin, then you'll step two feet back because the GAA take over from there.' At which he laughs uproariously, loving the idea, before going on in a more serious tone: 'It's a sense of belonging. You talk about tribal warfare: the pride of the parish is at stake. You'd rather die than not win. The fellows on the team would be prepared to put their head where another fellow wouldn't put his hand.'

A framed photo collage on the wall commemorates the titanic struggle at the Senior County final in 1997 between

Castletownbere and their arch-rivals, Castlehaven. It was 30 years since Beara had last won the title. Both sides are fishing communities, with a strong tradition of football, and there are good friendships between men who have worked on the same boats. Driving around west Cork in the summer of 1997, you could not fail to notice that every metre of the road passing through Castlehaven territory (Union Hall, Rineen, Castle-townshend, to the outskirts of Skibbereen) was decorated with the Castlehaven colours, blue and white, while on Beara, every telegraph pole on the peninsula and most of the windows were hung with red and white flags.

Like many Castletownbere fans, John loves to recall the big day: 'I stood in the tunnel before they came on to the field – we were letting Castlehaven on first. The Castlehaven door, it didn't just open, it burst open, it wasn't like soccer where they walked onto the fields, it was like the hounds of the Baskervilles, it was fierce. The door opened and their eyes were bugging out of their heads. They were beating their chests, they just flew out, and the man at the gate, they literally blew him out of the way, and he said they're animals! I went over to tell my fellows, they're just gone on to the field, and I knocked on the door, and before I knew where I was they were gone, out the door, just like the others, mark two, and the next thing the man was closing the gate and they bowled him over a second time...'

The photos of the team's victorious return to Castletown-bere are backlit by red flares, with swirls of smoke from the bonfires, every face jubilant with victory, and every hand a fist, punching the air. You can almost hear the klaxon horns. As John shows me the portfolio of large format photos he says: 'That'll give you some idea of what GAA is all about. It isn't just a ball game; it's a way of life. You meet people everywhere, in every walk of life, that make the connection, and are proud to be part of what you're doing.'

But, like many people of his age, John thinks that the younger generation are different. They are not volunteering for the organisational side of the GAA as readily as his generation: 'I think they're a lot more materialistic; they have a different way of looking at it. The young people play, but they're not getting involved in the running of the club. In the Church as well, they're involved up until a certain age, then they're gone. We're like any other rural church in Ireland. We have a hard core of older and younger people, but not much in between. It's sad in many ways, but you'd hope that people would come round. Religion is a way of life as well. A certain degree of affluence has affected people, and when they've got everything, maybe they don't feel the need for religion.'

I go up to my old familiar corner room overlooking the quay, knowing that I will be woken in the early morning by nautical clangings and the cries of seagulls. I am glad that some things don't change.

14

Amidst These Hills – The Gaeltacht, Saints and Scholars

For many people, west Cork is synonymous with the wild country to the west of Macroom: Inchigeelagh, Bally-vourney, Ballingeary, Gougane Barra. These are the ancient places in the Barony of Muskerry, isolated by the rocky geography, where the Irish language still survives and saints' 'pattern days' are still observed, as they have been since time immemorial. In the early years of the twentieth century it was to these places that Frank O'Connor, Seán Ó Faoláin and their contemporaries, encouraged by their teacher, Daniel Corkery, went to learn Irish. Corkery described in *The Hidden Ireland – A Study of Gaelic Munster in the Eighteenth Century* (Gill, 1925) the way people lived in the time of the last of the great Irish language poets of the old tradition. A new and revolutionary concept at the time, Corkery's 'hidden Ireland' came to be reviled as the source of all that was backward and stagnant in Irish society, as de Valera's new State imposed Catholic and conservative values.

These hills were the scene of much of the fighting during the War of Independence and the Civil War that followed, as the many roadside graves and monuments testify. Michael Collins and Eamon de Valera passed through frequently; they once stayed on the same night at Creedon's Hotel in Inchigeelagh, but the owners managed to ensure that they didn't meet each other. The biggest monument of all is at Béal na mBláth, on the back road from Clonakilty to Cork, where Michael Collins was shot dead by a sniper's bullet on 22 August 1922. Every year, on the Sunday nearest to the date, huge crowds gather to listen to a memorial speech. In 2007 this was given by an Englishman, David Puttnam. And not just any Englishman, but also a Lord – Baron Puttnam of Queensgate. 'He seems to be a down-to-earth sort of man,' someone wrote on a political website, 'I saw him having coffee with his wife in Field's in Skibbereen'. His speech, on the theme of 'Whither Ireland: living with the new prosperity', was well received. The occasion was generally perceived as a mark of the new maturity in the Irish State, and the shedding of the old assumption that the word 'English' is synonymous with 'Enemy'.

For me, the road west from Crookstown to Ballyvourney will forever be associated with the funeral of the poet Seán Dunne. It was Saturday, 5 August 1995. Seán had died suddenly in his sleep, aged 39, of a heart attack. At the time, he was Features Editor and Books Editor of the *Cork Examiner*, and had recently put together *The Cork Anthology* (Cork University Press, 1993).

The Lough Parish Church, a big Victorian church in an inner suburb of Cork city, was full to bursting that Saturday. I stood alongside journalist colleagues, hard chaws all, who made no attempt to hide the tears streaming down their faces. Priests, publicans, poets – Seán knew everybody, and they had all come to his funeral. Only during the funeral mass did most of us learn that Seán was to be buried near the shrine of St Gobnait in Ballyvourney, about an hour's drive away. As we milled around outside on another lovely, sunny day, I ran into an old friend, the architect Alex White, who was not driving. I was alone, and had not intended to go to the burial. But suddenly it seemed a good and noble thing to drive to

Ballyvourney for the final ceremony. I offered Alex a lift, and he, who had not intended to go to the burial either, accepted.

Alex's life had recently been transformed by a pilgrimage to Santiago de Compostela. On his return he grew his hair and his beard long, and wore a large cross on his chest. He did not say much and we drove west in silence, playing Peadar Ó Riada's music, *Amidst These Hills*, one of maybe 200 cars following the hearse. It was awesome to be part of such a large, spontaneous display of grief and affection.

Before Lissarda, just beyond the junction where the road from Crookstown joins the main Cork–Killarney road, there was a dead pigeon flattened on the hard shoulder. Alex saw me wince and raised his right hand in solemn salutation. He explained that he had learnt the salute from a colleague. 'It makes you feel better, to acknowledge the life that was there, to salute the spirit.'

I have used it ever since. It often reminds me of Seán Dunne, a serendipity he would have enjoyed. Lift your right hand off the steering wheel and hold it vertically in the air for a few seconds, acknowledging that there was life, and now there is life no more. No one else in the car knows what you are up to, unless you explain, which you usually don't.

Amidst These Hills is a suite of music which expresses Peadar Ó Riada's feelings about his home, Coolea, in the west Cork Gaeltacht. The recording was made at home, and deliberately includes the sounds of everyday life – Peadar's baby sons diddly-i-ng, birdsong, the screech of a peacock. *Suantraí*, a catchy lullaby, is played on the piano that belonged to Peadar's father, the composer Seán Ó Riada, complete with the occasional dud note where the felt has fallen off the piano key. Peadar plays all the instruments himself, some less well than others, but the point is not virtuosity: it is the freshness of what you hear, as if you were listening to music happening

naturally, beside a crackling fire, or in the hard acoustic of
Coolea Parish Church. Listening to its perennially fresh sound
is to discover that there is still a hidden Ireland, a place where
the language and the music are still alive and still part of
people's everyday lives, a heritage that is far more important
to them than material success.

The first time I went to Coolea, I drove straight through
it and out the other side. There is so little there – a church, a
few houses, a community hall – and we were expecting so
much. I was with Stan Gébler Davies, a friend and colleague
from London, a journalist known for his dry wit, author of a
biography of James Joyce, and also a trained musician. He
could read an orchestral score, a feat which greatly impressed
me. Stan had studied music in Toronto (whence his parents
had emigrated from Dublin when he was twelve), and had
intended to make composition his career, until he heard that
not even Aaron Copland could make a living from
composing. Stan idolized Seán Ó Riada, for *Mise Éire* and his
other orchestral compositions more than for his pioneering
work with Ceoltóirí Chualann, the traditional music group
that evolved into the Chieftains. Stan had recently met Ó
Riada's son, Peadar, and had been impressed by Peadar's stories
of life in the wild hills of west Cork, where people still fell to
blows over the satirical poetry that they composed (in Irish)
about each other to while away the long winter.

Peadar invited Stan to Coolea, to look at his father's
archive any time he was passing. So when Stan came to visit
me in Kinsale, the first thing he wanted to do was to go to
Coolea. It was a rainy Friday afternoon in January 1983. We
had been invited to stay the night. I had never heard of Coolea
and had no idea where it was, but when we reached the three-
arched bridge across the Sullane River in Ballyvourney, where
you leave the Killarney road, I recognized the place. I had
often stopped there for a picnic with my parents as a child, and
been entranced by the fast-flowing river.

Having driven through Coolea and realised our mistake,

we turned back, asking for directions to the Ó Riada house. We parked on the main road near a little gate and walked up the overgrown path to the front door – which was in fact the back door, but people were too polite to tell us. It was on the latch, and in we walked.

Peadar, a stocky, dark-haired man with blue eyes, was the eldest of seven brothers and sisters who had been orphaned when their mother, Ruth, followed Seán to the grave. His sister, Reitseal, had married and was living locally, and the younger children were at boarding school, returning home most weekends, where Peadar was the head of the household, organising bus and train pick-ups and making sure there was always food on the table. It was one of the most unusual and most welcoming households I had ever been in. There was no formality at all, yet the manners could be described as courtly. Irish was very much the language of the house, but when non-Irish speakers were visiting, care was taken not to make them feel excluded (neither Stan nor I had a word between us, let alone a *cúpla focal*).

Peadar was very much the boss, though there was much arguing and answering back. At the time there was a television advertisement for a cold remedy featuring a character known as 'the elder lemon', and this was the nickname Ali had given to his brother Peadar (not that they actually had a television). Ali was living at home full-time then, and Eoghan some of the time, and the younger teenage children, Cathal, Sorcha and Liadh, were there most weekends. Reitseal was a frequent visitor, and neighbours and their children passed through the kitchen at all hours of the day and night. There always seemed to be someone sitting on the bench at the big kitchen table, drinking tea. At meal-times there was always proper food, freshly prepared, and enough of it to feed whoever happened to be there. It was such a hospitable place that at first it was difficult to work out who was family, and who was just visiting. The large plain house was clean but unostentatious, verging on shabby, probably unchanged since the family moved in twenty years before.

Since Peadar had invited us over, an elderly neighbour had died, and he had to attend the removal. We said we would wait at the house, but instead we were told we would be very welcome, and were asked to give a lift to some neighbours. The deceased had been active in Cumann na mBan, and there was a large attendance at the funeral home down in Bally-vourney. The coffin was draped with a Tricolour. In spite of our protests, Stan and I were invited back to the house afterwards. Two people stood inside the front door of the modest bungalow, each with a tray of whiskey, one 'red', one 'white'. There was also tea and sandwiches and cake. Several people had travelled from Dublin for the occasion. There were a couple of TDs present, and a famous actor. Stan and I were introduced as friends of Peadar. I was amazed to be so warmly welcomed to such an intimate family occasion by total strangers. I wondered if there had been some mistake: did they think we were more important than we were? Had they mistaken us for someone else? I tried to explain this to a nephew of the deceased, and he told me not to bother myself: 'It's *who* you are that matters around here, not *what* you are. You're friends of Peadar. That's good enough for us.'

Peadar was only twenty-one when his mother died, but he was able to hold the family together and go on living in the family home with the approval of the guardians appointed by his mother's will: the poets Seán Lucy and Declan Tallon and the historian John A. Murphy. There were early attempts at commercial bee-keeping, a subject Peadar still cites as an interest. He has taken his duties as keeper of his father's archive and reputation very seriously, spending much time entertaining interested visitors and research students. In 2004 UCC acquired the archive. The presentation was attended by the Taoiseach, Bertie Ahern, the whole Ó Riada family, and a number of musicians, and was a joyful occasion that no one present will ever forget.

Seán Ó Riada was born John Reidy in Cork on 1 August 1931. His father, Seán, a sergeant in the Garda Síochána, was from Kilmihil, County Clare, and his mother was Julia Creedon from Kilnamartra in the Barony of west Muskerry. Both were from farming stock with strong cultural and musical traditions. When Seán was appointed Assistant Lecturer of Music at UCC in 1963, he moved his family to Coolea, to the house called An Draigheann, and commuted to the College, which is conveniently located on the western side of the city. Living within ten miles of his mother's birthplace, Seán Ó Riada felt he had come home. He wrote his first Mass for the choir in Coolea, and it is still sung at 10 a.m. Mass every Sunday in the parish church, where his son Peadar took over the duties of organist when his father died in October 1971.

I've been back several times to Coolea, with Stan (who died in 1994), then on my own, sometimes to attend Sunday Mass on my way to somewhere else, and on occasion to interview Peadar for some publication. I remember, many years ago, an angry Peadar telling me about a child from Coolea with meningitis, spending his first night in a Cork city hospital, and asking for *deoch* (drink). None of the nurses could work out what he wanted and they told him they had no ducks in the hospital.

In the early days there was always an excursion after Sunday lunch, either 'down' to Gougane, to Cronin's Bar, or 'up' to the Top of Coom: always with at least two car-loads of people, Peadar carrying a tin whistle and a melodeon. At other times we went to one of two pubs in Ballyvourney. We just took off in whatever direction, and once we got there other musicians materialised, and the music began, and went on and on.

I am not the only one to believe that Peadar is under-rated as a composer and has never been properly promoted in Ireland (he is perhaps better known in the USA). He is a regular broadcaster on Raidió na Gaeltachta, and has made films with his own production company, Dord. The Cór Chúil Aodha is in demand at arts and music festivals throughout the country, and he is often on the road. He has now seen several generations through the choir, and can make it sound as good with only five or six voices as it does with twenty.

Peadar is also an independent thinker, with a serious interest in contemporary philosophy, while at the same time being dismissive of the prevailing certainties. He says he believes in the culture of the individual rather than the culture of the masses. He often says he spends much of his time and energy swimming against the tide. In 2001, in the wake of 9/11, he organized a series of weekends in Ballyvourney, Éigse an tSúláin, which he described as a new school of experimental philosophy and independent thought, hosted in turn by himself, the philosopher and mystic John Moriarty, Desmond Fennell, and others. He said of the venture at the time: 'We believe that Irish thinking has become standardised, and dominated by ideas from outside. Neither the academics nor the media have any interest in ideas that are a bit different from the mainstream. You'd find the same ideas circulating in London or New York or wherever, as you would in Dublin.

'We do have independent thinkers living and working among us here in Ireland, and one aspect of the School is to give them a forum, where they can share their ideas with like-minded people, who, we hope, will help these ideas to percolate into the mainstream. For example, I keep asking people to name me an Irish philosopher, and they always think back to Burke. William Thompson is never mentioned, and he was fundamental to the birth of Communism. There have always been Irish thinkers. But rather than concentrating on those that are gone, we hope to pick up some ideas from the thought processes that are going on in the Irish psyche in contemporary times. To have philosophers working among us is a sign of a mature society, with its own thought processes, a society that does not have to imitate other people, and take its ideas and thoughts and leadership from other nations.' These days Peadar is involved with a movement called the Acadamh Fódhla, the Hedge-school University. Its aim is to 'decommodify' education, and return to deeper values.

Peadar still lives in his father's house. He is married to Geraldine, and they have their own family: twins Seán Óg and Seamus, Ruth, and Saibh. Seán Óg, a highly intelligent child, has complex special needs arising from a rare metabolic disorder, and caring for him has become a major part of the family's life.

When I first got to know Coolea and Ballyvourney, I was struck by the relative poverty of the Gaeltacht, in contrast to the surrounding areas. Everything seemed run down and crumbling. Just as the vegetation was wilder than elsewhere, so the pubs and shops were dustier and darker. I wrote at the time in a guidebook, 'Many of the bars and hotels in the Gaeltacht look (and, alas, probably are) rather poverty-stricken and can be a disappointment if you do not speak Irish.' That same simplicity and lack of ostentation is now what I like most about these places. When I went back to the Top Of Coom bar after an absence of about five years, Eileen Top (as the landlady is known), greeted me by name, and that meant a lot more than new upholstery. Joe Creedon, owner–manager of Creedon's Hotel in Inchigeelagh, quite rightly wrote and complained about my snooty comment. Joe's establishment has become a favourite bolthole. He is a large, affable man, passionate about watercolours and an expert on local history and lore – almost like a character from Robert Gibbings' *Sweet Cork of Thee* (Mercier Press, 1991). 'We have no need for foreign travel in these parts,' he says, standing outside his hotel's front door, pointing to the village's 'Pontevecchio', a modest hardware store ingeniously built of corrugated iron across a tributary of the River Lee, and then to their 'Fujiyama', a conical lookalike peak in the Shehy Mountains.

There have been big changes in the Muskerry Gaeltacht since the 1980s, and a marked increase in prosperity. Bally-vourney seemed to be dying when I first knew it, everywhere on the brink of closing down. Now, just like everywhere else, new housing estates are going up, there is a swanky new supermarket, two petrol stations, a coffee shop, and two thriving industrial parks. There is even a recording studio used by the likes of Christy Moore in preference to its big city counterparts. But I am told this is the way of the Gaeltacht: the people who have money don't like to make a display of it. 'The money was always there, but you didn't see it,' says Peadar.

In 1960, Seán Ó Riada was commissioned to write the music for a film called *Mise Éire* (I Am Ireland), directed by George Morrison. The film, which pioneered the use of archive material to recount historic events from the 1890s to 1918, was also the first Irish feature-length film to use an orchestral soundtrack. The stirring music took Ireland by storm. It made Ó Riada a household name and raised the status of Irish music amongst a section of society who had never taken any interest in it before.

Coolea Sunday, 30 September 2007
George Morrison and my husband, Aidan Higgins, have been friends since the 1940s, when they both used to attend the philosopher Arland Ussher's 'At Home' evenings in Dublin. So, when I rang Peadar to say I'd be at Sunday Mass on my way to Gougane Barra for the Feast of St Finbarr, I was delighted to hear that George, now 85, and his wife, Janet, were staying in Ballyvourney for a short holiday at the invitation of the Ó Riada family.

Getting out of the car up in the hills, as always the air is different – colder, damper – and there is birdsong, even in the village. I'm just in time for 10 a.m. Mass, and people are hurrying towards the church from all directions. The church fills from the back to the front, and, as one of the last to arrive, I have to sit near the front, with half a dozen almost empty benches in front of me. It's a simple country church, with cream-painted walls and wood-veneer floors and pews. The choir and organ are in the centre of the church. Already there are rasping winter coughs in the congregation. Signs on the main road through Ballyvourney advertise Polish coal on the pallet at last year's prices – still the preferred means of heating round here. People dress tidily for Mass, but most of the under-fifties wear jeans and cheerful chain-store tops, male and female. From where I sit I can hear babies and small children at the back: children are taken everywhere.

The great blast of male voices from the choir is a surprise at first, a jolt, though I know the music well, and this is what I've come for. Peadar is at the organ, three little boys sit at his feet – his sopranos? The strange harmonies, based on different intervals than the familiar European classical scale, are as mysterious and haunting as ever. The familiar paradoxical feeling returns, of being in the presence of living Irish, and aware of its rarity and importance, yet excluded from its content by ignorance of the language. The only words I understand in the sermon are Lazarus and Dives and *síochán*. People hang around outside the church talking after Mass, like they did in the old days. I say a brief hallo to George Morrison, and arrange with Peadar to meet up later at Gougane.

After Mass I buy a take-away cappuccino from the Ballyvourney supermarket and drive up to the graveyard at St Gobnait's. It seems a popular destination after Mass: there are half a dozen other visitors. Moss and ferns cover the stone walls by the road, but have been cleared from the sacred buildings and the walls of the cemetery. A large rosary is hung on Seamus Murphy's statue of St Gobnait, the patron saint of beekeepers; similar giant rosaries are hung on some of the gravestones.

A glazed board beside St Gobnait's grave outlines the prayers to be recited at each station – seven Our Fathers, seven

Hail Marys, seven Glory be to the Fathers. At the ruined church, the board instructs: 'When walking round the ruin, you say one decade of the rosary each time you go round five times. Then back to the Holy Well down the road.' I suspect the strange English is due to a direct translation from the Irish. The pole with the instructions on it has scapulars and ribbons – one with a laminated photo of a baby – tied around it. On the grave itself are rosaries, small statues, pens, a plastic souvenir of the Aran Islands, baby's socks, and a small, white, china rabbit.

The graveyard is in a natural dip, and sheep are grazing the hill above. Beyond the tidy, enclosed area there are small, rough fields, with gorse and bracken encroaching, and paths running through them. It has that deep peace often found in places of pilgrimage when there are no crowds. The place is very different from my memory of it during the crowded funeral of Seán Dunne. I find the grave of Seán Ó Ríordáin (1916–77), but not Seán Dunne's. Names recur on the tall headstones: Lucey, Cronin, Ó Tuama, Ó Céilleachair.

A short walk down the road, the Holy Well is in a railed enclosure, down three stone steps, under sycamore, ash, and hawthorn trees. The water runs beneath the stone slabs and emerges as a stream on the other side, filtered through beds of watercress and reeds. A tub of recycled empty plastic bottles is thoughtfully provided for you to take away holy water, and mugs are on hand to get it out of the well. The beech tree beside the well and a metal T-bar are hung with rosaries, ribbons, Immaculate medals – and socks again. The socks are puzzling. There are stiles for people arriving across country, presumably a traditional route.

Instead of driving on the mountain road from Coolea to Gougane, which I remember as unnervingly narrow, steep, and remote, I take the road from Ballyvourney through Reenanerree to Ballingeary. It's a beautiful drive, the crests of the hills on either side capped by pine trees (probably Sitka spruce, but from a distance they look good). The land has exposed rock faces with heather clinging to the edges, gorse in flower, and great stands of flowering Japanese knotweed. Though it's now a serious pest, you can see the decorative qualities that may have attracted nineteenth-century plant collectors. After the fork for Kilgarvan–Kenmare, two more series of mountain peaks rise up in front of me, another misty one looms on the right, and another one to the left, completely surrounding me. This must be one of the most beautiful drives in the county.

I arrive early at Gougane to have a look around before the crowds converge. The lake is as black as ever, the cliffs on the opposite side as steep. No wonder it is said that St Finbarr killed a hideous serpent that lurked in its depths: the only one to have escaped when St Patrick banished all the snakes from Ireland.

'This is a Holy Place. Here may you, pilgrim and visitor, find peace and the love of the Lord. Please – no camping or picnics.' The contrast to the inclusive homeliness of St Gobnait's shrine and well is noticeable. She'd probably be delighted if you ate a picnic, especially if it included honey. St Finbarr's Oratory has been cleaned up, de-paganised since I was last here. You are asked by a notice not to put money in the Holy Well. The tree that used to be studded with coins now has a notice on it: 'I am a tree. Please do not put coins into me! Please use coin boxes located in the church and grounds instead.' There are no ribbons or medals or votive offerings – no socks. (Next day I ring the Parish Priest, and he complains that, in spite of the notices, people will insist on throwing coins in the well.)

A few people are individually praying at the old stations, while outside the door of the Oratory volunteers test the sound-system rigged on top of a car: Count John McCormack sings Ave Maria. Cars with rosary beads hanging from the rear-view mirror mark the arrival of the devout. Most of those attending are from the surrounding parishes of Úibh Laoire. There are a few coaches, and hundreds of cars. A group from Kilgarvan traditionally walk the seven miles across the mountain. Robert Gibbings described the occasion in 1943: 'On the last Sunday in September, Gougane Sunday, masses are said in the oratory, and pilgrims come from far and near. In Daimler motors, in turf lorries, on horseback. Those who live near travel on foot, and many from far, too. Not only by road, but over the mountains they come, strings of them climbing down the hillsides, their faces and white feet glinting like the sparkle of waterfalls ...' (The white feet presumably are bare feet.)

Promptly at 2.30 p.m., the formalities begin. A group of nine clergy, including Cork's Bishop John Buckley, processes from the hotel to the causeway and on to the island, behind the Ballingeary Pipe Band who are playing the air of 'Faith of Our Fathers'. Most of the pipers are teenage girls, some in red kilts, some in black trousers, while an elderly man bangs the big drum. 'I'll be off to my prayers now', jokes a woman coming out of Cronin's Bar, hurrying down to the Mass.

Cronin's Bar is next to the Gougane Barra Hotel; both venerable institutions, still run by descendants of the same family as in Robert Gibbings' day, the bar and café by Breda, who was a small child in Gibbings' time, while the hotel is run by her son, Niall Lucey, and his wife, Katy. When you look out of the bar windows, all you can see is the sheer cliff face of the Shehy Mountains on the far side of the lake, continuing up where there should be sky.

George Morrison and his wife are having tea in the hotel lounge. Peadar orders more tea and sandwiches for us and his children, Seán Óg in his motorised wheelchair, and Saibh. Gougane Barra Hotel (Óstán Gúgán Barra) is a gracious, old-fashioned establishment, with a formal dining room, popular year-round for Sunday lunch. It was using the slogan, 'A Place Apart', long before West Cork LEADER adopted it. I congratulate George on recently being elected to Aosdána. He says it was all thanks to Bob Quinn, whose speech provoked such applause that he feels he was elected by popular acclaim. 'But the best thing about it,' he says, lowering his voice, 'is the income they give you. That has made a huge difference.' The 85-year old director of *Mise Éire* still teaches occasionally, and has recently taught himself to edit film digitally.

'I often wondered about Aosdána,' says Peadar. 'There was a time when I was about to be proposed, but people scattered, and it never happened.'

George says, 'Well, Peadar, we must see that you *do* get elected,' and starts to tell him how to begin. Peadar says 'No, I wouldn't worry about that. I'm quite happy as I am. I have other honours.' He changes the subject. When we call for the bill, Niall Lacey tells us it is on a stake down at the lakeside. In other words, it's on the house. We all protest, but he says firmly, 'It's just a small thank-you, Peadar, for all the things you've done for us over the years.'

As we are saying goodbye in the car park, I tell Peadar I've been writing about the old days, when he was the head of a household of brothers and sisters, and how nice it is that he is still in the same house, with a family of his own.

Then he explains that he was invited in 1976 to study music in Holland: the academics came down to talk to his mother, to get her to try and persuade him: 'I made a conscious decision then to stay here, never to leave, but to make my life in this place. The family has got bigger, and it's all around me now, it's the whole community. So that's why I'm not bothered about Dublin and Aosdána and getting on in the bigger world. I knew that wouldn't happen, when I made that decision, but I have it all here.'

'You are rich indeed,' I say, quoting the words Giana Ferguson had used to describe her daughter Clovisse's prospects as a vegetable grower: 'She may never get rich, but her life is rich indeed.'

I'd left the car door wide open, and my handbag on the seat. The keys were in the ignition, with hundreds of pilgrims milling around, and I was talking to Peadar around the corner, without a worry. I was in a place where everything is good, the old trust survives, where everyone knows who everyone is. There was a sort of grounding, a completing of the circle. Different though they may seem, this west Cork, with its wild hills and remote, unpeopled valleys – the 'inner' west Cork, as some call it – and the more conventionally pretty, lively coastal area are one and the same place at the core, thanks to the people who live here.

Index

Index

Index

Index

Index